Frederick's signature [Frch = Friedrich] is taken from a letter to d'Alembert of 1 August 1780.

Frederick in his seventieth year, painted by Anton Graff.

Gerhard Ritter

Frederick the Great
A Historical Profile

TRANSLATED, WITH AN INTRODUCTION, BY
PETER PARET

UNIVERSITY OF CALIFORNIA PRESS
BERKELEY, LOS ANGELES, LONDON

University of California Press
Berkeley and Los Angeles, California
University of California Press, Ltd.
London, England
This is a translation of the third edition of
Friedrich der Grosse: Ein Historisches Profil
published by Quelle & Meyer, Heidelberg, 1954.

First Paperback Edition, 1974
ISBN: 0-520-02775-2
Library of Congress Catalog Card Number: 68-15815
Printed in the United States of America

6 7 8 9 0

A Note on the Paperback Edition

GERHARD RITTER'S biography of Frederick the Great originated in a series of lectures, which were published with scarcely any revisions in 1936. In my translation, based on the third edition, published in 1954, I have tried to convey the hard and precise style that characterizes the German text, while eliminating some of the numerous adjectives and parallel phrases that a lecturer might have found useful for emphasis but which seem unnecessary on the printed page. With the author's agreement I have also excluded the brief introduction and epilogue of the original, since they are addressed specifically to the German reader and to German conditions. Gerhard Ritter died in 1967, shortly after the translation was completed; I shall always remember the kindness and tolerance with which he responded to my questions and suggestions. I am also grateful to Mrs. Fannia Weingartner of San Francisco, to the editorial staff of the University of California Press, and most particularly to Herbert F. Mann, Jr., now of the Oxford University Press, for their help in preparing the manuscript for publication. Some minor changes and corrections aside, the text of the paperback edition is the same as that of the original American edition of 1968.

Peter Paret

Stanford, California
April, 1974

Introduction

by

Peter Paret

FEW BIOGRAPHIES present convincing interpretations of their subjects. Even fewer add to our understanding of historical processes, and their number is being increased neither by modern techniques of research nor by today's psychological and literary fashions. In each biography the basic difficulties of the genre reappear, the solutions of which depend less on the historian's methods than on his insight and sympathy. In the past, biographers were occasionally advised to confine themselves strictly to their subject's personal and professional experiences. "Broad views," Edmund Gosse wrote in a famous article in the *Encyclopaedia Britannica,* "are entirely out of place in biography, and there is perhaps no greater literary mistake than to attempt what is called the 'Life and Times' of a man." This leaves the question open of whether the one can be understood without studying the other; indeed it was the weakness of Gosse's own biographical writings that they imbued such figures as Donne and Jeremiah Taylor with all the characteristics of Edwardian literary notables. Today few would agree with him. Far more common—among general readers, if not historians—is the assumption that biography is a particularly effective tool of general history. The hero's life-span gives the work its structure; he also provides it with its interpretive core by functioning as a prism in which the author captures and refracts the conditions of the age. And yet nothing is more ambiguous than the connections that exist between man and his environment; between his psyche and his actions. Man never fully becomes one with his affairs; no amount of documentation can ever wholly clarify the relationship between the external world and the thoughts, wishes, and fears of the individual.

Gerhard Ritter does not completely resolve the problems that Frederick the Great poses to historical analysis. Indeed his book does not even face them all, and its interest and force are derived partly from its evasions. The text is based on lectures Ritter delivered at the University of Freiburg in 1933 and 1934. Since he talked about a figure in the German pantheon, he felt no need to delve into details; he could risk developing his interpretations from a few allusions, certain that his listeners' reading and their school memories would enable them to provide a factual accompaniment to his variations. The result is an analysis of Frederick and the age of absolutism, which, although brief and even impressionistic, brings out with great clarity the themes that are of paramount interest to the author. Nor does his brevity lead to imbalance; on the contrary, one of the assets of the biography is its comprehensiveness. From the king's social conservatism to his theories of literature, every essential aspect of his life is at least touched on, and the syntheses, which often compress the result of generations of scholarship into one paragraph, are done with such skill that they end by becoming self-explanatory. The sparse treatment, originally dictated by the needs of the lecture platform, becomes a quality in itself, capable of existing in an alien environment. English and American readers, who do not bring to Frederick the emotional awareness of Ritter's German audience, may be more critical of his conclusions; the view of Europe from the vantage points of Berlin and Potsdam which he offers may seem strange to them, but should also be fresh and instructive.

Frederick the Great is less the product of its author's archival research than of his reflections on the history of political ideas. It deals with a subject which in different forms occupied Ritter throughout his long career as a scholar.[1] In the sequence of his writings, the volume followed books and papers on the Renaissance, on Luther, on Bismarck's domestic and foreign policies, and the splendid biography of Stein, completed four years earlier. It returns to questions that these works had raised: the differences between Germany's past and that of her Western neighbors; the role of power and its ethical problems, particularly in the development of political institutions and in the relations between states. At the

[1] A thoughtful introduction to Ritter's work is contained in Andreas Dorpalen's article "Historiography as History: The Works of Gerhard Ritter," *Journal of Modern History*, XXXIV, no. 1 (1962), 1–18.

same time the book served as a point of departure for Ritter's important achievement after 1945, the volumes on *The Political Art and the Craft of War,* with their subtitle "The Problem of Militarism in Germany," which range from eighteenth century Prussia to the end of the First World War. Power, its responsible use, and its abuse, was a permanent concern of Ritter, both as historian and as German citizen, and his biography of Frederick is a concise essay on one aspect of this general theme.

When Frederick ascended the throne in 1740 he fell heir to the accumulated resources of generations. It still required exceptional ability and ambition to give Prussia a voice in the conduct of international affairs that accorded with her political and military potential. The risks her ruler took were great, but by the end of the Seven Years' War Prussia had become one of the major powers on the Continent. This revolution in the affairs of Europe was achieved by means that were far from revolutionary. Frederick was rarely an innovator, and then only in relatively unimportant matters. He accepted Europe for what it was and he had a clear understanding of his own strengths and weaknesses; his success came from his willingness to exploit the potentials of both Prussia and the age to their limit. He himself later admitted that at the beginning of his reign he was too much influenced by personal ambition; soon, however, his feelings were sublimated into the demands of the state, as he interpreted them. His policies might still be ruthless, but now were subject to limitations imposed by his cautious evaluation of what Prussia could and could not achieve. His realism and his identification with the state—a sense of kinship in which responsibility and service played a role—saved him from copying Louis XIV's vainglory or the disastrous adventures of Charles XII. Gradually his youthful egotism was channeled into paths, which, while always dangerous to neighbors and rivals, at least proved constructive for the Prussian monarchy. In the course of his reign, so Ritter sums up the process, Frederick, as much as any individual can, came to exemplify the rational use of state power.

The interpretation of Frederick as the personified *raison d'état* is given urgency by an unhistorical concern on the part of the author. The direction Germany was taking under Hitler's leadership con-

firmed Ritter's deepest fears about modern totalitarianism. By un-
derlining the share that prudent government had in Prussia's rise
to power, he cautioned against the irrationality and irresponsibility
of Germany's new masters—a warning expressed with particular
force at the beginning of his discussion of Frederick's conquest of
Silesia. Ritter's audience could be in no doubt about the nature of
his message. The review of the first edition in the *Historische Zeitschrift* declared that the biography's "constant and one-sided emphasis of the rational element in the person and work of Frederick
can be interpreted only as a warning against policies based on emotion."[2] Looking back on the book's appearance, Walter Dorn later
wrote in the *American Historical Review* that its "scholarly tone
and critical temper were also designed to be a sharp repudiation of
the inebriated glorification of Frederick by the frenzied nationalists
of the Nazi era."[3] As might be expected, however, Ritter was not
content with simply confronting twentieth-century demagoguery
with Frederician absolutism; a comparison of two such dissimilar
epochs could scarcely do much to further our understanding of either. Instead he sought to establish a German tradition of rational
power politics, whose most successful exponents he found in Frederick and Bismarck. Not that joining these two figures was without dangers of its own. As one of the most acute reviewers of the
book has pointed out, Bismarck's *Realpolitik* differed fundamentally from the rationalistic policies of Frederick.[4] This is not the
only occasion that Ritter has been condemned for being vague in
his use of basic ideas—a criticism that will always find targets

[2] Gerhard Oestreich in the *Historische Zeitschrift*, CLXI, no. 3 (1940),
600.

[3] In his discussion of the third German edition in the *American Historical Review*, LIX, no. 4 (1954), 1006. In the same vein Klaus Epstein
describes the book as "the most interesting recent one-volume biography
in German . . . stimulating for its scholarship and for the parallels and
lessons that it draws for Nazi Germany." See Epstein's "Bibliographical
Note" in his edition of Sidney B. Fay's *The Rise of Brandenburg-Prussia
to 1786*, New York, 1964, p. 133.

[4] Eberhard Kessel, in his review of the first German edition in the
Forschungen zur Brandenburgischen und Preussischen Geschichte, XLIX,
no. 2 (1937), 413.

among scholars who develop the meaning of concepts in the course
of their analysis rather than establish it by early definition. For Ritter, comparing Bismarck and Frederick was a tactical device, demonstrating the effectiveness of reason in the intercourse of states,
which cannot support too heavy a weight of historical investigation. That, despite all the differences existing between the eight-
teenth and nineteenth centuries, a certain affinity does link the two
men has lately been reaffirmed by Otto Pflanze.[5] In the years when
Hitler was preparing the destruction of Western civilization, the
comparison possessed added political justification. Combined as it
is with references to the similarity between some of the problems
faced both by the Prussian monarchy and the German *Reich* it remains enlightening even in less apocalyptic times.

The work, then, is not a conventional biography, not even in the
expanded form of a "Life and Times," but fundamentally a study
in the history of political ideas and political attitudes. Ritter eluci-
dates the realities of Frederician absolutism carefully enough, but
he is more concerned with the ideas that shaped them and gave
them direction. Even the central figure—though neither his policies
nor his character and feelings are ignored—is represented primarily
as the carrier of an idea. Perhaps the greatest advantage of this approach lies in its avoidance of a danger common to all intellectual
history, which even in the best hands loses much of its vigor when
it does not remain attached to individuals and specific events. Ideas
are not purified by being lifted from their historical matrix; on the
contrary, their interpretation becomes schematic and unreal unless
they are seen in permanent interaction with the life that envelops
them. In turn, the biographical purpose of the book gains from the
attention the author devotes to such forces as Machiavellianism or
the political theories of the Enlightenment. By adopting a single
point of view, which regards Frederick above all as the agent of rational state power, Ritter achieves an exceptional unity of interpretation. An incidental benefit of this way of writing biography is
that it helps the author take a detached view of his hero's personal
qualities. It is an aspect of Ritter's biographical technique that can
also be seen at work in his otherwise very different lives of Stein

[5] *Bismarck and the Development of Germany: The Period of Unifica-
tion, 1815–1871*, Princeton, 1963, pp. 9–10.

and Goerdeler. More interested in ideas and in the state which gives them concrete and permanent expression than in the man, the writer feels little temptation to gloss over his subject's weaknesses.

There are moments, to be sure, when Ritter's detachment breaks down. Here and there in the course of the book a note of romantic overestimation is sounded in the depiction of the embattled king, contrasting strangely with the general sobriety of the text. Frederick's courage in the face of adversity, his energy and persistence, are evoked in glowing language. His attempt in his writings to rationalize the principles of his rule are praised as an ultimate intellectual achievement of absolutism, without noting that this kind of self-justifying theorizing is the only option available to an absolute monarch who is also possessed of strong philosophic interests and ambitions. In the quarrel between Frederick and Voltaire, it is the latter who is labelled "cowardly," though the relative power of the two men might have suggested to Ritter that if pejoratives were to be used at all, here was a case of the coward facing a bully. All this, while interesting evidence of a partiality of which the historian himself may not even be aware, would matter little if it did not have an effect on his interpretation of state power in the history of Prussia and Germany. But having turned Frederick into a symbol of political qualities that he admires, his biographer does not always escape the danger of romanticising the ideas personified together with the man who, in his view, personified them.

This is not to suggest that Ritter takes an uncritical view of Prussian absolutism. His biography of Frederick scrutinizes the defects and harshnesses of the system as well as its admirable qualities. But it is true that the range of his questions narrows when he approaches the central issue: the expansion of Prussia, and the mobilization of her society and government for this purpose. Despite Ritter's love for the supranational genius of Europe, the *raison d'état* at times assumes in his mind the same self-understood validity that he believes it possessed for Frederick. Here Ritter follows in the steps of the majority of German historians of the past hundred years. By the very existence of political authority—at least that holding sway in Germany—they were too often inhibited from asking all the questions, exploring all the paths, that awaited them. In the final analysis they always looked at the state from the point of view of the state. As the dean of Frederician scholarship, Reinhold Koser, wrote in the heyday of the Wilhelmine era: "To us absolutism is simply a historical phenomenon. When we encounter it, we ask only what were its political achievements." [6]

Such a statement signifies not only concentration of effort on the part of the historian, but also a surrender. The historian who seeks to reconstruct the essential elements of absolutism can hardly dismiss those of its workings that cannot be measured directly in terms of diplomatic and military potency. Both at the time and in later generations a price was paid for the expansion of the state's authority. In Prussia the long-term cost, among much else, was the fragmentation of society by the creation of state-preserving elites, and the maintenance of most of the population in a condition of severe political immaturity. The inadequacy of interpretations that did not take account of such factors was made increasingly evident to Ritter by the events of the 1930's and 1940's. After the war he admitted that in his writings he too had often uncritically accepted the necessity of states giving full reign to their drive for power. "Can it be denied," he wrote in the epilogue to the third edition of *Frederick the Great,* "that German historiography placed too much faith in the moral responsibility of German statesmen and in that rationality of the state which according to Hegel dominates history? Isn't it true that for too long German historians failed to recognize the [dangers of aggressiveness] with sufficient clarity, that they unhesitatingly praised violence, if violence was successful? Too often, in their admiration of decisive feats they failed to appreciate the 'demonic nature of power,' which entangles the political leader in a maze of personal guilt and impersonal fate . . . and which forces him into conflicts of opposing moral and political responsibilities, which almost always underlie great political achievements."

The insensitivity that such scholars as Koser evinced toward certain aspects of their topic does not, of course, render their work negligible. Ritter, too, was not prevented by his attachment to the state from subjecting Frederick and the Prussian monarchy to exacting investigation. In some respects his personal views on politics

---

[6] *König Friedrich der Grosse,* Stuttgart-Berlin, 1912, vol. 3, p. 553. The first edition of Koser's standard biography appeared in 1889.

and society limited his interpretation, in others they spurred it on
—as is shown by the influence that his opposition to National So-
cialism exerted on his analysis of Frederick. His biography, indeed,
is a good illustration of the way in which the circumstances of the
historian's existence affect, and even dominate, his work. Not only
academic interest, but the continuing crisis of Western civilization
caused Ritter in the 1930's, and causes us today, to explore the
genesis of the modern nation-state. That historians can rarely remove themselves to any great extent from the problems and pre-
conceptions of their own times certainly complicates their work;
but it is after all only their awareness of present reality, their experiences and actions, that equip them to be more than simple
chroniclers of what has gone before. They are agents in an endless,
reciprocal process. They face the past, but their interpretations reflect the present. Like every serious historical work, Ritter's biography not only sheds new light on its subject—Frederick and the origins of German power—but also adds to our understanding of the
course that events have taken since.

CONTENTS

1
Frederick and His Age: The System of Absolutism

TO UNDERSTAND the nature of absolutism, we must above all free ourselves from some common misconceptions of nineteenth-century liberalism. Measured by today's standards, the "absolute" power of the great seventeenth- and eighteenth-century courts was far from all-embracing. On the contrary, it was restricted to a very narrow area of sovereignty, hemmed in by a thousand different forms of legality, tradition, and political considerations, and equipped with extremely modest instruments of power. The authority of the princes was "absolute" only by comparison with the older feudal system, which it had overcome, not with the modern democratic national state, which it ushered in.

Former generations regarded princely absolutism as the unqualified opposite of liberty. Today, in the age of the "total" people's state which no longer recognizes any sphere of individual life as inviolate, absolutism appears to us simply as a transitional stage of development. It possesses the historical merit of having founded the modern, centralized nation-state, of having overcome the old feudal arrangements, without, however, as yet completely destroying them. Indeed, it is the resistance of members of the feudal nobility defending their traditional privileges against the monarchy, that gave rise to the seemingly absolute opposites "despotism-freedom" which dominate the older theories of English liberalism.

Basically the feudal system was identical throughout Europe. The splintered sovereignty of the state had passed into the hands of an entire hierarchy of individuals, families, and groups, the actual extent of whose public powers was more or less narrowly limited. They disposed over extremely varied and often overlapping types of authority: some proprietary, others more judicial in nature; some of private, others of public character and background. When—as in Germany at the end of the Middle Ages—the process of dissolution had gone very far, we can say that public authority was inherited as the fragmented possession of numerous families, all of which were permanently fighting among themselves over the enlargement of their power. No uniformly effective governmental will dominated the whole; there was no systematic royal dispensation of justice, and at least in times of peace no unquestioned power of command. The unifying force rested in the loyalty of vassal to liege lord, a bond made up of moral and legal strands. Uniform law, binding everywhere, was established only when the king could persuade his vassals at meetings of the Diet to agree on a common policy. In the German Empire this was only rarely the case.

Out of this chaos of authority the absolutist state emerged as forerunner of the modern nation-state. It developed first and most successfully in France, which came to serve as model for the entire continent. The French king was "absolute" insofar as he renounced the obligation of unconditional respect for the traditional prerogatives of his vassals. The late-Roman axiom *princeps legibus absolutus est* was given the new meaning that it was the liberties of the subject above all—or more accurately, the prerogatives of the nobility—whose binding authority was denied. The European monarchies attained absolute power in the state by systematically destroying or diminishing privilege. This end was not achieved without brutal compulsion. In France leaders of the nobility were executed; there were cruelties of all kinds, intrigues with foreign powers, and costly battles. And yet even in France the monarchy failed to vanquish the powerful feudal nobility completely; it neither leveled all class differences, nor could it entirely abolish provincial authority and reshape the nation into a uniform mass of subjects governed by a rational and centralized administration. All this had to await the great democratic revolution. Only then was the work of the monarchs completed. The truly absolute state, organized without regard for privilege and tradition, disposing over the property and life of all its subjects according to its own interests, was established not under the monarchies but by the modern democracies. Not until it appealed to the will of the people could the modern state become all-embracing, and finally grow even beyond absolutism to achieve totality of power.

In the development of the political institutions of Europe and of Germany, the historical position occupied by the subject of our study is defined by three factors: Frederick intensified and pushed to their logical conclusion the political traditions of monarchical absolutism, which French statesmen had originated in the seventeenth century. He overcame the backwardness of traditional German princely rule, and radically changed its character. Finally, by a process of spiritualization that raised the monarchy above the naïve enjoyment of power, Frederick completed the internal development of absolutism, and even pointed beyond it toward new political forms.

To understand these achievements we must consider the various methods by which absolutism overcame feudalism. They consisted of a gradual, systematic increase of the territorial ruler's liege, judicial, and religious rights, and of the expansion of his financial and military powers. Successes in diplomacy and war made this aggrandizement possible. Significant victories in these fields could, of course, be achieved only by the major powers; other states, particularly the lesser German principalities, were on the whole limited to extending their authority over the churches and to the careful nurturing and exploitation of their judicial institutions.

Let us first trace this development in France. In the Middle Ages, feudalism had shaken the structure of the French kingdom even more than it had loosened the unity of the German Empire. From this crisis the French monarchy freed itself only just in time by a determined retention of the rights of the supreme liege lord, by the expansion of his judicial powers, and by the establishment of a firm legal tradition that was carried by a body of professional royal jurists and by the beginnings of a modern bureaucracy. In the Hundred Years' War for the liberation of French territory from English occupation, the kings came to champion the common good against the treacherous egotism of the great noble families, which allied themselves with the enemy in pursuit of their particularist interests. The crown grew into a symbol of national independence. In the course of the fighting it succeeded in laying the foundations of a standing royal army, unaffected by feudal obligations, as well as of a permanent system of taxation for the maintenance of this force. At the same time, the decline of the papacy in the religious struggles of the Conciliar period enabled the monarchy to bring the rich Gallican church under a considerable measure of control. Henceforth bureaucracy, army, and state church became the most reliable supports for the royal power.

Not that the rise of the monarchy proceeded without serious reverses. During the religious wars of the sixteenth century the crown was unable to maintain itself above the raging fanaticism of the parties; it wavered back and forth between Huguenots and Catholics, both of whom called on foreign powers for help in the fratricidal struggle. But this very lack of stability made the need for a self-reliant, truly sovereign monarchy apparent to all. The modern French monarchy was born when Henry IV reconciled the religious enemies by returning to the old faith. With this step he finally cured the convulsions of sectarian conflict and raised the concept of the national state to unquestioned predominance. In principle at least—though still very incompletely in reality—religion and policy now were separated. The victory of Henry the Apostate proved to be the victory of the modern, purely secular Renaissance concept of the state over the semireligious rulership of the Middle Ages and of the Reformation. Jean Bodin's theory of sovereignty, the true beginning of modern constitutional law, at once gave this development articulate form. It was precisely the unalloyed secularity of the new approach, the nation's delivery from an unbearable intertwining of spiritual and secular forces, which lent Henry's reign a gloriole that sent its rays far into the eighteenth century. Voltaire praised the king in a magnificent heroic epos, the *Henriade,* a work that became a favorite of Crown Prince Frederick, and that together with Fénelon's humanitarian, didactic poem, *Télémaque,* helped kindle his political imagination. Frederick's reign was not to be a "Christian stewardship" nor his state a Christian state like that of his fathers; but purely secular, neutral in religion, "enlightened."

To be sure, Voltaire recognized that Henry IV was far from an enlightened spirit in the eighteenth-century sense, and that the separation of church and state, which had been achieved in principle, was by no means strictly observed under his successors. Particularly in the later years of Louis XIV's reign, the crown had again entered into the closest relationship with the Catholic national church. But while stretching its religious sovereignty to the extremes of a profound interference in the spiritual life of the church, and turning the hierarchy into a passive servant of the state, the monarchy itself became deeply ensnared in church interests, whose pursuit led far away from the concerns of sound state policy. The persecutions of the Huguenots, with their devastating effects on the intellectual, moral, and economic life of France, formed only a part of the harsh measures by which Jesuitical combativeness at Versailles repressed everything that seemed to oppose or to endanger official church doctrine. As a result, most of the great thinkers of French rationalism, always threatened by the censorship of the church, were compelled to live or to publish outside France, while French literature, deeply embittered by the universal religious intolerance, was filled with resentment and destructive criticism. In the first half of the century, this criticism found its most passionate and effective expression in Voltaire's writings. It goes without saying that in moderating relations between church and state Voltaire's friend and pupil, Crown Prince Frederick, sought to improve on the French model, and that he hoped to fulfill the true potential of modern absolutism better than the *roi soleil* himself and his successors.

Frederick was more favorably impressed with the French monarchy's approach to foreign affairs. Its tradition had been founded by Richelieu when he elevated the *raison d'état*—the pursuit of wholly secular, carefully assessed national interests—as the sole guiding star of foreign policy. Richelieu and his successor Mazarin had laid the groundwork of that artful system of European coalitions which under Louis XIV brought about a considerable increase in the power of France. On principle all action was to derive from the sober evaluation of the strengths of the several European states and of their naturally opposing interests. Sectarian enthusiasm was excluded, as were the personal ambitions and jealousies of the rulers. Counted as even less significant were national friendships or enmities: policy was still formulated and implemented in the detached sphere of the courts, far from the people and their national passions. The state, even the French national monarchy, was still essentially a dynastic construction; only rarely and from a distance could the subjects' wishes, longings, and fears make themselves heard in the realm of policy. National and dynastic interests nearly coincided; military or diplomatic laurels were prized above all as devices to increase royal glory and authority. Today the policies of the princely cabinets often appear soulless to us, little more than contests of mechanically driven forces, lacking the impetus of national passions and without the higher justification created by a sustaining, universal concept. In the years of Frederick's youth, this system was already weakening; after a century of more or less uninterrupted warfare had gravely sapped the strengths of the European states, it was becoming almost perfunctory and artificial. But if the maneuverings of the cabinets lacked strong passion, it was the easier to hope that they could be subordinated to the pure principles of the *raison d'état*. Since the days of the great French Revolution and of Napoleon we have learned how valuable such an achievement would have been, and what immense threats for Europe lie in policies dictated by national enthusiasm and hatred.

Even before his accession to the throne, Frederick had studied the rational principles underlying the theory of the state's natural interests, which long ago had become commonly accepted in European diplomacy and political literature. He tried to apply these concepts in his early political and historical writings, and soon came to realize that French foreign policy had by no means consistently followed the principles of the *raison d'état*. Here again the tradition of Richelieu, Mazarin, and Colbert had been broken by Louis XIV. Rather than remaining content with securing France behind strategically advantageous, fortified frontiers, Louis had drifted into an endless search for glory and prestige. Not the interests of the state, but added brilliance and renown for the royal arbiter of Europe had become the goal of his ambitions. A policy of prestige replaced the policy of valid national interest. The outcome was a serious depletion of the nation's energies from which France continued to suffer for decades.

Here again Frederick sought to go beyond the French model. Like Louis he was possessed by an extraordinarily strong desire for glory, the most characteristic expression of this drive being perhaps found in the words with which he himself, in the *Histoire de mon temps,* described the commencement of his reign: "Ambition, the opportunity for gain, the desire to establish my reputation—these were decisive, and thus war became certain." More than once he claimed "that the principle of aggrandizement is the fundamental law of every government," and that "the passions of the rulers have no restraint other than the limits of their powers." But he did not let the matter rest with these statements. The bitter experiences of the early years of his reign and of his first campaigns taught him to curb his temperament, and to place the needs of the state above personal ambition. "Princes necessarily possess ambition," he wrote in his *Political Testament* of 1752, "but this ambition must be wise, moderate, and enlightened by reason." He was prevented from naïvely trusting the blind instinct for power by the period's humanitarian ideals of the responsible state, by his genuine feeling for the horror inherent in any war, by recognition of the limits of his strength, and, above all, by his overwhelming need to achieve rational clarity in all aspects of life. He combined extreme psychic élan, a driving desire for power, the gift of making rapid decisions with sober, ruthless analysis, unaffected by any doubt and undeterred by any question. It is this remarkable union of qualities which seems to provide the essential clue to his political achievement. Throughout his life, certainly, he concerned himself with the question of how to reconcile such opposites as reason and passion, freedom and constraint, morality and politics, ideals of the common good, and the hard demands of national power. How far may the ruler's ambition and wish for conquest surge unchecked by considerations of policy and by attention to the people's welfare? Where lies the demarcation line between the interests of the state and simple longing for prestige? What are the limits to the statesman's obligation to be honest and to keep faith in political negotiations? How can the political reputation of the state be preserved, and how its vital interests? These are recurring themes of his political theory and his political practice. Together they form a serious attempt to fit the political realities of the absolute state into as rational a system as possible, and despite its many imperfections in thought and action it is an impressive attempt. In this field, too, Frederick developed the traditions of French absolutism to their logical conclusion.

Much the same may be said of his role in the expansion of the crown's power within the state. Here it was above all necessary to suppress the opposition of the feudal nobility and to establish a central government of unshakable authority. Louis XIV's rule had prospered by putting an end, in highly dramatic struggles, to the nobility's aimless factionalism. France was liberated from permanent civil war, a firm system of justice was imposed on the entire country; the old, powerful aristocracy became politically paralyzed. By force and seduction it was transformed into a servile court society, whose existence magnified the luster of the sun king without greatly interfering in his political designs. The instruments that had gained the crown this position were copied throughout Europe. We have already listed the most important among them: a standing army supported by regular taxes made available by a well-organized financial bureaucracy; royal courts administering the law in orderly hierarchies of jurisdiction and appeal; control over the state church. Added to these were sophisticated tariff and economic policies, a kind of state capitalism, which by providing impetus to trade and industry was designed to increase the nation's wealth. But the system of royal absolutism was not pursued to its full, logical conclusion. The nobility was now politically impotent, but to the exasperation of the bourgeoisie it continued to insist on social precedence, and retained significant remnants of its old dominance in rural France. Most damaging of all, it was condemned to lead a useless, dronelike existence, unable to justify its social superiority by significant achievements for the state. In Brandenburg–Prussia, on the contrary, the petty nobility, with its code of honor and the inherited capacities of an age-old elite, was mobilized by the crown for the royal service in army and administration. In Prussia the nobility became the firmest, indeed the absolutely essential, support of the monarchy. But, to be sure, in Prussia too it could not be the aim of the absolutist system, nor did it lie within its means, to take away the nobility's privileged position and to level all social distinctions.

The organization of the royal bureaucracy in France also remained incomplete, at least when measured by the standards of later times. The heads of the judiciary retained a good measure of independence, which they now and then exploited politically. In all areas of administration, the crown's executive power was limited by the purchase of offices and the leasing of sovereign rights to financial entrepreneurs; nor was the ancient coexistence of royal and feudal authority completely abolished. The internal administrative unity of the realm was far from having been radically carried through. Finally, France's economic and financial policies, whose course Colbert had masterfully mapped out, remained at a halfway point. A full development of the economic potential was first rendered impossible by the extensive campaigns of Louis XIV; under his successors the country's financial administration was at times carried on frivolously and even wastefully, or brought into confusion by the massive burdens of later wars.

By contrast, the manner in which—since the reign of Frederick William I—the officialdom of Brandenburg–Prussia had been molded into a completely acquiescent, orderly, and effective instrument of the crown, appears in its essential characteristics as progressive. To be sure, even here a genuinely rational, centralized administrative organization was not achieved. But at least supreme leadership of internal as well as external affairs rested in the hands of the king personally, not with numerous agencies and boards as was the case in Paris under the successors of Louis XIV. That the entire state administration found its ultimate unity in the person of the monarch signified, so to speak, the extreme rational consequence, the acme, of the absolutist system. In the great and powerful French monarchy such an arrangement would have been dangerous and in practice unworkable: dangerous in view of the personalities of the last Bourbons, and also because the pressures for economy and for the careful and frugal management of government affairs that existed in small and poor Prussia were not present in France; unworkable in practice, because this type of administrative structure could be effective only in relatively simple, circumscribed conditions. Frederick's successor already found the system unmanageable.

But even more important politically than the Prussian ruler's administrative leadership was his position at the head of his army.

The monarchy of Louis XIV was a court monarchy of the grandest type; Frederick and his father were soldier-kings. Louis permitted his marshals to fight his wars for him; he reserved to himself only the glory of brilliant but minor and carefully prepared engagements. The Prussian king personally led his troops in the field; he shared the discomforts of their life on active service, and he fought his own battles. If Frederick William I, according to the mature judgment of his son, possessed the military talents of a competent regimental commander, Frederick II himself was a master of strategy and tactics. And with this we come to the factor that gave Frederick's reign its worldwide significance. Really great political success can be achieved only when political and military genius work hand in hand. Alexander, Hannibal, Caesar, the great emperors of the Middle Ages, Cromwell, Napoleon—all were at the same time statesmen and soldiers. Bismarck, in the long run, would have remained unsuccessful without Moltke. Frederick the Great triumphed because he combined in his person all the courage, daring, and military expertise that could be found in Prussia. If the system of personal absolutism was to reach classic completion it required this union of all royal talents in one man.

2

The Brandenburg-Prussian Heritage

IN BROAD STROKES we have outlined the part Frederick played in the history of European absolutism. But the unprecedented novelty of his personality and rule, the breathless excitement he created, can be understood only when we consider him in the framework of German conditions. The German context will also explain the harsh and seemingly irreconcilable antagonism between his father and himself, which so embittered Frederick's youth. We must study Frederick's ideological heritage, the concepts and methods of German Protestant rule, whose barriers he was suddenly to break down.

During the fifteenth and sixteenth centuries the territorial dominions of the German dynasties had developed painfully and slowly into statelike structures. Most of these ruling families had only lately risen from the rank of second-class vassalage to princely dignity. Since the emperors had broken up nearly all the ancient dukedoms, grandiose provincial concentrations of power no longer existed, as they did in France, where the splendor of the Burgundian court far outshone that of the king. In petty quarrels with monasteries, vassals, towns, and neighbors over this claim or that title-deed, the German princes accumulated their patrimony—by force or cunning, feuds or litigation, by marriage, alliances, or testamentary contracts. For many generations the internal history of Germany seemed to dissolve into chaos, with bickering noble families fighting private wars that were devoid of any higher political aim. But in the long run this continuous feuding helped to create something akin to political self-awareness, at least among the greater principalities. The concepts of the indivisible territorial state and of irrevocable princely sovereignty gradually developed, sustained by a new, juridically trained civil service.

With the reforms of the fifteenth century, which strengthened the means for maintaining internal peace and created imperial agencies—particularly the Imperial Cameral Tribunal—for the legal settlement of disputes, feuding gradually declined. Besides, since the replacement of the feudal host by the mercenary and the firearm, waging war had become very expensive. The Religious Peace of Augsburg of 1555 spelled the end to feuding, even if it did not halt religious strife. The wild fighting cocks of the past were succeeded by a generation of peaceful princes, advised by councillors learned in the law, who showed greater concern for the careful preservation of inherited rights and properties than for daring adventures in pursuit of new acquisitions. The princes lacked the means for great undertakings even when, as occasionally happened, common interests led them to form an alliance against the emperor.

The course of the Schmalkaldic War and the fate of the Protestant party during the first decade of the Thirty Years' War proved that in the long run the Habsburg imperium possessed greater endurance. Whoever wanted to get ahead, whoever was prepared to add to his power by further weakening the structure of the old empire, had to make his services available to foreign potentates. It actually became legal to do so after the Peace of Westphalia granted members of the Imperial Diet full sovereignty as well as an almost unlimited right to form alliances. To be sure, this right was useful only to the larger principalities and only in times of major European crises. Most German petty princes remained peaceful and withdrawn, intent only upon developing their territories and increasing their incomes.

A good share of a prince's government was expended on nurturing his personal estate, caring for its conservation and growth, and defending it by legal measures. In addition, the prince strove to extend his ecclesiastical and judicial sovereignty. Clerical administrators and judicial councillors formed the core of every princely government. The welfare of the subjects' souls took precedence over all other duties. A Christian ruler's foremost obligation was to maintain the true faith among his people, to safeguard decency and respectability throughout the land through cruel, punitive laws. Furthermore he was to see that all classes obtained their "proper nourishment and necessities," according to merit and custom, without suffering from usurious prices; yet none were to be idle and wasteful. Peace, law, and order were to rule in the land. If the prince neglected these duties, if he indulged in excessive luxury, if there were the danger that he might swerve from the true Christian faith or plunge into foreign ventures, his loyal Estates would humbly remind him of his "obligations and duties to the country's common needs and necessities." There was a close connection between the rise of these Estates, which controlled the purse strings, and the peacefulness of the German princes. The princes' traditional sources of income, dating from the Middle Ages, had long since ceased to cover the monetary needs of court and administration; they could not manage without taxes and loans granted by the Estates.

The moral and intellectual influences of the Reformation led in the same direction. Luther had reminded the princes of the early Christian view that rulers are only God's officers and taskmasters, directly responsible to Him for all they do and fail to do, and he stirred their consciences so powerfully that the idea had acquired new and greater strength. Political life in Germany, the country of the semireligious imperium, had always possessed a more pronounced religious character than it did elsewhere. The Reformation deepened this trait. The Imperial Diets of the sixteenth century echoed and reechoed with theological disputes; at the same time concern for the pure word of God became the most important object of the princes' domestic policies. Without the cooperation of the secular authorities, the new Protestant church could never have organized itself. Inevitably, the church fell into the hands of the princes' jurists. Conversely, the Protestant theologians, though possessing no political ambitions of their own, had a profound effect on the political life of the country. Their preaching of Christian love set a limit to crude power politics. To wage war merely to extend dynastic power, without urgent reasons of justice or indeed self-preservation, seemed to them as much of a sin as it had to their predecessors, the scholastic theologians of the Middle Ages. Even the struggle against the reactionary Catholicism of Charles V had given the Wittenberg reformers serious pangs of conscience. As a result German governments followed a path very different from that of the West European dynasties with their unrestrained lust for power, let alone that of the Italian tyrants of the age of Machiavelli.

Only a very few German rulers of the sixteenth century remind us by their behavior that this, after all, was the Renaissance: among them is Maurice of Saxony, a ruthless power politician, and Otto-Henry of the Palatinate, the patron of a modern, purely secular culture. Far more common, however, was the type exemplified by Christoph of Württemberg—the "praying prince"—who would not go boar hunting without his court preacher so that he might dispute with him on delicate points concerning holy communion. Even the seventeenth century still saw many representatives of this type, particularly in Lutheran regions. The heroic figure of Gustavus Adolphus stands out in curious contrast to his German allies and coreligionists. He was driven to despair by their political passivity, especially that of the more prominent among them—George William of Brandenburg, and John George, Elector of Saxony, the so-called "Beer George," whose zeal in matters of the pure faith coexisted easily with extreme drunkenness and personal cowardice. Nobler personalities could certainly be found among the German rulers. But on one point most of them were alike, namely, in that never-ending desire for neutrality characteristic of the weak, who, fearing the great world with its rapid changes and risks, preferred to entrust the management of their affairs to God, and were content to educate their subjects in the love of God, honesty, and the true faith.

The ideal for this generation of princes was Duke Ernest the Pious of Coburg-Gotha, personally brave, conscientious, hardworking, and eager to improve the economy of his land, but politically powerless. His principles of government are faithfully mirrored in the treatise *Vom teutschen Fürstenstaat,* which his chancellor, Veit Ludwig von Seckendorf, published in 1656. The state is depicted as a vast private property, principal and income of which are carefully managed by the ruler, who seeks to increase and protect them against foreign avarice, without violating his obligations as vassal toward emperor and empire, and without forcibly abrogating the traditional rights and "liberties" of the nobility and burghers making up his Estates. In short, he protects rather than destroys the old feudal traditions! By an exemplary, pious life he best preserves the true religion and serves the glory of God. He will take up arms only in the most dire need. Even when his established rights are attacked he will think thrice before defending himself by force, "since to do so is a dangerous thing, which must be gingerly handled; particularly in such times as our own, cautious methods should be employed."

After the horrors of the Thirty Years' War the rule of the true Christian prince was seen in Germany as one strictly limited by the precepts of Christian morality and by positive law. The era of wild, fratricidal power struggles seemed finally a thing of the past; German life appeared thoroughly pacified, its tranquility closely hedged about by a thousand frontiers. The German people became accustomed to grateful reverence for the hereditary fathers of the country, who worked so eagerly to remove the debris of the great war, to revive agriculture, commerce, and trade, and who kept at a safe distance the ever-recurring fury of wars kindled by the major European powers. The peaceful subject hardly noticed that all the while the German Empire as a whole was decaying, that more and more territories on its borders were falling under foreign control, that the honor traditionally surrounding the German name among the nations of Europe was dimming, that German culture—almost suffocating in provincial narrowness and poverty—was now far outshone by the rising star of France. The memory of a proud common past uniting all German tribes under the forceful leadership of national kings, the Emperors of the West, was sinking into oblivion.

During those long generations of internal peace broken only by occasional outside disturbances, especially in the border regions, the Germans were gradually turned into nonpolitical, peaceful folk, loyal and servile populations of petty states, whose educated classes were much more inclined to think and feel in international than in German terms. Not until Brandenburg–Prussia rose to become a major power was this peace destroyed, and the nation swept from idyllic quiescence into the dangerous, glorious sphere of world affairs.

At first the Electorate of Brandenburg did not substantially differ from its neighbors, the petty Lutheran principalities of northern

Germany. Even the father of the Great Elector in no respect rose above the average Protestant princeling of the seventeenth century. The fragmentation of Hohenzollern possessions over the whole of northern Germany did provide a certain incentive to acquire more land, in order to round off territory; but Frederick the Great was the first to consider territorial aggrandizement as a geopolitical necessity and turn it into a clearly understood and deliberately pursued political aim. To be sure, the diplomacy of Frederick William, the Great Elector, appears far less scrupulous and restrictive than that of most contemporary princes. Yet fundamentally his were the usual methods: he rendered services to foreign potentates in order to rise with their aid. The only difference was that in contrast to the west and south German princes the peculiar geographic location of his core territories enabled the ruler of Brandenburg to change his alliances rapidly, and this flexibility in his loyalties and alliances permitted him a measure of political independence, or at least freedom to maneuver.

For their future it was also important that the Hohenzollern had since 1613 belonged to the Reformed Church, while most of their subjects remained Lutheran. This was conducive to a certain detachment from confessional strife, to a disavowal of the type of politics that fanatical court preachers had for decades successfully advocated in other states. But we must be careful not to overrate the practical implications of these facts. The religious policy of the Great Elector was not yet tolerant in the modern sense, that is, neutral between the confessions. Its Calvinist basis continued to be fairly apparent. His foreign policy, too, despite its greater flexibility, continued to be based on Protestant values and interests. Above all, the Great Elector remained firmly convinced that princely rule was not identical with the enjoyment of power, but was an office entrusted to the sovereign by God, who would demand an account of its use. Frederick William was far from completely renouncing the patrimonial, dualistic concept of the state.

It was not until the last decades of the seventeenth century that the effectiveness of the old Protestant ethic faded in Germany. By the turn of the century most German courts had become highly secularized. For the sake of brilliant political achievements, ambitious princes like Ernest August of Lüneburg–Hanover and

Frederick August II of Saxony did not hesitate to renounce the faith of their fathers. But what succeeded the old German probity and piety was not so much a new free spirit of secular culture that could vie with the progress of West European—particularly English—aristocratic society, but the partly frivolous, partly barbaric style of despots bent on enjoying themselves. They abused their power to exploit their subjects and to live in ostentatious splendor, in an excess of pomp that cannot be justified even by the most beautiful of the many palaces they built. The moral inhibitions of old fell away; their place was taken not by realistic and determined power politics, but by a superficial, often grotesque imitation of French claims of universal sovereignty, which revealed the hollowness of upstarts lacking any political understanding. The absolutism of these petty princes did not emerge from hard struggles for the pacification of the country, as had happened in France, but was solely the product of an exaggeration of the old traditions and rights of the patriarchal ruler. The luster of their courts was not created by glorious achievements in war and diplomacy, but by pure presumption. What these princes copied from Louis XIV was not his legislation—which was scarcely relevant given the limited means of the German principalities—but the pomp of his palatial architecture, the pageantry of his court festivals and ceremonial, of his dancing masters, opera singers, and mistresses.

Even the court of the first Prussian king, Frederick I, hardly rose above this level. It is true that Charlottenburg, the "court of the muses" of the gifted queen, Sophie Charlotte, served such distinguished minds as Leibniz as a refuge of independent, secular culture. Frederick I, with his vast building schemes and love of display, was fortunate to have discovered in Andreas Schlüter an architect of genius. At the newly founded University of Halle, where Thomasius taught, the first buds of the German Enlightenment began to appear. But the king himself and his intimate circle were not affected by the deeper intellectual trends of the new age. Blinded by the glitter of Versailles, Frederick I remained frozen in the forms of stale fashion, and could not move beyond a superficial imitation of royal ceremonial untouched by genuine dignity. His policies, domestic as well as foreign, offer a spectacle of pathetic weakness coupled with great pretenses and claims—entirely in accord with those of the average German prince of his day. Some of his advisors on foreign relations showed much intelligence and knowledge in their evaluation of international affairs; we may even say that on the whole they succeeded fairly well in guiding the state through grave dangers. But the king himself lacked any trace of genuine statesmanship. The same insubstantiality marked other areas of his reign. The promising beginnings of the philosophy of the Enlightenment in Prussia soon withered to decline into trite philistinism. Not until the days of Frederick the Great would German thought attain qualities of creativity and originality.

It was the personal accomplishment of Frederick William I that at the critical moment Prussia turned away from the seductions of French megalomania to seek the goal that the Great Elector had first advocated: to become a real power in Europe, self-sufficient and independent, and in this way to serve as the model for all of Germany.

Much like the absolute rulers of France, the Great Elector had begun the process of reshaping the state by changing his military instrument. In the upheavals that shook Europe, he needed a standing army to maintain his rule over the far-flung, fragmented territories of the Electorate. To support this force he overcame the resistance of his Estates, and secured for himself once and for all the necessary financial resources. This was only the first step. The new financial administration, originally established after the Dutch example, developed into the core of an altogether new form of governmental organization. In the course of time an extensive civil service came into being, whose spirit was hostile to the old dualistic traditions. His grandson, Frederick William I, who imposed a highly rational organization on this administration, and forced old and new state agencies into one unified, efficient authority, succeeded in increasing the army to such an extent that the ruler of Brandenburg–Prussia suddenly became far superior in strength to all other German princes. At the same time he was able to compel the now politically impotent nobility to serve him in the army and the civil administration, and to raise his own authority to the level of true sovereignty—that is to say, to absolute power.

Thus the military monarchy he left to his son was no longer the old dualistic state of the seventeenth century, an awkward construction in which the feudal privileges of the provincial Estates were loosely joined to the fragmented sovereign rights of the crown, but rather a well-organized whole: a modern, absolutist state, in which only the will of one man mattered. The Prussian army was not solely intended for court functions and parades, nor was it any longer simply a mercenary force, available—as in so many German principalities—to any foreign power. The army had become the core of the state. The entire monarchy has been called —with some exaggeration—an armed camp in the midst of peace. It would be idle to seek the essential reasons for this singular political development in the pressure of concrete necessity: the great external threats to the dispersed territories, the practical experiences gathered in the Northern War and the War of the Spanish Succession, the various failures of Frederick I's alliance and subsidy policies, which Crown Prince Frederick William observed at first hand. Certainly all these influenced his determination steadily to increase the military establishment. But in fact, an army of 80,000 men in a state of two and a half million inhabitants went far beyond purely defensive needs, and even the Great Elector had more often extricated himself from critical situations by diplomatic means than by war.

There can be no doubt that the military monarchy of Frederick William was a highly personal, deliberate, and in a sense artificial creation: the work of a strange, half-barbaric, but enormously strong personality. The oddest thing about him was that he created this modern power instrument without the slightest inclination or aptitude for modern power politics. Within the borders of his state, to be sure, he tolerated no limits to his authority: "I must be served with life and limb, with house and wealth, with honor and conscience, everything must be committed except eternal salvation— that belongs to God, but all else is mine." But this uncontrolled will to dominate knew nothing of the enjoyment of power that characterized the Renaissance tyrants and French monarchs, instead it consumed itself in boundless and energetic zeal in the service of the great machine of the state. He had even less feeling for the glory and pride of conquest, or for the demand of secular power that its vital interests be ruthlessly pursued in the conflict of nations. Naïvely he clung to the traditional concepts of duty and

"Christian rulership." In contrast to his predecessor, Frederick I, he was again the old-fashioned German Protestant father of his country, full of anxious and pedantic scruples in foreign affairs, full of eager concern for the morality and spiritual welfare of his subjects —although, living in the Age of Pietism, he lacked the older period's pronounced interest in theological dogma. In spite of its absolutist traits his concept of the state was anything but modern. Basically he regarded the whole state as a kind of benefice of the House of Hohenzollern—the view taken by the princes of the sixteenth century. He was so far removed from the ideological main current of his age that he deprived the most significant representative of the German Enlightenment, the rationalist philosopher Wolff, of his professorship at Halle and drove him from the state on pain of death.

Nothing expresses his mentality more clearly and directly than his *Political Testament* of 1722. He begins with the urgent admonition to his heir that he "ought to look to God, and keep no mistresses—or to give them their proper name, whores—and lead a godly . . . pure life." Comedies, operas, ballets, masquerades, and dances are not to be tolerated in the realm, because these "are godless and devilish, and increase the temple and kingdom of Satan." His finances he should "manage himself and the command of his army control himself, and these two chief concerns retain in his own hands," for "a ruler who wishes to govern honorably in the world must manage all his affairs alone, and therefore rulers have been chosen for a life of labor and not for a weak, lazy woman's existence." Like the owner of a great estate, who wishes to describe to his heir the various sections of his property and their income, he acquaints the crown prince with the land and the people, discussing first the nobility of the different provinces and the royal domains, then the finances of the state, the condition of the army, and the senior "royal servants," that is to say, the ministers and their personalities; further he talks of the general principles of judicial and ecclesiastical administration, of industry and trade, and similar matters. The grim zealousness that drove this man to raise his dynasty to true power and fame is apparent. But the principles of foreign policy that he puts forward are on the whole still those of the respectable, pious principalities of older times: all just aims of the House of Brandenburg must be supported, namely, the maintenance of all legitimate claims of succession, "which belong to our House by law and before God." On the other hand, he urgently and repeatedly warns against "unjust" wars: "Pray to God and never engage in an unjust war," for God deserts an unrighteous cause, as many examples from ancient and recent history show, and at the Last Judgment He will call to account those that spilled blood unjustly. The army must be constantly increased; not in order to be committed lightly in the great conflicts of the world, but primarily to enable Brandenburg–Prussia to appear as a "formidable" force in the midst of the great powers: "for whoever holds the balance in the world will be able to profit thereby." The Prussians should march only in the most extreme crisis: "if your army is abroad the tax returns will be reduced to less than a third; prices will fall, rents will not be fully paid, and there will be total ruin." Therefore one should seek to hire foreign troops to carry out the military obligations toward the Empire; one's own should be kept at home; friendship and peace should be observed with one's neighbors, whenever possible; under no circumstances should one enter into an alliance with France against the Empire, for that would transgress against the loyalty a vassal owes his emperor.

It was according to these principles that Frederick William actually conducted his foreign affairs. His loyalty to the Austrian dynasty was never seriously shaken, despite all his angry scolding about the ingratitude of the Habsburgs. Grave disappointments might push him closer to France, but never into a diplomatic conspiracy against the head of the Empire. On the whole he observed a fearful immobility in the midst of the great European alliances and their constant shifts—maneuvers that he regarded, with as much suspicion as helplessness, as "diplomatic buffoonery" and "devil's work." All the while the Potsdam soldier-king was being duped mightily by the clever policies of Vienna.

From this background of frightened, tame, and basically provincial attitudes of the Brandenburg Electorate, Frederick's genius rises one day, suddenly, unexpectedly, with an unbridled will to achieve universal glory. The story of his youth is the story of a bitter conflict between father and son. Originating in purely personal differences, their conflict eventually develops into an encounter between an old and a new epoch in the life of Brandenburg-Prussia.

3

The Development of
Frederick's Personality

i. Youth

THE STORY of Frederick's youth is known as a chronicle of suffering: psychological mistreatment and eventually physical abuse by his basically well-meaning but overly severe father; the tormented boy's desperate attempt to escape; his imprisonment at Küstrin; the threat of being sentenced to death; the execution before his eyes of his closest friend and ally in the escape; the boy's emotional collapse, followed by repentance, soul-searching, and finally submission to the will of the father. This, in outline, is the traditional picture.

Evaluation and interpretation of these events have varied. Humanitarian accusations against the brutal father, who could not comprehend his refined, intellectual son were followed by a more political view of the conflict. His mother, a princess of the Guelph House, had entangled the crown prince in highly dangerous intrigues of the English–Hanoverian dynasty against the policy of amity with the Habsburgs pursued by Frederick William and his minister, Grumbkow. The king's mailed fist was required to destroy this network of confusion, to guard the authority of the crown against all court machinations, and to save his immature son from committing high treason. Seen in this light, the terrible violence of the king's anger appears almost as an act of calculated political wisdom.

In the final analysis both views are one-sided. We should not overestimate the musical and literary interests of the young prince; basically they were little more than playful expressions of youthful energy, lacking discipline and clear direction. Nor can Frederick be said to have adhered to a particular political course in those early years. On the other hand, the father's blind rage and pedagogic folly can be denied as little as the inadequacy of his intellect when measured against the rich natural gifts of his son. The antagonism of these two personalities cannot be understood in purely political terms; but it is equally impossible to interpret their conflict simply as a family quarrel, devoid of political overtones. To us the struggle is important above all for what it reveals about the basic traits of the crown prince.

The starting point of the conflict was undoubtedly the political and personal animosity of the parents toward each other, into which their two eldest children—Frederick, born on 24 January 1712, and his favorite sister Wilhelmina, born three years earlier—were drawn at an early age. In northern Germany the Hanoverian dynasty, to which Queen Sophie Dorothea belonged, was the most envious rival of the House of Brandenburg. It had long been the ambition of the Guelphs to outdo Berlin in courtly pomp and cultural refinement, and their pride had increased since they had fallen heir to the British crown, whose brilliance far outshone that of the newly created royal dignity of the Hohenzollern. Though she lacked genuine education, Sophie Dorothea had come from Hanover with expectations that the military court of Frederick William could never fulfill. A true princess of the Baroque age, given the name Olympia because of her dignified and stately appearance—in later years especially wide chairs had to be constructed for her—she deeply regretted the absence of the stiff ceremonial, the great fêtes, the whole heavy pomp of her native court. She suffered from her husband's bad manners, and found his wild hunting parties as repellent and barbarous as his gluttony, his drinking sessions, and the crude jokes he enjoyed with his disgusting court-jester Gundling and his soldier-cronies in the Tobacco College.

The king, on the contrary, so much disliked the atmosphere of contemporary court life that he dressed the Berlin convicts in ceremonial wigs and laced hats, and in 1721 abolished court dress in favor of military uniforms of rough domestic cloth. He himself sat over his files wearing an apron and half sleeves to protect his uniform coat. The queen felt completely out of place in the company of this man, whose fits of anger and frequent quarreling made her life doubly difficult. She breathed easily only when he left on one of his inspection tours, and made the most of these opportunities by hastily improvising banquets and balls. Otherwise she was given to complaints and sneers and bitter outpourings about the family tyrant, whose zealous work, real abilities, and achievements she was unable to comprehend. At an early stage she disclosed her feelings to her children and naturally they were affected by this. Frederick was further influenced by Wilhelmina—a precocious, clever, but undoubtedly rather impertinent young lady. If we add to this the spying servants, gossiping ladies-in-waiting and governesses, and political schemers of all sorts, including no less a personage than the leading Minister Grumbkow himself, we can understand why the king did not trust his wife's apparent compliance and failed in his often touchingly awkward attempts to mold her and their fourteen children into an intimate and simple German family circle.

We must keep this atmosphere in mind if we wish to understand the psychological development of the young prince. Nothing would be less accurate than to picture him as a harmless, dreamy lad, or even as a youthful martyr of enlightened humanity and education. That he resisted his father's demand to live in strict preparation for his future reign was the natural reaction of youth. But in this environment his resistance became presumptuous stubbornness; it turned into egotism, precocious mockery and comfortable indolence in the secret knowledge that he was, after all, superior to his scolding, constantly angry father. Nothing is better suited to destroy the child's natural respect for his elders than the spectacle of uncontrolled temper. The less Frederick William was able to hide his emotions from others, the more the crown prince learned to do so. If we ask what character traits first became recognizable in the behavior of the adolescent boy, we discover above all an amazingly stubborn self-assurance, ambition which could not be deflected by any humiliation, the power to mask his feelings from others, and —to the seeming exclusion of any childlike openness—great cunning in getting his way.

Even as a boy Frederick differed strikingly from most of his contemporaries, and from his younger brothers and sisters, and almost more than anything else the impossibility of discovering "what goes on in this little head" angered and frightened the father. At times Frederick showed great mastery in using theological arguments to hide his opposition. Although he was closely watched he succeeded in secretly assembling a great library of French literature in a house in Berlin—less for serious study than for occasional dabbling. Since his state visit in 1728 to the opulent Dresden court he had acquired a taste for elegant clothes, musical scores, and other luxuries, all leading to debts, whose full extent he never dared acknowledge to his father. Instead he had the English government quietly advance him the money—demanding, incidentally, almost twice the amount that he actually needed. In return he promised that he would marry no one but his British cousin—contrary to the will of his father, who did not want this elegant family connection at the cost of changing Prussia's alliances.

It was almost inevitable that Frederick William should interpret his son's taste for luxury as voluptuous, dandified modishness copied from Dresden. He saw Frederick's aversion to the Potsdam barracks manner, the wild hunts, the crudity of the Tobacco College as symptoms of weakness and effeminacy. Repeatedly the king warned against "unmanly, lascivious, female occupations, highly unsuited to a man." He was convinced that like so many young princes his son was about to sink into a lazy and depraved existence. A sixteen-year-old daughter of a school principal in Potsdam attracted Frederick by her beautiful voice, and received some small presents from him. Although her innocence was established, the king had her whipped in public, and then locked into a workhouse. Actually the crown prince had no taste at all for being a spendthrift, dandy, or woman chaser. He went into debt because there was no other way in which he could satisfy his desires; as soon as he had full control over his income he proved himself to be as careful and economical a manager as his father. And what we are told of the prince's love affairs is based partly on court gossip, partly on the highly dubious boastings of the young man himself. About this side of his nature, which has always provoked much curiosity and sensationalism, there is in fact little of substance to report. Today we can say that Frederick's sexual life was in no way abnormal; but psychologically as well as physically his sexual needs were unusually limited.

In his relations with others the demands of the spirit, of a sharp, exceptionally vital mind, always in search of stimulation, generally outweighed the impulses of sentiment and sensuality. Up to a point this holds true even of the most tender of his friendships, the close familial bond with his sister Wilhelmina. From the outset their common intellectual interests played an important, stimulating role. Together they read forbidden books, performed duets, amused each other with malicious chatter and blurting out plain truths. Most other women simply bored Frederick. His need for masculine friendship was that much the greater. In his youth, to judge from some ecstatic letters, these friendships possessed a tender, even stormy character; but in these relationships, too, the requirements of the mind far outweighed the demands of emotion. Here lies the reason for his increasing loneliness in old age, when the friends of earlier days had disappeared, and the new generation could no longer enter into his intellectual world.

Frederick assuredly was not the rapturous "piper and poet" his father took him to be. It was scarcely accidental that in music he preferred the cool tone of the flute, a sound without hidden depths, to that of the violin. The large number of his flute compositions that survive—well over one hundred sonatas and concertos—clearly shows the type of music he liked to play. His compositions are models of sober school exercises, aiming at the proper variation of themes according to good Italian models. Their appeal lies not in sentiment but in the elegant play of figurations, runs, trills, and cadences, though now and then in the slow movements genuine feeling breaks through the stately development. Much the same may be said about his poems. No one will find Frederick's inner life adequately expressed in their conventional images, their derivative classicism and neatly tripping rhymes; but occasionally a verse does contain a few surprising lines that seem to spring from the depth of a passionate soul.

In Frederick's youth observers were particularly struck by the enchanting sound of his clear, modulated voice, and by the piercing gaze of his large, dark-blue eyes. Here was no gentle dreamer, but a wide-awake mind. People have often been astonished at the coolness with which this young man fought his father—his composure was indeed amazing. At the age of fourteen, during one of Freder-

ick William's illnesses the crown prince could coldly discuss the
prospects of an early succession to the throne with the French and
British ambassadors, and call upon their governments to support
his mother's political party. The information and assurances he
gave them were such that they did not dare include them in their
written dispatches. Even the letters he was able to smuggle to Wilhelmina from his cell in Küstrin, while awaiting court-martial, expressed only scorn for his judges. He was entirely unsentimental.
Certainly there was no need for his father to teach him how to be a
politician. Not that he was just unfeeling, matter-of-fact, ambitious,
and devoid of real need for affection. The expressions of friendship, of passionate sympathy for others, of emotional excitement
and conflict, which we possess from almost every stage of his life,
are too numerous and persuasive to justify such a view. Those who
dismiss these statements as insincere make the understanding of a
complex personality too easy for themselves. But there can be no
doubt that the innermost soul of this man was filled with a cold,
hard light. The young Frederick was not unfeeling, but there was
nothing demonstrative, warm, or good-natured about him. Even as
a child he lacked naïveté, frankness, and spontaneity. It is here,
perhaps, that he differed most from his environment. Possibly his
pronounced Latin inheritance, particularly strong on his mother's
side, helped detach him from the traditions of his dynasty, and
played a part in creating a sovereign with a completely different
outlook on life.

Individuals possessing such exceptional traits tend to be lonely,
and their close associates may find them difficult to fathom. Moreover, Frederick William possessed only the crudest and most primitive concepts for judging his fellow men. He thought that the boy's
failure to share his own pleasure in simple male companionship, in
carousing, and in the alcoholic delights of a true German bully betrayed a foreign, frenchified nature. How could someone like himself understand this young man, who was beginning to develop attitudes that had never before shown themselves in a German
prince? The slowness of Frederick's development to maturity made
a sound judgment even more difficult. The less the king understood his son and the less comfortable he felt with him, the more
violent became his educational methods. Just because he knew

himself to be secretly despised he resorted to brutal means to assert his parental authority, finally going so far as to slap his son or cane him in the presence of officers and servants. This treatment destroyed not only Frederick's last trace of confidence in his father, but also his unquestioning belief in dynastic power. The faith in the Godlike nature of kingship that infused the monarchs of the Baroque age could never take root with this upbringing. The mistreated boy learned more and more to think of himself as someone different and isolated, until he came consciously to oppose the traditions of his family.

We shall not trace the catastrophe of 1730 in detail—neither the inadequate, indeed childish, preparation and execution of the flight and its disastrous end; nor the link between these events and the schemes of English marriages for Frederick and Wilhelmina, which their mother had long championed; nor the influence exerted by the conflict between the Habsburg and English–Hanoverian factions at the Berlin court. Actually all these connections were insubstantial. Frederick knew that his escape would not be welcomed in England, since it destroyed all prospects of one day shifting Prussia's policies from the Habsburg alliance to the Anglo-Dutch course. Driven by despair, he acted without any assurance of foreign support—indeed, even against explicit British warnings—fleeing not as a traitor, but as a private emigrant. It was this knowledge that gave him his self-assurance and clear conscience at the trial. But he should have realized that, whether he liked it or not, a fugitive Prussian prince would be a figure of major political significance. Even worse, he had engaged in intrigues with the French and British ambassadors. For years he had exploited his potential political power by having them assist him in his financial difficulties. In spite of all extenuating circumstances, the disaster that befell him was not undeserved. Without question he had deserted.

Most significant about his court-martial was the unerring political instinct of the eighteen-year-old, who despite fear and confusion deciphered his father's real intentions, and cleverly opposed them. It is unlikely that Frederick William ever seriously meant to have his son shot for high treason. Politically it would have been a most dubious act. Apparently the king hoped that terror and the threat of death would lead Frederick to renounce his right to the throne in favor of a younger brother. The endless interrogation to which he subjected his son pointed in that direction. But after an inquisition of 178 parts concerning the details of the escape, Frederick was still able to reply with great diplomatic art when asked "whether he merited becoming a sovereign prince?" and "whether he was willing to renounce his claim in order to save his life?" His evasive answers to these decisive questions left full responsibility with the king. Later, when he had reason to fear life imprisonment, he showed himself prepared to renounce the throne. But as soon as he sensed that this punishment was never seriously considered he regained the courage and even the derisive arrogance he had shown during earlier interrogations. Only the unexpected execution of his friend Katte before his eyes—a sentence that the king imposed in defiance of the court—his inability to save his friend even at the cost of his own life, suddenly brought about Frederick's collapse. The direct presence of death finally broke his pride and his will.

He passed through a severe psychological crisis. For days he struggled against despair. In the end he decided to stop fighting fate and to feign submission to the will of his father. In reality—as became apparent soon after the catastrophe—he remained unchanged, except that his taciturnity and reserve grew even more pronounced.

The traditional and widely accepted historical interpretation has it that after the king's pardon, Frederick underwent a change of heart. Engaged in administrative duties in the Küstrin provincial government, taking part in the work of the Prussian administration, he learned to admire the great material achievements of his father, and their official reconciliation was soon followed by a genuine meeting of minds. But matters were not that simple.

The introduction of the prince to the practical business of the Küstrin war-and-domain chamber, and his administrative training under the guidance of its intelligent and learned director, Hille, was undoubtedly of some benefit. The first letter the king addressed to him after his pardon might also have had some effect: he should now learn from the course of public business that the ruler himself must understand all details of administration so as not to be dependent on his officials. Once the disdainful stubbornness of boyhood had melted, such warnings might meet with a better reception. At any rate, during the next years Frederick acquired an understanding of the problems of government. In particular the rehabilitation of East Prussia, laid waste by epidemics, seems to have made a strong impression on him. Later as king, Frederick referred to his father's internal policies with great admiration. With conspicuously strict conservatism he retained the administrative organization he inherited. But on no account should the change of his opinions be interpreted as a sign that he had passed through a period of contrition and soul-searching. Not deep remorse, but an indestructible, almost inexplicably tough spiritual strength is the dominant impression we gain even from this most critical personal tragedy of his life.

After Katte's execution, Frederick passed several days in theological dialogues with Chaplain Müller; scarcely in order to find spiritual solace in religion, but to persuade his father that he was sincere in his remorse and his religious "conversion"—a fact on which his future depended. He was prepared for every concession if it could save him from Katte's fate. Willingly he permitted himself to be instructed in the dangers inherent in the teachings of predestination concerning human freedom, which to his father's horror he had hitherto championed—without in reality abandoning them. Aside from that, he was particularly anxious to hear details of the last days and hours of his executed friend. His awareness that in the final analysis he bore responsibility for Katte's death was a terrible burden on his soul. But this responsibility was purely personal, not to be understood in religious terms, and it could never bring about a moral conversion of the kind his father expected. From childhood on Frederick had proved unreceptive to the terror and solace of Christian preaching. There is no evidence to lead us to believe that a change had taken place.

It is an essential aspect of Frederick's character that his highly developed self-assurance could not be shaken by any experience of personal inadequacy. For that reason he also wanted nothing to do with a search for religious salvation. His was an iron, unbending nature, which tenaciously held on to life and survived all tempests and disasters with amazing buoyancy. A few weeks after Katte's death he was again on top of things, "gay like a chaffinch," Hille reported. As host of a cheerful circle of secretly invited guests, he wrought daring plans for the future, when he would finally ascend the throne. He enlivened the sessions of the war-and-domain chamber of Küstrin with the humorous tone of his reports. With sovereign disdain he dealt with the subaltern lessons that his father had assigned to him—copying documents, estimating the budgets for estates, and other such affairs. He wrote comic verses about his superiors, the councillors of the provincial administration:

> La chambre et les commissaires
> qui font le métier des corsairs.

He considered their daily round of duties as little more than scribbling; later on he would have his servants take care of such insignificant matters. Yet that did not prevent him from learning his assigned tasks rapidly and with surprising thoroughness. But unlike his father's ambitions, his own did not lie in the economic sphere; the various projects for improved trade policies on which he worked for a time under Hille's guidance could not fully satisfy him. The earliest stirrings of his political imagination of which we know concerned instead great deeds in foreign affairs.

Plans of this type are developed in an extraordinary letter that Frederick wrote to his trusted chamberlain, von Natzmer, in February 1731. In a manner characteristic of Frederick's maturity, this early statement already links an ambitious, daring imagination to realistic arguments. It is a preview of the political musings contained in his later political testaments when we read that Prussia must seek to enlarge her territories, not according to whims or accidental historic traditions, but by following a systematic plan. Her situation in the center of Europe is threatened from many directions, her territories are badly fragmented. But for these reasons true statesmanship will not remain on the defensive: "he who does not advance, retreats." In a systematic development Prussia must seek to enlarge her territory so that her scraps of land are firmly connected. Therefore, the most important goals are Polish Prussia (West Prussia) and Swedish Pomerania (Lower Pomerania). Their acquisition would bring the greatest military and economic advantages. Mecklenburg, which by inheritance would one day fall to the House of Brandenburg, would round off the state; as would Julich and Berg, possession of which would make possible the defense of Cleve and Mark.

Frederick claims to be speaking "only as a statesman"—without considering the legal justifications, which to be sure, are essential (as means to an end, it seems). In the final analysis the "political necessity" of conquest is always decisive. Prussia must "seek major goals, and leave minor ones aside." Then the King of Prussia might one day "cut a fine figure among the great powers of the world, and play a significant role." Then he would possess so much power that he could keep the peace, "not out of fear, but purely for love of justice," and only so long "as the honor of the dynasty and of the country permit it." "I wish for the Prussian state to raise herself out of the dust in which she has sunk, to bring the Protestant faith to flower in Europe and the Empire, to become the refuge of the oppressed, the shield of widows and orphans, the support of the poor, and the terror of the unjust." As long as obedience to God and the desire for justice suppress lack of faith, party strife, greed, and egotism, the state need not fear the anger of Heaven.

The utopian fantasies of the young prince reveal a mixture of influences: the traditional, knightly concepts of honor of the German rulers, the humanitarian ideals of the literature of the French Enlightenment, and even significant remnants of the old Protestant ideals of Christian authority. When he was twelve or thirteen years old, Frederick had cited at table a passage in Luther's pamphlet *Of Earthly Authority,* which dealt with God's pleasure at the reign of Solomon, whose name meant in German *"Friedrich* or peaceloving, he who ruled a peaceful realm." This sentiment is still distinctly echoed in 1731. But by then it is submerged by what strikes one as an overwhelming love for power which, confident of victory, bides its time.

This remarkable young man possessed seemingly inexhaustible sources of energy. His will to live and to reign broke through all the barriers of duty, work, and pedantically arranged routine, which his father continued to impose even after their reconciliation in August 1731. No sooner was he released from the fortress than Frederick began an elegant flirtation with the young and beautiful wife of a neighboring squire. In numerous French sonnets he declared his admiration; more out of joy in the triumphant impression made by his own glowing youth than out of genuine love. He wished to please, he wanted to be victorious. His indestructible optimism even survived a grave new violation by his father—the enforced engagement of the nineteen-year-old crown prince with a princess of Brunswick-Bevern, whom he did not love. An exceptionally distasteful political intrigue formed the background to this affair.

For years Frederick William's foreign policy had almost slavishly followed Habsburg leadership. The imperial ambassador, Count Seckendorff, who had served with Frederick William in the War of the Spanish Succession, was deep in the king's confidence, and was fully supported by Grumbkow, the first minister of state, whom a secret Austrian pension tied to the Habsburg interest. Both men opposed the British influence at court, which centered in the queen's entourage. Shortly before Frederick's flight the British government, using captured letters, had tried to unmask Grumbkow's treasonable activities and bring about his fall. The attempt failed, thanks to the king's repugnance for diplomatic intrigues; at the same time the failure rendered the prospects of Frederick's marriage to an English princess most unlikely. Under these circumstances, the prompt discovery of his attempt to escape constituted another triumph for the Austrian party. Now an English marriage was entirely out of the question, and efforts were redoubled to tie the son as well as the father firmly to imperial policy. Seckendorff managed to persuade Frederick that his pardon was due to the intercession of the emperor, to whom he thus owed a debt of gratitude. At the same time, Grumbkow forced himself on the prince as confidant, in part to secure his own position should a change of reigns occur. Since his imprisonment Frederick had been cut off from his mother and from British influence; to evade the constantly reawakening distrust of the king he was dependent on the minister's friendly counsel and offer to act as intermediary. Grumbkow further strengthened their relationship by passing on secret political information to satisfy Frederick's curiosity. Now exploiting Frederick's powerless situation, Grumbkow artfully maneuvered him into the hands of his crony Seckendorff. For some time the prince had received an imperial pension to improve his meager budget. If he were quickly bound by a suitable marriage he would be forever kept out of the nets of the British. To be sure, the bride was not to be a Habsburg princess, as Frederick himself wished for a time, but a member of the minor House of Brunswick, a niece of the Empress, whose marriage would leave Vienna uncommitted.

Frederick William placed himself completely in the hands of his advisors. With the English project out of the question, he was less concerned with the political than the personal aspects of the marriage. Above all his children were to be Prussians, nothing but Prussians, and therefore should not become politically obligated through foreign marriages. He saw Frederick's marriage primarily as a means of educating his son, of saving him from a disorderly life. He didn't bother himself much about the wise choice of a bride for such a singular and discriminating personality. The Brunswick princess was well trained and decently brought up— that was the main thing. "She is neither ugly nor beautiful—she is a God-fearing person, that is all, and she suits both you and her parents-in-law." And so he ordered his son to marry her.

The anger and despair caused by this decision need not be detailed. Not only did Frederick find the princess hard to bear: she was kind, but shy, provincial, docile, boring, anxious, and awkward—"she dances like a goose," he wrote after their first meeting —but it outraged his sense of freedom that on such an important issue he was subjected not only to prohibitions but to direct commands. And who could deny that an unconscionable game was being played with human beings? The wire-pullers in this intrigue themselves disclosed its ugliness when on the eve of the wedding they suddenly demanded that Frederick William break the engagement in favor of a connection with a British princess—because Vienna had come to hope for a British alliance, which this marriage might help bring about! That in the end Seckendorff's whole marriage policy turned out to be a bad miscalculation goes without saying.

There were times in the period leading up to the wedding when Frederick seemed close to complete despair. In the end the tenacity of his will to survive won out in this situation too. Without agreeing to the marriage he could never hope to escape from the "Küstrin galley." With icy self-control he forced himself to play the obedient son and happy bridegroom. His true feelings remained closely hidden. He tried to impress the old roués whose diplomatic intrigues had pushed him into this desperate situation with his cynicism. He made frivolous allusions to the manner in which he intended to conduct himself in this arranged marriage, and cracked malicious jokes about his bride, and about marriage in general.

These then were the fruits of his brutal upbringing and of the conflicts of his youth: he had been taught to dissimulate, to hide his feelings and thoughts. At no time had his experiences been able to break down his self-confidence. But he had lost his trust in people. He had learned to know the limits of his will, and to take account of circumstances that were beyond his control. Undoubtedly a man of his qualities would have been able to carry on the work of his father even if he had not gone through this hard school. But perhaps, without its discipline, his will might have expressed itself even more violently after his accession to the throne than it actually did. He might have become a gambler like Charles XII of Sweden—whose story he read with such enthusiasm as a boy—had he not learned to control himself, to become a cautious schemer and diplomat.

He was ready to cope with life. But whatever youthful naturalness he once possessed had been destroyed, while his penchant for cool, rational analysis had been strengthened and fully developed. Eventually the gay scoffer would turn into a bitter cynic; the intelligent observer of man would become contemptuous of mankind. No one can say how, given different circumstances, the warm, lovable side of his personality might have developed. His daemonic qualities, on the other hand, are revealed with exceptional clarity in the story of his youth. They would raise him to the heights of historical glory. But they would make him lonely, particularly among Germans.

ii: Rheinsberg and Sans Souci

FREDERICK'S unwanted marriage at least had the advantage of freeing him from the fortress and giving him his own household. At first his court was extremely modest. From 1732 on the crown prince resided in Neuruppin as colonel of a grenadier regiment, his days in the little garrison town barely filled with his regimental duties and various economic projects in the local war-and-domain chamber. He was carefully watched, his companions were limited to officers of the regiment, mostly rough fellows, unsophisticated and without education. For the time being his wife lived apart from him, in Schönhausen, a château that the king had given her. Gradually, by the careful execution of his duties, Frederick quieted the king's suspicions, though he never succeeded in removing them completely. His deepening military interests were an important factor in the improvement of their relationship. He had always had a military bent—an inheritance from his ancestors as well as a natural condition of his position. But he had repressed it out of stubborn resistance to the philistines in uniform whom he saw in his father's entourage, particularly in the Tobacco College, and out of distaste for the mindless drill that had made up his military education. Now his antipathies began to vanish. In 1734 he was permitted to accompany Eugene of Savoy, the most famous general of the age, on his campaign along the Rhine, a tour that awakened dreams of future generalship and military glory. Then on his return from the field it seemed that at last he was about to exchange his harsh apprenticeship for the plenitude of power.

On several occasions since 1730 Frederick William had fallen seriously ill with the dropsy. By the autumn of 1734 his condition appeared hopeless. Certain governmental matters were already being entrusted to the crown prince, who thought himself near the intensely desired goal of power; but an unexpectedly successful operation saved the king's life once more. For another five years Frederick William's bearlike constitution was to resist the repeated onslaughts of his incurable disease.

In confidential letters to his sister Frederick openly expressed his anger and disappointment at the turn of events which the "athletic health" of the king had brought about. He remained unreconciled to his father. To the end he resisted the latter's tyranny with deep hatred. And yet it was a kind fate that kept Frederick from taking over the reins of government before he had fully matured. It seems likely that under the press of affairs the harsh features of his personality would have hardened early, and that his rich psychic gifts would not have developed as fully as in fact they did. For only now, when he could expect his father's rule to continue for some years to come, did Frederick resolve to put aside his ambitious hopes for the time being. He sought relief in intensive study, in eager and even passionate devotion to learning and culture. The monotony of garrison duty came to be dispelled by the bright rays of enlightened humanity, which gradually opened to him new views of life and of the world.

Soon after his father's recovery the twenty-three-year-old prince launched upon a tremendous reading program. But he lacked sufficient independence until he was able to quit his bachelor existence in Neuruppin in August 1735 and settle with his wife in Rheinsberg. At his new court he gathered a company of intelligent and highly educated men; to someone whose education was as incomplete as Frederick's, their company proved to be priceless.

In the four years he lived at Rheinsberg, years not yet burdened with the vast concerns of government, he experienced all the happiness of which he was capable. To be sure, he continued to be under the surveillance of his suspicious father, who feared him as rival and successor. Their clashes never ceased entirely. Military reviews were precarious occasions and the annual weeklong visits to Potsdam and Wusterhausen were periods of horror, or at least of deadly boredom. Nevertheless, the king was obliged to recognize his son's achievements; his confidence in him gradually increased and with it Frederick's independence. An element of joy now entered the prince's life. Again and again during these years Frederick's natural optimism and the elasticity of youth dispelled all sorrows; they lent a gay note to his letters and transfigured the new community at Rheinsberg. The graceful late baroque château, its best sections the work of Frederick's friend Knobelsdorff, aptly expressed the psychological needs of the owner: a forbidding medieval keep is altered by the addition of Mediterranean arcades into a cheerful, harmonious structure. Its center is a concert room; on the ceiling Antoine Pesne's young Apollo, victoriously ascending through clouds, announces the coming of day, whose splendor vanquishes a world of dark shadows. In this newly created environment Frederick's sparkling intellectual vigor could fully unfold.

Frederick's life at Rheinsberg shows how completely Frederick William had mistaken his son's character. The court in no way emulated the self-indulgent debauchery that marked so many German reigns in the heyday of absolutism. The usual brutal excesses of hunting, drinking, and gambling were absent, as were the tasteless theatrical pomp and the mistresses of the fashionable Dresden court. The pleasures of Rheinsberg are diffused with the light of the spirit. They are characterized by masculine friendship, clever conversation, expertly played chamber music, and above all by constant reading. The four years at Rheinsberg form Frederick's great educational experience—that is their true significance. During this period the young officer, whose formal schooling was highly defective, developed into the best educated, most knowledgeable, and sophisticated prince in Europe.

This result could be attained only by enormous energy and application. Frederick's achievement is the more admirable since he had been deprived of nearly all the usual guidance. His formal instruction had been kept within modest limits, and had ended in 1727 on the day of his confirmation. The grand tour of the great European courts, the method of education most popular among his caste, and had been denied him, since his father considered such a voyage unecessary and even dangerous. Apart from the short incognito trips he was to take to Strassburg and Holland during his reign, Frederick never left Germany. He knew no cities outside Prussia besides Dresden and a few south German capitals, and on the whole his direct knowledge of people and societies remained limited to Prussia's provinces east of the Elbe. And yet the political writings of the crown prince already evince a high degree of judgment concerning the most important states of continental Europe, their strength, historical traditions, political principles, and the personalities of their leaders. The critical certainty that was still lacking he quickly gained in the first decade of his reign. Only the British Empire with its far-flung overseas interests remained a mysterious world that he could never entirely comprehend, but he knew the courts and the political conditions of the Continent much better than any grand tour could have taught him. Not travel nor the teaching of others but his own studies were the sources of his political expertise and of his general education.

At times during the years in Rheinsberg this program of studies must have been pushed to extremes of compulsive asceticism. From four in the morning until noon he would sit over books in his tower chamber, and in the evening he often continued reading beyond midnight; once he was even supposed to have attempted to forego sleep entirely. His literary interests knew no limit: classical and contemporary literature, history, philosophy, the natural sciences—all were devoured; the classical authors he read in French translation since his father had forbidden him to learn Latin. And he read pen in hand; he was involved in an extensive exchange of literary-philosophic letters with the best minds that were available to him—the well-educated Saxon diplomats Suhm and Manteuffel, and later Voltaire. Added to this was an almost uninterrupted, voluminous political correspondence with Grumbkow, who kept him informed on the most important developments in Prussia's foreign relations, and at times even sent him official files. Carefully Frederick prepared himself for his duties as ruler, inspired with the ambition to surprise the world with well-thought-out deeds as soon as he assumed power.

When we later come to survey the result of these years of study, our analysis will not be restricted to the period of Rheinsberg but will include Frederick's entire literary achievement. What he began at Rheinsberg he continued throughout his life, as much as time and energy permitted. It was his unchanging ambition to face the literary greats of his age not simply as an amateur but as an independent creator. He always sought to find in his own understanding the answers to the great questions posed by history, nature, and life, and to illuminate with the highest attainable measure of rational clarity the darkness that envelops the active man. Science, poetry, and art became essential elements of his existence. As much as in later years the practical duties of governing drove him into routine work—at times almost beyond human endurance—his scholarly and literary interests always retained their vitality. In the midst of administrative business, and even on campaign, he played his flute, lost himself in the works of great poets and philosophers, or transformed his ideas into graceful or pathetic verse. Especially on the eve of making major decisions he liked to escape and seek relief in the liberating realm of the muses.

The sociability of Rheinsberg also continued in later years, though its character changed. After his return from the first Silesian campaigns its setting was in one or the other of the newly built palaces in Potsdam, among them his favorite Sans Souci, the most beautiful of retreats. Here he repeated the light, brilliant decorations and the furnishings of the rooms dearest to him at Rheinsberg—the study and the library in the tower. But now his mode of life had changed. The royal dignity had elevated him above all men, even over his closest friends, his brothers, and other relatives. From the first day of his reign a vast distance separated him from his companions of Rheinsberg, the majority of whom were young officers, clever, experienced, fashionably educated, but lacking true political interests and professional training. If they had expected high positions and political influence they had all miscalculated. Frederick was as far removed from showing favoritism as from harboring misplaced gratitude and loyalty. Concrete achievements he rewarded, real abilities he exploited—but always according to strict standards of usefulness, without regard for personal feeling. The interest of the state came before everything, it even took precedence over supposed obligations to friends. Frederick knew very well that the absolute ruler is always in danger of becoming dependent on flatterers, gossips, and schemers of all sorts —and in defending himself against this threat he did not spare even his closest friends.

And so intimacy and trust disappeared between him and his old companions, some of the most superior of whom, incidentally, died during the early years of his reign. During the long wars he grew entirely estranged from his wife. His environment reverted to one of unrelieved masculinity. Elizabeth Christina never dared to enter the Potsdam palaces, while Frederick only reluctantly spent a few weeks each year, around Christmas, in the palace in Berlin. Even here he rarely appeared in public with his wife; he seemed almost like a stranger at court, "spreading awe and coldness." With the natural self-defense of the intellectual who is absorbed by concrete problems, he hated all official pomp and unnecessary waste of time. Once returned from his reviews and parades and from his great inspection tours, he fled into the silence of his study from which he usually emerged only in the evening hours. Then he sought compensation for his exhausting work in the daily concerts and in dinner conversation. It was the strangest court imaginable.

The magic of this singular assembly at Sans Souci has often been depicted—its intellectual brilliance, its freedom, the sovereign assurance with which its philosophical view of life rose above the daily struggle for existence. And surely Frederick's historical figure includes the image of the mocking wit in the midst of aesthetes, who savors repartee and bon mots and unsparing personal maliciousness, while touching lightly, without pedantry, on all questions of human understanding. But we should not assume that his heart belonged to this group or that even here he bared his true character. We will repeatedly encounter the marvellous duality of his nature. What he showed his friends at dinner made up only one side of his personality, and not the more important one at that. It was indeed a circle of companions rather than of friends. Voltaire, whose mind he most admired, most deeply disappointed him as a human being, and rewarded his hospitality with cowardly abuse and slander from afar. That in the end Frederick conquered his disappointment and resumed their correspondence with repeated expressions of admiration for Voltaire's genius, shows how indifferent he really was to the personalities of his French associates. Basically they were no more than a means of self-education. If that was his attitude toward Voltaire, it held even more true for the braggart Algarotti and the adventurer Lamettrie. Even that superficial *bel esprit,* the Marquis d'Argens, on whom he squandered some of his most beautiful letters, was nothing more to the king than a kind of intellectual sounding board. He felt more warmly toward the demanding, never satisfied invalid, Maupertuis, the President of the Royal Academy, whom he treated with a strange mixture of paternal, friendly care and inner detachment. Among the foreign guests only the brothers Keith, Scots nobles who had wide experience of the world and were absolutely loyal, gained his true friendship.

In the end the world of Sans Souci was only a beautiful world of appearance, not of Prussian and German reality. No doubt Frederick needed this world to help him endure life. Under the figs and orange trees of his garden, surrounded by marble figures of antique beauty, he might feel himself transposed for hours to Augustan

Rome, the longed-for city that he never saw. And during the best hours of cheerful and skeptical conversation with Europe's most emancipated minds, awareness of his responsibilities might vanish from his spirit. But the real fulcrum of his life lay elsewhere: in the hours of intense work, of great decisions, in his service as monarch. Frederick was not a crowned philosopher, but a king who required philosophy to make himself aware of his own humanity. That he also possessed an unreflective instinctual side, a heart wanting love, he showed least of all to his philosopher companions. This side of his nature emerged in the only relationships in which he could be tender, those with his mother and his beloved sisters. And in different form it also appeared in the passionate comradeship, particularly with soldiers, that could mean so much to him. For such Prussian officers as Keyserlingk, Rothenburg, Winterfeldt, and Fouqué, he did feel genuine friendship based on a harmony of personalities and of professional, not solely cultural, interests. And finally even the simple routine of his daily life could nurture faith and mutual confidence of the kind that binds an officer and his orderly. In later years the strange, half-trusting, half-paternal attachment to his servant Fredersdorf seemed to express a longing, a desire, which elsewhere the lonely man could no longer satisfy.

4
The King's View of the World

FREDERICK'S mind developed rapidly during the last years before his accession to the throne, and reached maturity during the brief interval between the Silesian campaigns and the Seven Years' War—the periods of Rheinsberg and Sans Souci. The aesthetic achievement of his vast and many-sided literary output—much of which stems from these years—interests us less today than does its psychological and intellectual content. What can his writings tell us about his personality, his view of life, and his ethical principles?

His poetic efforts in particular, which from his youth on formed a great part of his literary work, should be read from this point of view. We will probably best do them justice if we regard them as reflections of an energetic and inquiring intellect, and consider their arguments rather than their artistic qualities. Writing verse appealed to Frederick primarily as a challenge to overcome the problems of language, to achieve the utmost in clarity, precision, and elegance of expression. He acted in truly royal fashion when he chose Voltaire not only as his stylistic model, but also as his personal teacher and helper. Eventually he penetrated so deeply into the spirit of the French language that according to modern French critics a reader might forget that here was an author not writing in his native tongue. It was not surprising that on their first appearance in 1750, the selected poems of the "Philosopher of Sans Souci" gained the approval of a small circle of connoisseurs. To us they almost all seem cold, elegant rhetoric rather than true poetry, and every recent attempt to interpret them as important manifestations of literary genius has failed. A few odes and rhymed epistles, composed in the field during the Seven Years' War, and in general the patriotic poems, contain passages that sound the note of true feeling; but even these are not entirely free of rhetorical posing, and lack the simplicity that appeals to the heart.

Poetic talent is a gift of nature, which cannot be compensated for by any amount of effort. But Voltaire's poems, too, have long since shed their luster. One reason lies in the remoteness to our day of the baroque and rococo styles; their deliberate formality, their didactic and reflective character, classical garb, and opulence of mythological decoration are foreign to us. Yet these qualities are equally present in the great tragedies of the age of Louis XIV, whose monumentality continues to delight and move us. The difference must be that Voltaire was an epigone of French classicism, who despite his eager emulation of the masters of French baroque poetry could not genuinely accept their ideals of courtly pride and heroic virtue, of the divine right of kings and the nobility's elevated concepts of courage and sacrifice. The realism and unheroic humanity of the English Enlightenment had already penetrated the thinking of this completely bourgeois figure too deeply for his classicism to be convincing. The born skeptic was hardly suited to write epics and heroic tragedies; his attempts to express enthusiasm and faith too easily slid into false pathos. Voltaire was great as a critic, philosopher, and historian of culture, not as a creative poet. In his school Frederick would never learn to translate his feelings into poetry. And yet Frederick clearly differed from his model and master in that to him the ideals of royal humanity, knightly greatness, and heroism, which Racine had once proclaimed from the stage, still held a genuine magic, so that again and again Racine's verses aroused his enthusiasm and moved him to tears.

Here we come to a question of particular concern to us: Was Frederick in his writings simply an imitator of the French, or did he retain his individuality as a German? Did his acceptance of French values wholly estrange him from German ways?

It has always pained Germans that the man who ushered in their country's rise to new political significance so completely ignored the reawakening of the German spirit that occurred during his lifetime. Lessing, who among the founders of the classic age of German literature stood closest to the Frederician ethos, was only the first to be hurt by this alienation. And ever since the appearance of Justus Möser's pamphlet in defense of German literature, complaints against the king's criticisms have not ceased. Down to the period of the Weimar Republic every opponent of Frederician and Prussian policy in Germany, every champion of the *grossdeutsch* and Catholic factions, has exploited this estrangement.

No good purpose is served by trying to lessen the impact of historical realities through reinterpretation, or by pointing to extenuating factors. It is argued, for instance, that during Frederick's formative years at Rheinsberg, German literature was still in an immature stage, while later the king no longer enjoyed the leisure to occupy himself with new writings. Or we are reminded that at times Frederick praised the achievements of such German philosophers as Leibniz and Wolff. Actually in his youth he had already become so thoroughly acclimatized to the language and ways of thought of the French that he declared himself incapable of understanding Wolff's metaphysics in the original German, and had the text translated. And, indeed, Frederick not only found it difficult to read and write German, he also spoke it—according to his own scoffing words—"like a coachman." To some extent this onesidedness was due to his having been educated by a Huguenot émigré, Duhan. As monarch he continued to observe carefully the progress of French scholarship and literature, he even participated in the discussions of the French *philosophes* through his pamphlets and letters; but the works of German authors remained so foreign to him that in 1780 he found it possible to publish with few changes an essay *On German Literature* that he had written as long ago as 1752. In spite of Herder, Winckelmann, Lessing, and the young Goethe, he still regarded German literature as pedantic or barbaric, and considered its language as being as verbose, awkward, and dissonant as it had been in the days of Gottsched. He had no feeling at all for the language of the Lutheran Church. The efforts of German scholars to prepare editions of the middle-high German epics he found ridiculous. By his command the proceedings of the Royal Academy in Berlin were conducted in Latin or French—German was to him the tongue of the uneducated. He appointed mainly Frenchmen and French Swiss to his Academy, and continued to do so even when the candidates recommended to him in France were second- or third-rate scholars and men of letters while exceptionally able Germans waited in vain for admission.

All these are facts that cannot be fully explained by the dominance of the French style at the beginning of the century, and by the use of French as the language of aristocratic society. Frederick William I had received a fashionable education, and had nevertheless always shown a violent dislike for "Gallic ways" and felt himself to be a "German prince and man of honor." German Pietism, with which he strongly sympathized, firmly and consciously opposed French intellectual influence in the country, and thus did its share to awaken German self-confidence. But Frederick always found his father's kind of Germanness barbaric and backward. It was spiritual affinity, not his education, that turned him into an admirer and pupil of the French. Whether his Latin antecedents played a part in this need not be investigated here. It is more important to discover the historical meaning of this affinity, and to determine whether it was something superficial or whether it reached to the depths of his soul.

Frederick's sympathy for French thought was certainly not an unimportant and accidental factor, which historical analysis can afford to ignore—a blemish that does not really matter. On the contrary, central to his kingship was the fact that it did not stand foursquare among the German people, that it neither represented Germans nor spoke in their terms. Instead it was isolated and detached. Frederick knew the people only as "population" of a state's territory, the primitive basis of state power, a mass of subjects whose nationality had no political significance. His state was not yet the living expression and political form of a particular popular consciousness, it was not yet the carrier of a national idea. Seen from the present, the Frederician state was an abstract system of power, the creation of a dynasty whose goal was European rather than national significance, a dynasty with numerous international connections which it nurtured with great care. Frederick fulfilled the potential of the monarchical state in the age of absolutism to its last logical consequence; he did not go beyond it. When we come to analyze the events of his reign we will see that his policies show not the slightest awareness of national responsibility.

But must the absence of national ties represent only a weakness, a failing? It might be argued that the Prussian monarchy—equally independent in domestic and foreign affairs—was able to shape its policies with a freedom that is difficult if not impossible to achieve for a nation-state with its compelling passions and prejudices? The history of Europe since the French Revolution seems to confirm this view. And surely there can be no doubt that without the influx of foreign ideas, drawing solely on German political traditions, Prussia could never have acquired those freer concepts of the world and the state that became vital to her. We have seen the limited extent to which the modern theory of the state had been developed in Germany before Frederick's time. By comparison with the growth of great national power complexes in Western Europe, Germany had fallen centuries behind. Had Frederick followed the wishes of his father and grown up to be a well-meaning, pious, and paternal German ruler, conditions in Prussia presumably would have remained unchanged. No doubt life would have been peaceful; but the state would never have risen to great political power. Only by tearing himself away from his native tradition was Frederick able to gain the inner freedom to set out on the dangerous and glorious road that carried him far beyond his predecessors. And he achieved this liberation only with the help of the ideas of the European Enlightenment. If we consider the broader implications, we may no longer find the king's preference for French culture quite so strange. The political and cultural history of Germany contains more than one period in which stimulus from other countries was needed to encourage progress—as well as times, to be sure, in which German development was disturbed and inhibited by outside forces. Frederick himself was convinced that Germany, having been held back in her course by severe political catastrophes, now needed to emulate as closely as possible the nations of Western Europe, so that she could catch up with them and achieve new stature. His essay on German literature is filled with zeal for the greatness of the German name; but at the same time with enthusiasm for the triumph of the Enlightenment and its humanitarian ideas, and with hope for the liberation of the Germans from the delusions of prejudice and ancient superstition, and from the barbaric formlessness of their language and culture. The notion that he could defile the nation's honor by openly criticizing its cultural standards would have been incomprehensible to him; on the contrary, he believed he was rendering an important service. "I love our common fatherland as much as you do," he wrote to an admirer of the new German literature, "and for that reason take good care not to praise it before praise is deserved."

With obvious sympathy he described the difficulties with which the German people had to dig their way out of the destruction and misery of the Thirty Years' War: "While the Turks besieged Vienna and Melac laid waste to the Palatinate, while houses and towns burned to ashes, while undisciplined mercenaries desecrated even the preserve of death and tore dead Emperors from their tombs to rob them of their miserable coverings, while desperate mothers fled with their starving children from the ruins of their country—were sonnets to be composed and epigrams wrought in Vienna or Mannheim?" If at such times the nation failed to achieve the splendor of more fortunate civilizations it was certainly not due to lesser abilities but to bitter anxiety over the necessities of life. External security and political strength must be attained before the intellect can flower. But now the time had come to make up for past neglect.

Today many of Frederick's suggestions strike us as mistaken or inadequate: the smooth and cold elegance of Voltaire's prose style and the aesthetic ideals of French baroque poetry could not simply be transplanted across the Rhine. He failed to recognize the great merits that lay in the thoroughness and penetrating search for certainty of German scholarship. And some of the wishes he expressed for Germany were already answered as he made them, or were near fulfillment. Nevertheless, taken as a whole his criticisms deserve more serious consideration than they usually receive. Frederick warned the German writers against wallowing in emotion, against their tasteless turgidity of language, extravagance of expression, servility of attitude, against the obscurantism, empty verbiage, and schoolmasterly heaviness of scholarly exposition. A concise and clear language, definite yet possessing charm, without unnecessary circumlocutions and universally understood—that was his ideal. With it he sought a philosophic system that established firm principles for our behavior, faced the problems of life with clarity and cheerfulness, and overcame them with sober reasoning.

In literature, Dilthey has written, Frederick "sought gaiety and the dominance of the intellect; but the songs of his people offered him only the gloom and depth of emotion." And he would have been equally disturbed by the works of Klopstock, Wieland, and of the young Goethe had he known them better. The Rousseauan spirit of boundless emotion that they expressed was profoundly distasteful to him. He was frankly shocked by the demonstrative formlessness of the imitators of Shakespeare among the German dramatists. He could not know that the greatest of them would one day free himself from the turgidity of *Sturm und Drang* to attain classical grace, discipline, and clarity. But he did sense the approach of a new and better age. Sometimes, he said, "a later generation surpasses its predecessors. . . . We shall have our classic writers; everyone will want to read them and profit from their works; our neighbors will learn the German language, it will be spoken at court, and the time will come when thanks to our good authors the refined and perfected language will spread from one end of Europe to the other. These beautiful days have not yet arrived, but they are drawing near. I predict their coming, they will appear; but I shall not see them, my age deprives me of this hope. Like Moses I see the promised land from afar, but I shall not enter it."

Being a statesman, he believed that royal patrons could do much to raise the level of culture, particularly by helping universities and the secondary school system. But he recognized that while the state might stimulate and encourage intellectual life, it could never actually create thought nor determine its direction, since the mind can prosper only where freedom reigns. In the final analysis, he felt, all depended on the emergence of able men, who are always unpredictable gifts of Heaven. And though he urged the Germans to learn from French models, he did not lack the historical awareness that every nation possesses its indestructible individuality and its own national spirit. Education might alter the character of a nation, but could never abolish its fundamental features since these were the product of unchangeable forces of geography and history.

He himself, despite his French education and culture, never lost his specifically German characteristics. The native features of his mind become particularly clear when we consider his philosophic and moral concepts as they developed from his studies and experiences. It is true that he differed sharply in his ideas from the traditions of his dynasty, from his predecessors as well as his successors, and indeed from the traditions of German ruling houses in general. But neither did his views simply reflect the concepts of the French and English Enlightenment: they were the expression of an original and unique personality.

In his youth Frederick confidently dove into the sea of metaphysical problems that in those days formed the favorite topics of every philosophic salon: the nature of the world, of man, and of the creator; the relations between natural law and freedom, between body and soul. He gloried in having escaped the theological narrowness of his paternal training. To his new friend, Voltaire, he naïvely and eagerly praised the most ponderous of all philosophic treatises, Christian Wolff's *Rational Ideas on God, the World, the Soul of Man, and on All Things in General,* as the key to every mystery of the Universe. But he was soon sobered by Voltaire's skepticism, and even more by his studies of the critical writings of Bayle and the English empiricists. He recognized that there can be no limit to discussions of the general and universal, that human understanding is too weak to attain certainty about ultimate truths. Without hesitation he turned away from speculations about the unknowable. He was interested only in those questions that we must answer if we wish to master the confusions and dangers of practical life.

The philosophy of his age was the doctrine of rationalism and of determined secularism. The more deeply he penetrated this body of thought, the more strongly he came to accept the belief that lay behind every aspect of the Enlightenment: with the help of reason it should be possible not only to reach a sounder understanding of the world but also to make it a better, freer, and happier place. Few men of his century held this hope with such enthusiasm and avowed it so confidently as the optimistic philosopher of Rheinsberg and Sans Souci. Theological dogma and positive Christianity he dismissed forever. At the beginning of a new epoch in the world's spiritual development, he felt himself called on to assume a royal charge which would enable him more than any of his contemporaries to turn the ideals of the new age into reality. Society,

economic life, the church, the state, government policy—all were to
be newly ordered according to the principles of human understanding. The remnants of the Middle Ages and of centuries of
stifling illusion were to be cleared away. The new well-being and
happiness of his subjects, education, religious tolerance, the flower-
ing of science and the arts would make the world forget the period
of medieval barbarity.

His new state of mind was completely secular. The world had
become entirely temporal—or, perhaps, not entirely? Frederick
dared to deny the existence of God as little as did his teachers, the
English and French Deists. For some time the traditional proofs of
God's existence were able to set his mind at rest: since the world is
a wondrous achievement of perfection, the best of all possible
worlds, a perfect being must have created it. Let us delight in this
perfect world, and give thanks to its benevolent creator. Let us enjoy its beauty with all our senses, without fear of any supposed
hereafter:

> Si comme Thèbe, hélas! notre âme avait cent portes,
> J'y laisserais entrer les plaisirs en cohortes.

But slowly he came to doubt the perfection of this world. Is it
really the best of all possible worlds? Does not the technical won-
der of the cosmos contain far more horror for man than joy? Does
not the sum of evil and suffering outweigh by far the good and
beautiful? His study of history acquainted Frederick with the
tragedy of human fate; his own experiences, his bitter youth, the
pressing sorrows and dangers of his reign, the horrors of war, the
early deaths of those closest to him—over and over these things
made him aware of the questionableness of human existence. What
is the human spirit? A flame that dully flickers amidst the gusts of
passion and soon dies in the storms of fate. If an all-benevolent, all-
wise creator does exist, he stated to his friend d'Alembert in 1782, it
remains a puzzle why he created this disgusting world. In reality,
he argued, this God is nothing more than an impersonal concept, a
mysterious, unintelligible essence, which inconsistently enough
Frederick interpreted now as world intelligence, now as motivating
principle inherent in nature, now as the external originator of the

Universe. To the end of his days he sought to defend his faith in this intelligent, spiritual God against the materialism of the last generation of the Enlightenment. He could not accept the world as a simple and soulless mechanism. At the same time he recognized, not without irony, that crusading for God was a role for which he, the radical free spirit, was scarcely suited.

The existence of this God—how little did it actually mean to mankind! The Heavens are silent, without pity for our distress. God is a being whom no human cry can hope to reach. The concept of divine providence is as foreign to Frederick as the immortality of the soul. Certainly, the world as a whole is designed according to the scheme of a supreme intelligence; but the individual human life plays no noticeable part in this enormous context. Even the conflict between Austria and Prussia is "far too insignificant a matter to interest Providence." In the most critical period of the Seven Years' War he wrote to d'Argens, "I save myself by looking at the world as a whole, as though from a distant planet. Then everything appears unbelievably small to me, and I pity my enemies who take so much trouble over such insignificant things." Here we touch the core of Frederick's convictions—the idea that everything in human existence is preordained.

Proceeding from the Calvinist concept of predestination, Frederick from youth on defended the belief that in reality human freedom was nothing but self-deception. The life of man is governed entirely by the play of natural forces, whose paths we cannot deflect. Even God cannot change them without destroying his own work. He is the cause of the universe, but he does not intervene in human life, which is ruled by causes of a secondary order, derivative causes, which themselves are products of the unchanging general laws of nature. Accident does not exist; but we do not always recognize the true connection of things. Even human will is inextricably bound by this causal chain. The soul itself is no more than the function of biological realities, of nerves and of the brain, with whose destruction it ceases to exist. Once Frederick had shed the Christian belief in immortality, he took pleasure in speculating about these questions as soberly and ruthlessly as possible—always in the sincere hope that in his way he might free himself from illusions that could prevent him from seeing things as they are. The belief that we determine our own actions he held to be as much an abortion of human vanity as the concept of immortality. "I shall never be dissuaded from my conviction that regardless of how much noise he makes in the world man is only an infinitely tiny creature, an unnoticeable atom in relation to the universe. . . . Instruments of an invisible hand, we move without knowing what we do; statesmen and warriors are no more than puppets in the hands of providence, which guides the world as it will."

At first Frederick also denied the freedom of human volition; in tenacious disputes with Voltaire he claimed that the behavior of man was no more than the product of natural preconditions. But how could such a condition be combined with man's ethical responsibilities? This proved to be a difficult and for the time being insoluble problem. Only in old age, in reaction to the frightening consequences that revolutionary materialism was drawing from the concepts he himself had championed, did Frederick give up the rigidity of his earlier beliefs. Now he admitted that it was possible for us to choose between reason and our passions. From various options our imagination could help us select one specific course of action: "Everything is caused, but not everything is inevitable." But even then he retained his faith in the predestination of human fate.

The belief that all our actions are under the control of an unlimited power, before which human greatness turns to dust, has never robbed determined men of the courage to act. On the contrary, it stimulated the Calvinists of the sixteenth century to ensure their eternal salvation by redoubling their zeal to fight for God. Bismarck thought he could not bear the heavy burden of political responsibility without the assurance that in the end all human action was governed by a higher power, and that *sub specie aeternitatis* all kingdoms were nothing but "dust on the moving wheel of world history." As a freethinker Frederick did not believe in a just, or, indeed, in a personal God; but as a true son of the Enlightenment he did believe in the complete rationality of a world order, whose working determined our fate. In the face of this rationality, the sorrows or joys of the individual were without true significance. And even more important, he believed in the intelligence of the universe; that is, he held reason to be the creative principle of the world. He remained untouched by the confusion of modern free-thinkers, who seek the most general principle of our behavior and the highest concepts of justice, goodness, and truth in the accidental configuration of the individual—in the instinct either of creative man who lives according to self-made moral laws, or even of the organized mass, which simply trusts its time-bound opinions and feelings, rather than obeying the eternal laws of truth and justice. By contrast Frederick conceived of a force of universal reason, far above human arbitrariness, which imposed a binding, eternal, unchanging, timeless truth and an equally eternal moral law on our consciousness. This made up his "natural" religion. Assured of this "natural" truth, and certain of the ability of his intelligence to comprehend it, he could be confident in his power to master life for as long as he succeeded in bringing his own passions under the rule of reason. After all, he was only acting in agreement with the conditions of this rationally organized world.

With this attitude the young prince faced life. He was cocky and sure of success. He had no need of a helping hand from another world, he had the self-assurance that he could manage his royal calling on his own. He would know how to govern Prussia according to the principles of reason, and to reshape the state wherever this became necessary.

But just as the experiences of his life diabused him of his cheerful belief in the rationality and perfection of the universe, so he came to lose his optimistic confidence in the ability of the human intelligence unfailingly to recognize what was sound and sensible. If we wish to understand Frederick's philosophizing we must always seek to distinguish those aspects of his thought that he simply took over from the intellectual fashions of his day, and those ideas and ultimate convictions that grew out of his personal experiences. How fully he trusted his ability to see through the secret intentions of the courts of Europe, and to predict their future maneuvers with certainty at the beginning of his reign! His first disappointment came when at decisive moments he repeatedly miscalculated and, as a result, found himself in the gravest danger, enmeshed in apparently inextricable difficulties. The deeper his entanglement, the more painfully he recognized the limitations of human knowledge and ability in the presence of nature and fate. He asked: How much can one man achieve in constant struggle against exhaustion, illness, and death? How can the general evade the blind fury of nature, which makes a mockery of his strategic plans? What can the enlightened prince achieve against the force of traditions that rule the minds of man? Does it make sense to destroy these traditions, to replace irrational belief with rational disbelief, if faith makes men happy, obedient, and industrious? Might not the majority of mankind decline into fear and weakness because it could not bear the light of pure truth?

Frederick no longer shared Voltaire's sacrilegious confidence that turning the battle cry *ecrasez l'infâme* into reality and destroying the Christian church and its superstitions would suffice to bring about the triumph of reason and make the world both freer and happier. Of course, he joined Voltaire in ridiculing the senselessness of church dogma. And though—being Protestant by birth—he thought he could discern the beginnings of more liberal attitudes in the Protestant camp while these remained completely absent on the Catholic side, he directed his criticism without favor against the teachings of both confessions. But he was convinced, as he wrote in his *Political Testament* of 1768, that these denominations "could never damage the state, so long as their priests were kept within the limits that are presently drawn for them. They can do an immeasurable amount of good—but they must be disciplined as soon as they interfere in things that do not concern them." He was far from sharing the narrowness of the French *philosophes,* who in their struggle against religious intolerance themselves called for extreme measures, for the help of the political power to establish a reign of reason—help which later, during the French Revolution, was to be freely given. He was not interested in utopias. Because he knew the natural limits of state power, he wanted no part of state support for turning enlightened philosophies into substitute religions. In his Prussia, everyone really should become "happy after his own fashion."

He sharply rejected the crude forms of antireligious behavior that began to spread in France on the eve of the Revolution—the disruption of religious processions, for instance, or the defacement of holy images. He coolly rejected Voltaire's suggestion that he should offer an asylum on the lower Rhine to the radical *philo-*

sophes who were being persecuted in France, and permit them there to establish a center for their literary campaigns against the church. D'Alembert's notion of erecting a temple to the new religion of reason in Potsdam met with the same refusal. Frederick knew that religions could not be improvised, that they could not be distilled out of abstractions. All application of force in intellectual and spiritual affairs seemed suspect to him. He considered it as a denial of the principle of freedom, which alone sustained all true thought: "Let us beware of introducing fanaticism into philosophy."

And he differed on yet another point from the propagandists of the Enlightenment. In his heart he did not share their faith that man was naturally good, that he was capable of every great deed, and that he needed only to be liberated from the delusion of his prejudices to become happy and charitable. Obscured now and then, his belief that most of mankind is dumb and mean—"le gros de notre espèce est sot et méchant" eventually always comes to the fore. As he grew older his behavior was increasingly influenced by the conviction that we are part of a "cursed" race, whose natural instincts must be met with the sharpest distrust.

This sentiment, which all his experiences—including his intimate dealings with "that fool" Voltaire—seemed merely to reinforce is not part of the European Enlightenment. Unless we interpret it simply as the personal characteristic of a lonely genius, we can seek its roots only in his Lutheran and German background. The orthodox Lutheran belief in man's complete sinfulness might well take on secular garb in the form of a sober recognition of the wretchedness of existence and of the permanent inadequacy of thought and action. The cheerful optimism of rational philosophy is invaded by a foreign and tragic element, which came to affect and finally dominate Frederick's entire view of life.

It was not difficult for men to be optimistic, to believe in the triumphant clarity of the Enlightenment and pass easily over the mysteries of our existence, so long as they stood detached from life, so to speak as reflective observers, and did not act with the full weight of authority. None of the French writers with whom Frederick surrounded himself ever felt the burden of responsibility that is imposed by great political actions. They avoided life's most violent storms they substituted gallantry for true passion, cosmopol-

itan declarations of solidarity for patriotic sacrifice, irony for con-
suming doubt. They hoped to overcome emotion by means of self-
criticism, to master sorrow by understanding its pointlessness, and
by rejecting on principle all feelings of regret. In the abstract
sphere of literature all this might succeed. But that was not Frederick's world. He had to answer for his people, his army, and his
state. The passion, sorrow, exigencies, and hopes of an heroic existence swept over him with undiminished strength. When uncontrollable ambitions spurred him on to take risks, and when the
massed misfortunes of the great war shook him to the depths of
his soul, he tried with cold reasoning to persuade himself and
others to remain calm, realistic, and stoically indifferent. But in the
end he had to admit, "we always fool ourselves when we seek the
basis of human action outside the passions and outside the heart."

A permanent dialogue between reason and emotion ran through
his thoughts. He knew himself to be free of physical cowardice:
"Not to exist is no evil. . . . The breath of life that animates me I
willingly and without plaint return to the benevolent being that
had bestowed it upon me, and my body to the elements from
which it was formed." Since evil is inevitable in this world we
must accept it with "generosity" and decency. "To grumble or
complain is to go against the laws of the Universe. One misfortune
more or less does not affect the world. . . . Is there no age of man
in which we should be ashamed to play with hopes like a child
plays with dolls? . . . He who cannot support misfortune does not
deserve happiness." This last is a truly royal thought; the expression of a heroic will that rises above fate and death. Frederick's
spirit, to cite Dilthey once more, is "the spirit that rejoices at
having escaped the rule of imagination and of religious passions
. . . he takes pleasure in life—and has the strength to disdain it." A
lively temperament, a sensual nature that seems made to enjoy happiness fully, and that loves the good in this world—friendship,
beauty, intellectual grace—forces itself to renunciation, to the hard
service of the state on campaign and in administration. Fate throws
him into the whirlwind of endless wars. For years he sees no way
out of his predicaments, he can maintain himself only by the most
intense force of will, and when peace finally does come he returns
home prematurely aged, without pleasure or happiness. All his feel-

ings are dammed up so that nothing can weaken his energy and will. Is it to be wondered at that this man hardens his soul, that he grows lonely, and at last seems to petrify into a heartless statue?

In his poems Frederick repeatedly praised the classical Roman ideal of the Stoic philosophers. But for him this was a desirable fantasy, not reality. In the end, Stoicism implies relinquishing—hardly the natural attitude of a man who is out to change the world. His Stoicism never weakened his urge for glory, and it never fully stamped out his passions. He suffered more—not less—than most men from sudden changes of mood, from anger, and from depression. He himself was sufficiently concerned about his temper and sharpness of tongue to dislike giving audiences to diplomats, and preferred to deal with his ministers in writing. His self-control and deliberation were not inherent, but achieved by willpower. And it is not surprising that in the life of this unyielding, self-contained man there were hours when he was truly beyond control, and when despair threatened to overcome him. At such times he remained firm not by demonstrating to himself how useless it is to give in to feeling, nor by the optimistic faith of a man of the Enlightenment in his own intelligence, which would find a way, and least of all from a belief in abstract, universal rationality and in a higher purpose to all events. He kept his courage out of a simple, irrational, but totally compelling sense of duty. Even though he recognized the supremacy of fate and the predestination of all human action, he saw it as his duty to face life stubbornly, despite the mystery of God's intentions, and despite the danger that death might suddenly erase everything that gives purpose to life. It remained his task to fulfill his historic mission, without illusions and without fear: "It is not necessary that I live, but I must do my duty."

This sense of obligation, which nothing could shake, was no doubt derived from Stoic traditions; but it also possessed original characteristics. All experiences to the contrary, Frederick did not become resigned, but continued to welcome life. His concept of duty was not mobilized for the sake of humanity, for an abstract world empire of rational sages, but for concrete service to the concrete state. The French philosophic literature that he admired so greatly had no room for this attitude. Nor can his position be called Christian, since Frederick did not recognize a personal responsibility to a personal God. Instead he drew his vitality from the ideals of self-determination and purely secular greatness, which are self-sufficient and independent of the need for God's help. And yet, in the unconditional nature of its demands and in its disregard of human happiness this attitude was closely related to the ethics of Christianity. In his moral philosophy Frederick most inadequately sought to explain ethical behavior as the product of a refined egotism. As a man of action he outgrew this theory. And he was aware that in his unconditional obedience to the voice of duty he was the true heir of his father. We need only compare the kingship of Louis XV with that of Frederick to recognize the historical significance that lay in the continuing strength of Prussian and Protestant traits in his background.

5
The King's View of the State

COMPELLING personal ambition and the strictest adherence to an abstract concept of service, refined egotism, and a selfless devotion to duty—these characteristics are combined in Frederick's work for the state. The more he wore himself out in this service the more the abstractions were charged with ethical values: the rigid performance of duty turned into patriotic fervor, the state—metaphysical power structure and dynastic possession—evolved into the fatherland. What he understood by the commitment to political service he nowhere expressed more beautifully than in the collection of letters of his last years *On Love of the Fatherland*.

There he explicitly rejects the Epicurean teaching that man is born to happiness, that the individual has the right to "exist in the obscurity of private life." The true function of man, he writes, is to work for the common good, for the fatherland; only those individuals who fulfill the obligations and responsibilities embodied in the social contract are entitled to respect. The ideal fatherland is a state "in which all citizens show strength and energy, all are active," in which "repose is permitted only to the mentally and physically ill, the blind, and to the aged." To combat private selfishness and cosmopolitan attitudes, Frederick has the personified fatherland address its children. The nation reminds them of the duty of grateful loyalty, and receives the answer: "Yes, I acknowledge that I owe everything to you; I am closely and eternally tied to you; my love and gratitude will end only with my life; this life itself is your gift; should you demand its return I shall sacrifice it with joy. To die for you is to live forever in the remembrance of men; I cannot serve you without covering myself with glory."

Patriotism was the fundamental attitude from which Frederick developed his concept of the state. Here again he was indebted to the teachings of French and English philosophy. But the very fact that he was both philosopher and statesman gave his political ideas a distinctive character. Early in his life, abstractions gave way to practical experience, and speculation to responsible action. He spoke as an expert, not as an amateur.

In marked contrast to the writings of most French political philosophers, Frederick's political works are based on a broad and intensive study of the past. As a boy he had been thoroughly schooled in the background of his family as well as in recent European diplomatic events, and from youth on he was an ardent reader of historical books. Those works in which he tried his hand as a historian—*Memorabilia of the History of the House of Brandenburg, History of my Time,* as well as others—constitute the most valuable and lasting of his writings. He labored over their style and took great pains to achieve analytic precision. Even so they exhibit numerous technical flaws, errors in interpretation and inaccurate details, betraying the negligence of a princely author, who, writing in his spare hours, could not call on the same patience in dealing with minutiae as the professional scholar. But what they lack in reliability and scholarship is on the whole compensated for by their clear and vivid presentation, expert judgment in political and especially military matters, and in general by their forceful and realistic political character. These qualities were totally lacking in the academic historiography of his day. They enable Frederick's works to hold their own even in a comparison with Voltaire's histories.

It is generally agreed that their chief merit lies in the astonishing candor and even ruthlessness of their author's self-portrayal and self-criticism. Their frankness, which sets them apart from most memoirs, is closely related to Frederick's rationalistic outlook, and brilliantly demonstrates its special qualities: it is not emotion that has its say in these pages, but—on the whole—a cool and discerning mind. Frederick writes not to defend himself or to accuse others—though he can be maliciously and even brutally ironic about his antagonists—but to learn from the events he describes. He unsparingly criticizes the rashness and other errors in war and politics during the first part of his reign; he openly admits his ambitions. With equal frankness he acknowledges the diplomatic achievements of Maria Theresa, and soberly and fairly judges the motives underlying her policy. He remains entirely free of hollow self-glorification, propagandistic phrases, and arrogant superiority toward other nations.

Frederick studied the past and wrote about it as great statesmen have always approached history—not to intoxicate themselves, but to clarify their own political tasks. It goes without saying that history never provides political recipes. It may, however, assist the political leader by acquainting him with the background of his state and its position in the world, as well as with the potentials, aims, traditions, strengths, and limitations of other powers. By Richelieu's time the theory of the natural political interests of the state —one of the most important sources of modern political history— had developed into a special branch of political literature. Frederick contributed significantly to this body of thought—there is for instance his grandiose survey of the European courts and the political forces of the age that introduces the *History of my Time,* or the *Reflections on the Present Political Condition of Europe* of 1738, the earliest of all his works. What inspired these studies was Frederick's desire to give firm shape to the everlasting flexibility of politics, to master the affairs of states with the aid of historical insights, and raise them out of the sphere of uncertainty and chance to the realm of rational calculation. As the mechanic has exact knowledge of the workings of a clock, he wrote in the essay of 1738, so the politician who understands the *raison d'état* knows "the permanent principles guiding the European courts, the mainsprings of every ruler's policies, the sources of all events." This knowledge is acquired through the study of history, since "the minds of men and the passions governing them are always the same, and must necessarily call forth the same results." Above all, "the policies of the major powers are practically unchanging." Their actions can therefore be predicted by historical analogy.

The note of youthful exaggeration in these sentences is obvious. To interpret the present from knowledge of the past is difficult enough. Frederick proved this, incidentally, in the main section of the essay, a delineation of France's means and political goals more applicable to the era of Louis XIV than to that of Cardinal Fleury. But if the present is hard to gauge, how much more difficult is it to predict future policies on the basis of the few facts that are available at any given time. It would be simpler if the true interests of the state, which can be rationally calculated, alone determined policy, without the intervention of emotions, of hate and sympathy, of the drive for power and prestige. Frederick was to discover soon enough—and more than once—that despite all his calculations, war and policy were affected by chance and by continuous surprise. Later he openly admitted this fact. And yet, his repeated brave attempts to narrow as much as possible the area of the fortuitous, to cast the light of reason as far as he could into the darkness of the future, remained an essential aspect of his statesmanship. To act from mere political instinct seemed to him the mark of a barbaric age, which happily had been overcome.

He was convinced that to follow the guide of true *raison d'état* not only secured political success but also benefited the cause of humanity. Although this highest form of political realism might not immediately rid the world of blind violence and chaos, its aim had to be the establishment of judicious policies and a durable political order. Frederick stated this thought most vividly in the second work of his youth, the *Anti-Machiavel,* which following its appearance in 1740 rapidly became famous. From the biographical point of view this study is particularly interesting, since it shows the boundless optimism and confidence with which the young author awaited his accession to power, an event that would enable him to help bring about a new age of happiness for mankind. Beyond that the *Anti-Machiavel* expresses a new sense of purpose of the European monarchical system.

The monarchies of the early sixteenth century, which Machiavelli had in mind when he wrote *The Prince,* had just begun their ascent to political power and moral prestige. The Italian princes were petty rulers, who advanced themselves through the use of violence, deception, fraud, and crimes of every kind. They lived surrounded by immediate threats to their existence. Under such conditions all means of self-preservation seemed permissible. Even in the seventeenth century the monarchical system still fought to assert its authority against powerful cliques of the nobility and against the passionate hostilities of the various religious faiths, which tore society apart and prevented the emergence of a unified nation-state. By the time of Frederick's youth all this seemed to have been overcome. Supported by his standing army and disciplined bureaucracy, the monarch no longer needed to fear a rebellious nobility; and religious conflict had long since subsided in the mild atmosphere that a new view of life, free of prejudice, had brought to the world. Enlightenment, tolerance, and reason rather than ungovernable passion seemed the watchword of the new age. The new attitudes drew most of their strength from England. In the fortunate isolation of their island realm, Britons had long nurtured the ideals of a state devoted to welfare and justice, and had often looked with distaste, and perhaps also with some sense of moral superiority, at the violent struggles for power on the European Continent. During Machiavelli's lifetime Thomas More's *Utopia* had presented a bright picture of the peaceful realm of pure humanity. These ideas, intertwined in the English philosophy of common sense and pure empiricism, now spread to France. The *Abbé* de St. Pierre outlined a new utopia—the vision of "eternal peace." During Louis XIV's last years the reform groups at the court of the Duke of Bourgogne demanded that the unremitting pursuit of war and dynastic prestige which was ruining France, be curbed. Instead the nation's economy should be nurtured, the arts and sciences promoted, the level of civilization raised. Fénelon in his *Télémaque* —which Frederick enthusiastically read in his boyhood—depicted the ideal prince as a virtuous, just, and peaceful shepherd of his people, while Voltaire's historical studies concentrated on cultural progress, rather than wars and politics, as the main content of history. In his heroic poem, the *Henriade,* Voltaire praised moderation, conciliatory mildness, promotion of economic wellbeing, and cultivation of the arts and sciences as the highest qualities of the perfect prince. Frederick eagerly absorbed these favored ideas of the age; his *Anti-Machiavel* is filled with them.

But was Prussia actually in a position to take the lead in bringing these ideas to reality? Could Prussia really be compared with the mature, cohesive national states of Western Europe, which could now afford to think about furthering the peaceful work of civilization for a time instead of pursuing aggressive, expansionist policies? Wasn't Prussia, exposed to the greatest dangers in the heart of Europe, still a rising state, an unfinished, dissatisfied, and fragmented political organism? Had it yet progressed very far along the dangerous road to power and prestige? In her situation could Prussia completely renounce all Machiavellian means for self-preservation and conquest?

Assuredly it was not Frederick's historical mission to become the apostle of humanity of his age. Tame acquiescence had long been Prussian practice—not exactly in the sense of the new humanitarian ideas, but in response to the older religious view of the state, with its ideals of charity and justice. The two concepts were indeed closely related. It has always been considered strange, and rightly so, that it was the conqueror of Silesia who publicly expressed indignation about Machiavellian power politics. Almost simultaneously with the anonymous appearance of his *Anti-Machiavel* in 1740, its author outraged Europe by his particularly ruthless use of force. He was the same man whose diplomacy soon acquired the reputation of being unusually shifty and marked by disloyalty to allies, and who throughout his reign did little to ameliorate the barbaric system of conscription and military justice that had become the practice in his state. Was Frederick's enthusiasm for humanitarian ideals superficial, or was it seriously felt? Was it in fact no more than a cynical mask with which a man of particularly Machiavellian cunning attempted to deceive the world about his true intentions?

Nothing could be further from the truth. There was so little cunning in the author of the *Anti-Machiavel* and the *Reflections on the State of Europe,* that in one and the same breath he could warn his fellow princes against the "criminal rapacity" of wars of conquest, and declare that "at all times it was the principle of great states to subjugate all whom they could and to extend their power continuously. Throughout history their wisdom had consisted in forestalling the artifices of their opponents, and in playing a more refined political game." That Frederick did not perceive the inherent contradiction of these statements demonstrates the naïve honesty of his beliefs. For the time being the primitive drive for power of a dominating personality coexisted in equal measure with enthusiasm for the ideal of humanitarian reform. And for both he found historical models as well as numerous stimulating allusions in contemporary literature. The glory of daring conquerors, such as Alexander and Caesar, had by no means disappeared from the printed page. French drama and historiography in particular had never ceased to praise their valorous deeds, as the heroic and virtuous ideals of French baroque literature continued to influence later authors. Even in Voltaire's writings these qualities are still clearly discernible despite all the praise for the virtues of humanitarian princes. Only the future and the reality of governing, would show which of the two ideals held the stronger attraction for Frederick: Caesar, the martial hero and conqueror, or Marcus Aurelius, the philosopher and prince of peace.

The course of the Silesian Wars soon provided the answer. But it is not true that as king, Frederick forgot the humanitarian ideals he had worshipped as crown prince. Throughout his life he seriously attempted to reconcile the eternal opposites of morality and policy, humanity and political necessity, love of peace and need for war. In the arguments of his historical works, in his political testaments, and in the reflections of his old age, his thoughts always reverted to these conflicts. We have already seen how he labored not only to justify Machiavellian methods in foreign relations on moral grounds, but also to restrict the use of these methods to cases of compelling necessity. The result of his meditations was that policy should be governed by the self-evident requirements of the state, and not by the personal ambitions of the ruler. Calm reason, not recklessness and passion, should determine policy, and restrain and constantly guard the potential of violence. In his view ambition could not be a quality of true heroism unless it was disciplined by self-control, wisdom, and moderation.

To be sure, these were generalizations. In his actual conduct of foreign affairs Frederick never shied away from breaking the moral laws that he propounded as humanitarian philosopher—if he thought that it was in the interest of the state to do so. But even then he retained a clear awareness that the possession of power imposes obligations. He had to answer for his actions to the court of pure reason. He never sought to rid himself of responsibility for the consequences of his policies; on the contrary, he suffered from his failure to achieve this detachment. His kingship no longer was an office granted by God, as his predecessors had considered it to be; but it was even less like the rule—characterized by pure enioyment of power, simple force requiring neither moral nor philosophic justification—of the Italian tyrants for whom Machiavelli had written. Frederick saw his rule in terms of duty and service. From the time he wrote the *Anti-Machiavel,* he never ceased to re-iterate in new formulations his thought that the prince should be the "first servant of his state"—or, as he originally put it, "of his peoples." Behind this view lay a concept that he had taken from the natural law theorists of his day and from the historical and po-litical literature: the monarchy had originated in a contract. Free individuals combine to form the people of a state, and voluntarily transfer their self-determination to a ruling authority appointed by them.

Frederick drew the consequences from this fundamental concept with his customary determination and clarity. In his *Anti-Machia-vel* he states that the prince should consider his subjects not only as equals, but also in a sense as his masters. The ruler is the means for their happiness, as they are the instruments of his glory. An essay on *Forms of Government and Duties of Princes* of 1777 argues that if he does not wish to neglect his duties the ruler should frequently remind himself that he is only a man like the least of his subjects. Despite his disdain for the human race, Frederick remained un-touched by dynastic arrogance. As a true son of the Enlighten-ment he was convinced that men "in the final analysis are equal," and that "high birth is chimerical." From this point of view, king-ship appears essentially as an accumulation of duties, and Frederick never tired of analyzing these duties anew. In the great *Political Testaments* of 1752 and 1768, in which the political ideas of his ma-turity are given masterful expression, he explicitly and systemati-cally described the duties of the prince, and earnestly urged his successor to take them to heart. The demands he placed on the knowledge, ability, energy, and character of the ruler are so exten-sive that it hardly seems possible for one man to fulfill them. Cer-tainly they exceed by far the capacity of the average individual. But these high expectations are part of the nature of enlightened des-potism. Even in the eyes of the monarch his kingship had lost the mysterious, religious splendor derived from having been established in authority by God. The awesome dignity of ancient historical de-scent could not stand up to the sober critique of the Enlighten-ment.

Frederick found it possible to demonstrate dispassionately the theoretical advantages that republican or parliamentary forms of government enjoyed over the system of royal absolutism. If the monarchy was to retain political authority in this completely altered intellectual climate, it must constantly prove itself by supreme achievements in politics and war. Here is the source of the almost anxious eagerness of the great didactic essays that Frederick addressed to his successor, by which he sought to insure that his work would be carried on after his death. This too explains his strong warning not to depend on ministers, councillors, and other assistants—in the end, the fate of this kingship depended on its remaining absolute in the highest sense. Carrying a heavy burden of responsibility it also needed to assure for itself a full measure of glory. What mattered above all, he constantly repeated, was to govern not recklessly but according to a firm and comprehensive plan. "I am not master to do as I wish." The king must govern according to a system that "arises from the intelligence of the ruler like armed Minerva from Jupiter's brow. . . . This system must not be the product of haste and frivolity, but of serious thought, deep knowledge of state affairs, prudence, calculation, and real wisdom." All branches of government must be harmonized: "They must be guided in straight flight, all abreast, like the quadriga in the Olympic Games, in which each steed covered the course with equal energy and equal speed and gave victory to its driver."

With such impressive imagery he sketched the character of modern absolutism. Frederick's belief in the rational origins of his dignity and his references to the social contract in no way shook his self-confidence: on the contrary, they increased his strength and pride. After all, men did not act capriciously when they agreed to subordinate their individual freedom to the common good, but obeyed the commandment of rational necessity. There would be no social order without this original contract, and therefore subjects of the state are firmly bound by it. It never occurred to Frederick, nor to the generation of French political philosophers with whom he exchanged ideas, that one day the people might demand the return of their original liberties. But obviously, the unselfconscious kingship of earlier times was a thing of the past. No longer was the state dynastic property, nor was the royal dignity any longer granted by the grace of God. Though he occupied the highest rank a king no longer stood above the state, but in its midst, as a participating, serving member. The king's claim to authority was no longer a self-asserted right, his dignity no longer came from eternity; both derived from the right and dignity of the state.

The purposes of government had also changed. No longer was its highest aim what it had been in the early period of German territorial organization: the primitive exploitation of economic and human potential in order to increase the power and wealth of the ruling dynasty, or—as during feudalism—increase of the power of the great noble families, of the prince, and of his mightiest vassals. But neither was government mainly concerned with the well-being of the people—at least not in the manner of later liberalism, which turned the state into little more than a guardian of private property, and proclaimed the watchword "The greatest possible happiness for the greatest possible number"—nor in the sense of modern democracies, which, faced with the material desires and political demands of the masses, follow, at least theoretically, the course that "best serves the people." In Frederick's state neither the personal interest of the prince and his dynasty, nor the desires of his subjects ultimately decided the government's actions. Domestic and foreign policy were guided exclusively by the *raison d'état*, by the interests of the state. Both prince and people were its servants. Never before or again was the concept of state individuality and state interest grasped so clearly—and with almost abstract purity—and never was it as politically effective as in Frederick's enlightened despotism. Its influence can still be seen in the thought of such statesmen as Metternich and Bismarck.

The interest of the state primarily centers on power. The state exists necessarily on the basis of combative power—though in Frederick's view this force must not take the form of blind violence, but should be guided and limited by reason. His state was a historical power structure, whose right to exist derived from past events, a right that Frederick never doubted, all accidents and even artificiality of Prussia's development to the contrary. The first and most urgent aim of Prussian policy must be to turn the state into a major power. Other considerations, even the well-being of the people, are rigidly subordinated to this purpose. The state insists that all subjects do their "duty" and serve it. The Prussian state is neither a union of expediency as revolutionary humanitarian ideals would consider it, nor an organization for the furtherance of the general good of the individuals within its borders, whose private interests determine its institutions. The state has its own life and its own purposes, which stand far above the wishes and opinions of the individual. It demands service from ruler and subject; it demands sacrifices, and in some circumstances the renunciation of happiness and even of life. But Frederick was far from ignoring the humanitarian question of the ethical justification of these demands. On the contrary, he took it for granted that in the end all concentration of power must serve the establishment and continued protection of a peaceful social and political order. This view was already suggested in the memoir that he had written to Natzmer at the age of nineteen: Brandenburg–Prussia should rise from the dust, become a true power whose might can maintain peace— not a weak peace but a peace of justice and of the general welfare. The simple existence of state power was by no means sufficient reason for men to subject themselves to it voluntarily. Power is not sufficient unto itself, it must be justified by higher moral purposes. It must seek to serve the progress of mankind by furthering justice, economic well-being, morality, education, and culture. In Meinecke's words, "Frederick considered it a serious and sacred obligation to give his subjects the greatest measure of happiness, material well-being, intellectual vitality, and moral energy that could be combined with the purposes of the state. We should not permit the jarring notes of his cynicism to drown out his deep, instinctive conviction in these matters." Frederick knew that Prussia could not be a paradise on earth. But so far as possible his reign was to be "philanthropic" not "despotic." It would be unreasonable not to recognize that in his economic and social policies, for example, he was seriously concerned with humanitarian ideals of the general weal as well as with the fiscal and military interests of the state. Exaggerating the concept of sacrifice was as foreign to him as indulging in the pleasures of power. Regardless of the enormous sacrifices the Prussian military state demanded of its inhabitants, and regardless of the frequently harsh nature of its institutions, in the eyes of its architect it was not simply a despotism. On the contrary, the state was turned consciously onto the path of justice and culture.

This intention becomes most apparent in the limitations of tolerance and justice that Frederick imposed on the expansion of state power. The underlying principles of his legal reforms were: absolute legal security for all, even the most lowly, protection of the subject against the arbitrariness of government, abolition of cabinet justice, separation of administrative and judicial functions, and assurance of the strictest observance of the laws. His views on the protection of the intellectual liberties of his subjects can be learned from his essay of 1777 concerning the duties of rulers: "A poor unfortunate may be forced to pray according to a set formula, but he can refuse to believe in it; thus the persecutor has achieved nothing. If we consider the origins of society it becomes quite apparent that the ruler possesses no authority whatever over the thoughts of the citizens. We would have to be insane to imagine that men once said to one of their own kind: we shall raise you above us because we like to be slaves, and we give you the power to form our thoughts according to your will. On the contrary, men said: we need you, to insure that the laws by which we wish to be governed will be maintained, and that we will be wisely ruled and defended; for the rest we demand that you respect our freedom." In the clear awareness of its purely secular task the absolutist state did not aspire to absolute power.

6
The Conquest of Silesia

SINCE Nietzsche proclaimed the theory of the superman with his creative instincts, it has become commonplace to consider true heroism and realistic thought as incompatible opposites. According to this doctrine the hero must not only be without conscience, but he is necessarily also "always without consciousness." He must be unjust not only toward past and present, but at the same time blind, closed to reason, driven only by the creative daemon of his passions. Rational thought, so runs the common complaint, threatens the forcefulness of action. It makes men insecure, ambivalent, skeptical. The truly heroic decisions are born not in the sobering daylight of rational consideration, but in the twilight of dreams, in intoxicated enthusiasm, in the fever of a fanatical urge to act.

Frederick the Great is the most striking refutation of this false antithesis. He would never have grasped the idea that the statesman could see the reality of things too clearly to reach a decision. On the contrary, at times he was troubled because in spite of everything he still lacked the insight to evaluate the effect of his policies with certainty. It was not the cold and clear light of reason that disturbed him, but the cloudy twilight of doubt, the opaque play of chance, which distorts our analysis. As ruler he lacked neither conscience nor knowledge. As we know, he thought seriously about the inescapable conflict of duties, about the schism between the demands of humanitarianism and the demands of the state. We will see that he carefully analyzed in advance all possible dangers and every conceivable effect of his political and military actions. He mistrusted pure instinct; at the same time he was sufficiently clear-minded and free of illusions to recognize the uncertainties inherent in all political calculations. But his energies were far too great, his faith in the power of intelligence was much too firm, and his creative imagination too spontaneous and natural, for him to be handicapped or even delayed in his decisions by rational or ethical reservations. No "creative mood," no willful illusions or moral excitations, were needed to goad him into action. His letters and poems show how widely his moods ranged between jubilation, despondency, and even despair; but in the midst of emotional turmoil his will remained firm, and his mind sober, realistic, and penetrating. If any great German can be called a "rationalist" it is Frederick. And his example shows that rational thought does not necessarily have to mean debilitating criticism and skeptical equivocation. Stronger by far than his skepticism were his will and readiness to act; and these were not weakened but purified and hardened in the flames of rational analysis.

To be sure, Frederick did not possess this level of maturity at the outset; he had to educate himself to achieve it. If we study his political and military decisions during the first years after his accession, we find a good deal of youthful rashness, violence, and lack of foresight; not infrequently he gave way to moods of the moment, and alternated sharply between bravado and insecurity. On assuming the powers of government at the age of 28, he does not at once prove himself a polished master of statesmanship, as Bismarck was able to do when he was called to high office at the age of 47. The change that tore Frederick from the suspicious surveillance in his Rheinsberg retreat to the plenitude of power was too sudden. His contemporaries were certainly struck by the personal magic of this young king, who from the first day of his reign played his part with such assurance: a genius who did not doubt for a moment that he was setting out on the road to eternal glory. But at first his behavior was not without vanity and egotism, the inevitable products of a self-consciousness that has been overly stimulated. Extremely sobering experiences during the first two Silesian wars were needed to cure him. That he could be sufficiently severe with himself to turn these experiences to good use forms an essential part of his historic achievement.

His friends confidently expected that he would reign as a new Telemachus or Pericles. They saw in him the ideal humanitarian ruler, who would usher in a new golden age of peaceful morality and a renaissance of the arts and sciences. Nor did he disown these ideals in his new situation. The philosopher Wolff was recalled from the banishment that Frederick William I had imposed. The

Prussian Academy was thoroughly rejuvenated under its new head, Maupertuis. The reform of criminal justice was begun, torture was abolished, the principle of toleration of all confessions introduced into the state's religious policies. The personal relationship with Voltaire commenced. Knobelsdorff prepared plans for a new opera house; singers were hired to create a strong permanent ensemble. Nevertheless the friends of his Rheinsberg days were disappointed at the sparsity of the funds expended on cultural purposes, and at the modest tone of the new court in general. On the other hand, moneys flowed copiously to augment the army. And soon enough it became clear that this young prince wished to do more than garner grateful poems and speeches as the admired patron of writers, actors, and scientists.

From the first day his foreign policy sought to make it quite clear to the world that a new epoch had begun in the history of Prussia, that with Frederick's accession a new and disturbing power had joined the concert of Europe. Frederick was convinced that above all Prussia lacked reputation—the respect due to a state which needed to be feared. He was well aware that Vienna had considered his father as nothing more than a poltroon, whose threats and outbursts of anger need not be taken too seriously. He had personally experienced the mixture of cunning and disrespect with which the imperial ambassador, Seckendorff, manipulated Prussian policy in the intrigues that led to his marriage. Later Grumbkow had enabled him to learn some details of Prussia's negotiations with Austria and the western powers over her claims to Julich and Berg. Indignantly he saw that again and again Frederick William let himself be duped with false arguments, or was intimidated by collective notes sent by the various courts. Forty treaties or agreements were signed by the king, Frederick angrily wrote in his *History of the House of Brandenburg,* "which we refrain from listing since they are meaningless." It was his burning desire to avenge this chain of snubs and humiliations—as he interpreted them—and to let other powers at last feel the full weight of Prussia. Nothing better characterizes his attitude than the famous instruction to Colonel von Camas, sent to Paris as special envoy at the beginning of his reign: Camas should describe the new monarch as a hothead with incalculable ambitions. He should call attention to Prussia's military preparations, which were intentionally carried out with a good deal of fanfare and hint that in his uncontrollable urge for glory the king was prepared "to put all of Europe to the torch." In this calculating manner he turned his energies into diplomatic pressure. To underscore the message he terminated a long-drawn-out dispute with the Bishop of Liège by abruptly occupying the object of the quarrel—the abbey of Herstal. The impotent anger that spread through Europe as a result was just what he wanted. The two ministers heading the department of external affairs, who had dared to raise modest objections, were brusquely silenced by the young king: "When the ministers talk of policy they are quite competent men, but when they talk of war it is like an Iroquois discussing astronomy."

For Frederick's desire "to acquire reputation" as soon as possible, it was a great stroke of fortune that in October 1740 Emperor Charles VI died prematurely in Vienna, an event that shook the entire international system. Charles VI was the last Habsburg in the male line, and Europe had long awaited with suspense the moment of his death. At the cost of great sacrifices he had prevailed upon the major courts to recognize the Pragmatic Sanction, which imparted the succession of all Habsburg dominions to his daughter Maria Theresa. But what help were paper contracts against the ambition and avarice of powerful neighbors! For years Frederick had been convinced that every state would find different reasons to free itself from its commitments, and to lay its hands on a part of the Habsburg heritage. For Prussia, which stood in particular need of increasing her territory, it seemed important to move more rapidly than the others. A new situation must be created before negotiations began. Repeated experience had shown that otherwise the youngest of the great powers would in the end be left empty-handed.

This simple train of thought led to Frederick's sudden occupation of Silesia. At the time he himself assured his Italian literary friend, Algarotti, that the death of Charles VI caused him few headaches: Prussia's moves had long been prepared for this eventuality; it only remained to carry them out. This was juvenile exaggeration. Nothing at all had been prepared. The invasion of

Silesia was not carefully planned for years, but essentially a daring improvisation. Otherwise it might never have come about. But from the first Frederick was certain that he must not miss the opportunity to make important gains and avenge old wrongs that the Habsburgs had inflicted on Prussia. He was convinced that Prussia, squeezed between powerful neighbors and always threatened by hostile coalitions, could move ahead only if she quickly seized the right moment and exploited it by prompt and purposeful action. Frederick felt strongly that a missed opportunity would never recur. In his evaluation, the present condition of Europe seemed to hold out particular promise for a daring stroke.

Two principles—developed largely from his historical studies—dominated Frederick's view of the relations of the European powers. France's constant drive for hegemony; and the irreconcilable enmity between the French continental power and the naval and colonial power of Britain. He still saw in France the paramount, steadily expanding military state of Louis XIV, as Voltaire was to depict it in his historical writings, the great rival of the Habsburg dynasty, the ally of Sweden and Poland. Indignant with French actions in the reversion of Julich-Berg, he had recently, in his *Reflections* of 1738, warned the German princes against the deceitful schemes of Versailles. But now he felt certain of French assistance in his struggle with Vienna. It was inconceivable to him that the heirs of Louis XIV would fail to exploit Austria's difficulties by reducing her imperial power, solidifying and extending French influence in Germany, and possibly acquiring the Austrian Netherlands and the rest of Alsace. The French could not achieve this without Prussian help. But if Versailles should really misjudge the true interests of France so badly that it rejected the aid of the enterprising, young Prussian monarch—which was hardly conceivable—and should France remain faithful to the recently signed treaty with Austria and the Pragmatic Sanction, then Frederick believed that there was still the possibility of a rapprochement with England. It appeared certain to him that England, which was just becoming involved in the opening phases of a lengthy trade and colonial struggle with France and Spain, would always be on the opposite side of Bourbon alliances. How often during the last dec-

ades had the English sought Prussia's friendship! Wasn't this
friendship at one point to have been sealed by the crown prince's
marriage to an English princess?

This, essentially, was Frederick's evaluation of matters when he
began the conquest of Silesia. And on the whole he did not deceive
himself. Nevertheless his analysis contained some important errors.
Above all, the France of Fleury was no longer the France of Louis
XIV. She had passed the zenith of her power, her energy and determination having been sapped in the horrors of the War of the
Spanish Succession. The effects of this last great European catastrophe spread slowly; they were recognized far less clearly by contemporaries than by later generations. The prestige and might of
the French monarchy, her army and her finances, very gradually
decayed, while England imperceptibly rose to the position of first
power in Europe—though being a colonial empire she was never
involved as deeply and directly in the affairs of the Continent as
was her French rival. The ambitious, warlike France of old had
weakened and grown tamer. Several times in recent decades, in
quickly changing diplomatic combinations, she had allied herself
with her great rivals Austria and England. Her last duel with the
Habsburgs—the so-called War of the Polish Succession in the
1730's—had been conducted with little energy on either side, and
had ended with a complete reconciliation, indeed, even with signs
of amity between the two courts. But France's reputation had diminished. Her protégé, Stanislaus Leszynski, had finally been
compelled to give up the struggle for the Polish crown. Since then
Poland, which for so many years had been France's ally in the east,
had been hopelessly enfeebled. And Sweden, the other eastern ally,
had long ago lost her former power. The French government was
headed by Cardinal Fleury, now 87 years old, who seemed to have
no aim other than to secure the painfully achieved gains of his administration: the conquest of Lorraine and the rehabilitation of the
state's finances, and not to let them be compromised through new
wars. It was his doing that the most passionate enemy of the Habsburgs at the Versailles court, Chauvelin, the secretary for external
affairs, lost his post. If it was in Fleury's power, peace would long
prevail on the Continent. And France stood the more in need of it
since in September 1740 for the sake of her international prestige

she had reluctantly joined in the Spanish naval and colonial campaign against a threatened English trade monopoly.

It seemed that the second major Continental power—the Habsburg empire—had also aged and become weary. The diplomacy of Emperor Charles VI had sought security above all. Instead of consolidating Austria's eastern conquests, he made important sacrifices to gain paper guarantees for his Pragmatic Sanction. Rather than seeking security in military power, the emperor allowed the army to decay after Prince Eugene's death. The strength that still remained he squandered in a badly planned, pointless, and languid campaign against the Turks, which benefited Russia more than Austria. At the conclusion of his reign, the state's finances were exhausted to such an extent that it was scarcely possible to find money for the upkeep of the court. Finally, since the death of Peter the Great, the new and rising power in the East, the Russian Empire, was severely handicapped in her foreign affairs by repeated conflicts over the succession to the crown. For a moment Europe really might hope that the great continental struggles had finally ceased, and that the balance between the leading European states was at last fairly well established.

This international constellation offered favorable prospects to a young and ambitious power like Brandenburg–Prussia. However, the newcomer ran the danger of appearing as an unwanted meddler, who disturbed the balance of power that had been created with such difficulty, an intruder who released a new wave of wars over Europe, and once again called into question the entire international order established in the last decades. From the outset Frederician Prussia bore the handicap of being considered a brutal, presumptuous upstart. Her ruler believed that this newest power could succeed only through surprise attack. For this reason Prussia was soon decried as ruthless, warlike, and "militaristic." Weakness often obliged her to change alliances rapidly, to exploit new situations without scruple—and the state soon gained the reputation of being especially sly, faithless, and Machiavellian.

Frederick found it much more difficult than he had expected to disturb Fleury's policy of peace, to arouse the ambitions and warlike instincts of the French nation against the pacific system of her leading minister. Before he succeeded, his Silesian project nearly

failed. He was even more disappointed with England. Not for a
moment did the possibility of a genuine alliance present itself.
George II was also Elector of Hanover, and in this capacity observed the dangerous progress of his north German rival with envy
and hate. He did all he could to form a coalition that would encircle Prussia and bring her to her knees. His motives, however,
were not shared by his British ministers. As in the past, the British
Empire had no greater interest on the Continent than to prevent
the hegemony of any state that might become a threat on the seas
and in the colonies. France fitted into this category, but not Austria. Indeed, a strong Austria was desirable for the maintenance of
the European balance of power. Consequently Frederick's attack on
Silesia appeared in England as an assault on the most sacred principles of European politics. Since this island power is never directly
involved in the territorial conflicts of the Continental states, she
finds it much easier to let her special interests coincide, in reality or
in appearance, with the common interests of Europe. And in general English thought and attitudes were entirely opposed to the
policy of Frederician Prussia. The genuine Briton is repelled by the
idea that the fate of peoples, the decision for war or peace, could
depend on the ambition, the lust for glory, or even the conscien-
tiousness of a single individual. Moreover, to this day England re-
tains from the Middle Ages something of the old faith in the invi-
olability of eternal principles of right and justice, which are un-
touched by the passions and policies of the moment. The English
have not lived through as many catastrophes and wars, which
shook this faith and dulled the instinct of justice, as had the continental states since the Renaissance. Therefore they are more prone
to condemn acts of power politics as atrocities, and as violations of
humanitarian ideals. Finally, the manner in which Frederick executed his Silesian project presented him to the world as a criminal
and a malevolent aggressor.

Decisive in creating this impression was the fact that he attacked
Silesia without warning, and occupied it before he so much as
opened talks with Vienna. We already know the reason for his decision: he believed that negotiations over his Silesian claims could
not succeed until he had created a *fait accompli*. No doubt he was
correct. But if we wish to understand Frederick's historical image

completely we must recognize the unprecedented and daring quality of this action. The principles of strict justice that his father and,
indeed, most of his predecessors had observed in foreign affairs
could not have been transgressed more sharply and suddenly. What
now remained of the pathos-laden assurances in his *Anti-Machiavel*
that violations of laws and treaties were unnecessary to truly enlightened policies? Completely isolated, without allies, without diplomatic preparation, he faced Europe, trusting only in the logic of
the situation and in his army. Even though he conceived and justified his actions to the world as necessary for the good of the state,
as an emergency measure, as retaliation for former transgressions
—all of Europe felt challenged. His own close advisors, General
von Schwerin and Minister von Podewils, considered the enterprise
a dangerous adventure. Without success they sought to postpone or
modify it. He listened to them, but he followed his daemon. They
foresaw what would happen: his entire life was to be spent in
overcoming the consequences of this adventure, in meeting the
dangers that resulted from it. But overcome them he did. With his
success he laid the foundation of Prussia's greatness. As long as her
rise continued, his policy could be justified as the dangerous but inevitable breakthrough of a state which violently shook off narrow
and petty conditions to achieve worldwide significance.

There is little point in pursuing the question of whether or not
Brandenburg's claims to Silesia were legally well-founded. Originally they extended over great parts of the province; but wars during the latter half of the sixteenth century threw their validity in
doubt, and in the seventeenth century they were superseded by new
treaties. Only the dishonesty with which Austria had secured these
agreements now made it possible to renew the old demands. Frederick's predecessor had no longer raised the claims. But the young
king decided that the Silesian "pretension" was far more advantageous to Prussia than her much-contested Rhenish claims. They
were more significant economically, and incomparably better suited
to round off the Prussian heartlands. They provided an excellent
strategic bridgehead for a policy that had to contend with both Poland and Austria, far removed from the sphere of interests of the
west European powers. Frederick would have liked nothing better
than to exchange all claims in western Germany for Silesia. On

several occasions in later years he showed himself ready to relinquish sizable parts of his West German possessions to France or England in return for acquisitions in the East. His desire for expansion was guided by considerations of practical usefulness, not by historical accident and antiquarian "legal claims." At bottom, the appeal to venerable dynastic treaties of inheritance had no place in his diplomatic style. He left this sort of thing to his jurists and ministers—let them see how far they could convince the world. On the margin of a legal argument that Podewils had drafted, he wrote the arrogant and cynical comment: "Bravo: the work of an excellent charlatan!" He scarcely expected legal documents to make much of an impression in Vienna.

He counted far more on the effect created by the facile occupation of Silesia, which took place in December 1740. This event, he hoped, would persuade Vienna to give in, especially if the occupation were combined with offers of a financial indemnity, of Brandenburg's vote for Maria Theresa's husband Francis of Lorraine in the imperial election, and of a guarantee for the rest of Maria Theresa's heritage. He counted on the weakness of the foreign prince-consort, on his indifference to Austrian possessions, as well as on the isolation and inexperience of the young queen and on her helplessness in the midst of enormous dangers. He did not know that this woman possessed more courage and a greater sense of honor than all the men at her court. That she had been robbed of Silesia without so much as a warning made it impossible for her to acquiesce. She would rather risk extreme peril than accept such an insult. In her person, Habsburg's ancient imperial pride rose up against the faithless vassal, who after stealing a province dared to insult the dynasty even further by extending an offer of assistance.

That was only the first of Frederick's disappointments. More serious ones followed. With what bravado and assurance he had left for Silesia, for the "rendezvous with Glory" as he had proclaimed to his officers on the eve of their departure! For a time the quick initial achievement threatened to deprive him of all calm and vision. After occupying Breslau he felt himself to be "Fortuna's happiest child," and was certain that this success would bring him and his helper, Podewils, eternal fame. Although now even he thought of the Silesian enterprise as a "great folly," he saw it as "a folly that is very difficult to shed once you have been possessed by it." But winter passed and he was unable to find a single ally. All hopes for the success of the Prussian intrigues in St. Petersburg proved to be vain. England–Hanover evinced a remarkably cool reserve. Then, in March 1741, word came that a great European alliance for the defeat and destruction of the aggressor was almost completed: England and Austria were to be joined by the Dutch Republic, Russia, and Poland–Saxony. Cardinal Fleury said he was prepared to accept the Pragmatic Sanction, now he hoped to deprive the Habsburgs only of the imperial dignity, and bestow it on the Bavarian Elector, who was to serve as a pawn of French policy. Frederick's speculation that the European powers were avidly waiting to join Prussia's attack and share in the inheritance of Charles VI appeared to have been quite mistaken.

The political crisis was intensified by military developments. The thin screen of Prussian detachments was unable to prevent the advance of Austrian forces across the Bohemian mountains into Silesia. Rather than concentrate his troops immediately for a counterattack, Frederick was misled by his advisor Schwerin into spending far too much time protecting his depots in Upper Silesia. He recognized too late that the main Austrian army under Neipperg was endangering his communications with Lower Silesia and with Berlin. Suddenly everything hung on the outcome of his first battle—the battle of Mollwitz on 10 April 1741. If he failed to break through the Austrian envelopment, his position would be extremely grave. It cannot be said that he showed himself fully equal to this crisis. Instead of attacking the surprised and numerically inferior Austrians in their camps, he wasted time—as he himself subsequently admitted—on complicated and methodical approach marches, as laid down in the regulations. A sudden, massive cavalry attack disrupted his advance. The Prussian formations fell into disorder, the cavalry failed to do its duty. For a moment everything seemed lost; the king himself was in danger of being taken prisoner together with his entire army. No one had expected anything like it. How long had it been since a Prussian ruler had personally fought in battle? The fate of Gustavus Adolphus and of Charles XII may have flashed before the eyes of the Prussian generals, and the natural excitement of their young commander-in-chief probably interfered with their tactical dispositions. At any rate, Schwerin urgently advised Frederick to escape; he himself would see what could be done to save the situation. And his advice was taken. Frederick rode over fifty miles that night, searching for the Prussian reserves; only chance prevented his capture by Austrian hussars. When he was called back to Mollwitz the following morning, he returned to victory. Under Schwerin's determined leadership the methodically advancing Prussian infantry had defeated their badly trained and inadequately disciplined opponents.

Frederick was saved, but the campaign was far from won. Upper Silesia remained in Austrian hands, and despite their great numerical superiority, the Prussians did not risk a second battle. For an entire summer the two armies faced each other, scarcely moving, while Frederick was busy improving the discipline and ability of his troops, especially—in light of the experience at Mollwitz—teaching his cavalry how to attack. The political consequences of the successful battle were stronger than its military effects. The diplomatic situation finally became more flexible. On the one hand, the planned Anglo-Russian alliance failed to coalesce. The English government recognized how dangerous Prussia might become, and much against the wishes of George II now worked for a compromise solution of the Austro-Prussian conflict, which would free Austria to move against France. By contrast, the party led by Marshal Belle-Isle became dominant in Versailles, and on 5 June an alliance was concluded between France and Prussia. At first Frederick had spun out the negotiations; he was not prepared to fight as the vassal of France, as though he were a mere German princeling. Eventually, he succeeded in having the alliance impose far greater obligations on France than on himself. In the meantime the small German states were becoming restless. Under the leadership of France the majority of the Electors combined to support the Bavarian Elector for the Imperial throne. In the fall Saxony joined them. All were reaching out for the possessions of the Habsburg princess; everyone wanted to take part in the easy looting. French and Bavarian troops penetrated into Upper Austria; Vienna itself seemed in danger. Almost despairing, Maria Theresa fled from her capital to Hungary. On 11 September 1741, in a speech before the Hungarian Estates, she implored the nobility to take up arms for her and for her child, and to save the throne and the realm. With this address began the rise of the Hungarian element in the Habsburg monarchy, which until that day had been dominated by Germans. It laid the seed of that later dualism, which was finally to destroy the Habsburg state—a tragic consequence of Prussia's growing power in Germany.

But with the invasion of Austria, the Franco-Prussian party had passed the apogee of its achievements. The characteristic flaws of all coalition warfare had long since become apparent: in the final analysis each ally thought only of himself. The military efforts of France fell far short of Frederick's expectations. Fleury had no intention of bearing the major burden of the war. An advance on Vienna, which Prussia advised, was not carried out; instead the French tried to occupy Bohemia, possession of which would strengthen the Bavarian Elector. Why should they help Frederick conquer Austria? How would that benefit France? Her aim in the war was not the establishment of a new, powerful German Empire, but the perpetuation of the strife of antagonistic German leagues possessing relatively equal strength. Frederick did not remain ignorant of this policy, and was deeply disappointed. Nothing troubled him more than the prospect of having the war drag on. What he needed were quick, sharp blows and rapid decisions. His finances could not support long campaigns. He was impatient to end the war, to secure his conquests, to gain Upper Silesia as winter quarters for his army, to block inconvenient Saxon claims on Bohemian and Silesian territory by means of secret negotiations—above all, he violently resisted being nothing more than a satellite of French policy.

For these reasons Frederick secretly concluded an agreement with the Austrians—the Convention of Kleinschnellendorf of 9 October 1741—which was intended as a preliminary to a separate peace. Neipperg was permitted to withdraw unhindered from Silesia, while after a pretended siege Frederick occupied the fortresses of Neisse and Glatz. This put all of Silesia under his control; on the other hand, Maria Theresa could now deploy her one sizable field army for the defense of Austria. To deceive Prussia's allies, the advance guards of the two armies staged a few skirmishes. Frederick promised that in the coming peace talks he would limit his demands to Lower Silesia; a clear decision between the two powers had been avoided. But in spite of all attempts at justification, which continue to be advanced even today, Frederick's step was politically as rash as it was morally doubtful. He himself recognized the Machiavellian character of his act; he tried to justify it by the political and military emergency in which he found himself. But even if there had been no collusion, Neipperg could not have held the fortresses much longer. And in the political realm, Frederick simply lost the trust of his allies, who could not be kept ignorant of his arrangements, and made no concrete gains in return. By removing the pressure from his great antagonist Maria Theresa, he ruined the prospects of his own party. His decision was prompted not by a true crisis, but by his youth and impatience, and perhaps also by a kind of quizzical desire to see whether he could outdo all others in the refinements of a ruthlessly cunning diplomacy, and cheat the Saxons of their spoils. It was no accident that his ministers were never consulted.

And yet in the long run it was not possible for him to withdraw from the war unilaterally. Austria would now make peace only if the Bavarian imperial candidacy were renounced. On the other hand, the important military successes which the French and Bavarians were gaining in Bohemia evoked the fear that by remaining inactive Prussia would go empty-handed in the division of the spoils. Only a few weeks after the agreement had been reached at Kleinschnellendorf, Frederick rejected the Convention.

We need not follow the further diplomatic negotiations and military developments in detail. Frederick's basic aim was to maintain Prussia's independence from France. This was the motive behind his insistence that he would reenter the war only at the head of a separate Prusso-Saxon army. For this reason, too, he at once reopened talks with the Austrians after his daring thrust at Vienna through Moravia had failed, and the deliberateness of French strategy once again threatened to prolong the war. To be sure, he did not accomplish his purpose until a second victory, the battle of Chotusitz on 17 May 1742, had reaffirmed his military prowess. In the Peace of Breslau, concluded on 28 July, he again unexpectedly deserted his allies, and after stubborn negotiations over the exact location of a new border, he succeeded in retaining all of Silesia.

But was it really possible to bring the spoils to safety before the struggle, now grown into a European war, had come to an end? Could the originator of this war withdraw before the ultimate decision had been reached? Weren't his policies creating an impression of weakness and unreliability? Wasn't he personally. destroying the renown that had cost so much blood to establish? Frederick might well fear that the final peace negotiations would exclude him, and that, discredited, he would then have to face the vengeance of his great Austrian opponent in isolation.

His fears were fulfilled soon enough. As might have been expected, the Bavarian Elector, now Emperor Charles VII, was unable to maintain himself against Austria without the help of Prussian arms. Soon his army was compelled to surrender. In the meantime England harvested the fruit of her peace mediations. The English had hesitated to take an active part in the war on the Continent; they feared that Hanoverian concerns might involve them too deeply in conflicts that were remote from their true interests. But the political climate changed in February 1742. The Walpole Ministry fell, the activist party became dominant, and soon was given completely free scope by Prussia's withdrawal from the war. Europe witnessed a development that it was to experience repeatedly in centuries to come: England's will to fight grew slowly, and not until numerous attempts at compromise had failed, but then with tenacious and sustained force. Under the command of George II a large army was assembled in the Netherlands to support the Pragmatic Sanction. The fight against France was proclaimed a national war, waged to restore the European balance of power and international justice as well as to achieve British rule of the seas. Combined into a "Pragmatic Army" English, Hanoverian, Danish, and Hessian contingents drove the French across the Rhine, and soon after entered Alsace. Bavaria was flooded with Austrian troops, and the unhappy emperor hurried from place to place, a fugitive in serious danger of losing his native land to the Habsburgs. At Hanau, in the summer of 1743, peace negotiations were already getting under way, from which the Prussian ambassador was excluded.

In this situation, Frederick first tried vainly to reestablish his position by diplomatic means. For the first time he employed a device that he was subsequently to use more than once when Prussia could not find support beyond Germany's borders: he made himself the champion of the German Estates against the Habsburgs, the protector of the Empire's constitution and of the privileges held by the German princes. He sought to range the south German courts behind the emperor, and to strengthen Bavaria by secularizing ecclesiastic territories, and by organizing an imperial army. He played with the idea of a new constitution in which Bavaria would assume the symbolic leadership of the Empire, while Prussia controlled its military forces. In short, he was thinking about a new Empire, founded with French help, a realm dependent on French protection. It is a significant fact of German history that such a scheme could no longer be carried out. Not only were most of the smaller courts far too firmly attached to the Habsburg imperial tradition, but even more important, in the last century France had become Germany's "arch-enemy." Frederick knew that even his closest advisor, Podewils, resisted a Franco-Prussian alliance with all his soul. In the German courts he encountered the same opposition to an even greater extent, coupled with a pronounced suspicion of Prussia. His policy could lead only to failure.

Frederick's concern increased when King George's "Pragmatic Alliance" was joined by Sardinia and Saxony. Was it possible that a new coalition was being formed to attack him and deprive him of Silesia? His suspicions made the threat seem even greater than it actually was. Frederick's attitude was the natural one of a man always in danger, to whom only a constant readiness to fight seemed to guarantee the permanency of his power. His quick decision to take up arms is characteristic: once again he must surprise and forestall the enemy. Nevertheless, this time he was unwilling to attack without being certain of having allies. Otherwise France might make a separate peace with Austria, especially since she was now fighting to defend her own territory. Frederick quickly negotiated a new alliance with France. Fleury had died, the young Louis XV longed for martial glory, and felt disposed to go to war. Frederick succeeded in inflaming his ambitions to such a degree that the recent disappointing experiences with Prussia were forgotten at Versailles. He also initiated alliances with Russia and Sweden, though in the end these came to nothing. But further delay was impossible if the enemy was not to triumph. He broke the peace of Breslau. Eighty thousand Prussians—"Imperial Auxiliaries" for Charles VII fighting for the "Liberty of the Empire" —invaded Bohemia in August 1744.

Frederick's hopes for military victory were greater than ever. He had carefully used two years of peace to replenish his war chest, to increase his armies to 140,000 men, and to train his soldiers in field maneuvers—at that time an important innovation. He counted on sizable assistance from France. But rarely were proud hopes disappointed as ignominiously as in this campaign. In the first Silesian War the fortunes of war had repeatedly passed from one side to the other; in the second they brought Prussia close to disaster. That in the end Prussia was saved was due only to the fact that Frederick's psychic energies and military abilities kept pace with the increasing dangers.

In the military sphere it was nearly his undoing that his strategy —as in the first campaign—was too daring for the capabilities and supply systems of eighteenth-century armies. He hoped to advance rapidly, carry the war as far into enemy territory as possible, defeat the main enemy forces, and in conjunction with the French possibly even reach Vienna. Accordingly he invaded Bohemia without paying attention to the Saxon threat at his rear. He captured Prague, and continued his rapid advance to the south while his own generals secretly criticized the risks he was taking. His plan could succeed only if his French allies fully occupied the Austrian forces along the Rhine until the trap was sprung. But at the decisive moment an illness of Louis XV immobilized French leadership, and the Austrians were able to turn east. Unexpectedly they appeared on Frederick's open right flank. Their generals maneuvered perfectly and could not be forced to give battle. Some tactical errors committed by Frederick, the desolate condition of the country, roads made impassable by the fall rains, the breakdown of supply, failures of the commissariat, of the medical services, and above all of reconnaissance—everything combined to complete the disaster. A terrible retreat began across the mountainous Bohemian border, through swamps and forests, with the troops harassed by enemy fire. Epidemics thinned the ranks; no fewer than seventeen thousand men deserted. Totally demoralized, the proud army finally returned to Silesia. Every weakness of troops trained to unquestioning obedience but incapable of independent action had been laid bare. Even the officers began to lose faith in the generalship of their young monarch.

The enemy in his turn crossed the Prussian border, and it seemed impossible to retain Silesia for long. Maria Theresa triumphed, the situation of 1741 had been reversed. An anxious winter began. Emperor Charles VII died, and Bavaria came to terms with the Habsburgs. France was kept busy in the Low Countries, and lost interest in German affairs; the energy of her war effort seemed gradually to decline. It was in vain that Frederick appealed to England's good offices—the English were busy strengthening Austria and Saxony by creating a new European alliance, in which even Russia might participate. The Prussian treasury was empty. Attempts to negotiate a loan in Holland failed; the contributions paid by the Estates of the old provinces of the monarchy were far from sufficient to finance another campaign. Frederick seriously considered selling England the harbor of Emden, which he had recently inherited together with East Frisia. He was ready for the worst. Toward the end of April he gave orders that in a crisis the royal silver treasure, the court, and the royal archives be moved to Spandau. Based on the fortresses of Spandau and Küstrin he would defend the Mark Brandenburg once Silesia was lost. The first major crisis of the state had arrived. Had Frederick miscalculated? Had he lost his game?

He still possessed one potential which seemed inexhaustible: his courage. The exceptional psychic energy, which he had demonstrated as an eighteen-year-old in the conflict with his father, now underwent its first great historic test. In amazingly little time he was able to overcome the army's demoralization. He inspired his troops with the same optimism and will to succeed that possessed him, and in the spring of 1745 he was again ready to fight. Assisted by the refined maneuver strategy of Prince Leopold of Dessau, a "mentor" whom he personally disliked, he greatly improved his positions in Silesia. But only a decisive battle could really save him. Finally his opponents gave him his opportunity when they descended in eight columns from the Silesian border range to the plains of Hohenfriedberg. Seventy thousand Austrians and Saxons

faced sixty thousand Prussians. Frederick deceived the enemy with
feints, surprised him with a night march, and attacked him in an
oblique order of battle. All this belongs to the highest achievements
of his generalship. It is apparent how much Frederick was learning
from one clash to the next. At Mollwitz, Schwerin alone had saved
a critical situation. At Chotusitz, Frederick decided the issue by a
clever outflanking maneuver, which had been planned and already
partly executed by the younger Dessau. Hohenfriedberg was Frederick's first great personal achievement. He was particularly proud
that his formerly ineffective heavy cavalry now proved itself equal
to every test.

The battle of Hohenfriedberg rid Silesia of the enemy and re-
stored Prussia's hopes for victory, but it was far from bringing
peace. The Austrian army had not been destroyed, it moved into
strong defensive positions in Bohemia, which Frederick did not
dare to attack. Maria Theresa's fighting spirit was undiminished;
her political position in Germany excellent. Even without Brandenburg's vote she was now able to carry through the election of her
husband, Francis of Lorraine, as German emperor. England at last
agreed to try mediation, but English policy remained ambiguous,
and new dangers threatened from Russia and Saxony. Seduced by
George II and backed by Russia, Saxony entered into a military
pact the object of which was the partition of Prussia. In the meantime operations in the field almost led to a new catastrophe. While
returning from Bohemia to Silesia, Frederick's own carelessness led
his army into a trap near Soor, from which no escape seemed possible. His amazing calm and the courage of his troops transformed
an apparently certain defeat into a brilliant victory. From this day
on dated his European reputation as a military leader, and the belief in his invincibility. But even this success did not yet suffice to
bring about a reasonable peace. Maria Theresa was too embittered,
and she still hoped that her forces might effect a juncture with the
Saxons for an invasion of Brandenburg. Her fighting spirit broke
down only when this prospect was ruined by Leopold of Dessau's
hard-fought victory on the snow-swept fields of Kesselsdorf, after
the Saxons were decisively beaten, and Dresden was occupied by
Prussian troops. Under strong English pressure, peace was concluded at Dresden on 24 December 1745. Frederick recognized

Francis as Emperor of Germany, but retained all of Silesia, which was gain enough. He had never intended to weaken Austria to the point of assuring French predominance in Germany.

Above all, the peace released Prussia from a political and military situation which in the long run was insupportable. The Prussian treasury had been exhausted months earlier, a Russian invasion was imminent. Frederick deserted his French ally once again, but this time his justification of dire necessity was more convincing. In the dreadful experiences of the last campaigns he had finally recognized the limits of his power. He returned to Berlin determined never again to challenge Europe with a war of aggression: "Henceforth I won't bother even a cat," he said, "unless it is in self-defense. To my mind, more true greatness lies in working for the happiness of my subjects than fighting for the peace of Europe. In one word, I want to enjoy life. What are we poor humans, that we devise projects that cost so much blood? Let us live, and let us further life!"

By retaining Silesia, Prussia had established her position as a major power in Germany and in Europe. Now the ambitious warrior on her throne again gave way to the enlightened, peaceful prince, to the humanitarian shepherd of his people. While the European war dragged on, to end at last in exhaustion and compromise, the issues never clearly settled, Frederick turned his undiminished energy to the internal development of the state.

7
Maintenance of Prussia's New Power

i. The Diplomatic Encirclement of Prussia

CONQUEST and retention of Silesia completely changed the character of the Brandenburg-Prussian state. The "mongrel, part electorate, part monarchy," as Frederick called it, had joined the ranks of the leading European powers, and now shared with them the responsibility for the political fate of the continent. With the acquisition of Silesia, the population of the state, which in 1740 had numbered approximately two and a half million, increased by nearly half. The treasury gained 800,000 taler annually from the surplus of the Silesian administration—about half of the amount contributed by the royal domains in all the central provinces together. Still, even with these additions the potential of the newest of the major powers remained relatively modest. In 1756 the state's 4 million inhabitants compared with over 16 million Frenchmen, 12 million Austrians, and the more than 8 million inhabitants of the British Isles. What was even more important, Frederick remained —in Voltaire's derisive phrase—a "King of the Border Zones." Apart from the few core provinces around Berlin, his state consisted of widely distributed territories. East Prussia was entirely isolated. The Saxon border ran less than 35 miles from the gates of Berlin. The only connection between Silesia and Brandenburg was a corridor 25 to 35 miles wide. In any major conflict the Prussian possessions along the Rhine, in Westphalia, and the recently acquired territories in East Frisia on the North Sea were outposts that could not be defended. The inhabitants of these scattered areas were still so far from sharing a sense of national community that at the beginning of the Seven Years' War, preachers in Berlin could refer in their sermons to "all these provinces, which together we must revere as our fatherland." It was the experience of the Silesian wars that created the concept of a common Prussian state, and, indeed, it was during these wars that the name Prussia began to be used as the collective term for all Hohenzollern possessions.

Even after her expansion in the 1740's, Prussia unquestionably remained an incomplete state; the addition of Silesia only intensified her problems. Prussia still had not achieved the territorial cohesion that Crown Prince Frederick had longed for in the days of Küstrin. During the peace negotiations of 1742 he had sought to exchange East Frisia for a strip of northern Bohemia in order to improve his strategic position vis-à-vis Saxony and Austria. The later years of the War of the Austrian Succession had taught him that Saxony would be the most desirable of all future conquests; farther down the scale of usefulness came the Polish province of West Prussia, and Swedish Pomerania—all territories which his political testaments of 1752 and 1768 urged his successors to acquire, either by diplomacy or by war. However, he considered these to be ultimate goals, not attainable perhaps for generations to come. It was "chimerical" to think of them seriously since Prussia could never embark on such ambitious schemes unless international conditions were exceptionally favorable, and he hardly dared hope that this could ever be the case. In any event, for his part he was determined not to pursue fantasies, but do what was reasonable and possible. Prussia's weaknesses might be compensated for by sound economic and financial policies, by an efficient administration, by increasing and fully exploiting the monarchy's human and other resources, and above all by strengthening the army. With this resolve he returned to Berlin at the conclusion of the War of the Austrian Succession.

It was this time that he was first acclaimed "the Great." Actually it was only now that he entered into his full political maturity; the preceding years had in many respects still been a time of apprenticeship. The ten years of peace between the second and third of his wars, however, showed Frederick at the peak of his ability to shape Prussia's domestic affairs. And it was only now that the institutions and procedures of the state took on a characteristic "Frederician" cast. These years were also the golden age of Sans Souci, and the period when in his actions Frederick came closest to his ideal of the humanitarian, peace-loving prince. Not that he renounced his ambitions, or in Delbrück's words, became used to the "comfortable and uneventful life of an industrious administrator, who devotes his free hours to philosophy, poetry, and music." Not for a moment could his life or the situation of his state be considered comfortable. But his ambition to strengthen Prussia could take paths other than that of military conquest. He did not want to be a saber-rattling daredevil as epitomized by Voltaire's depiction of Charles XII. He had learned to place the interests of the state before his personal desire for glory. And consequently it was not a new urge to conquer but his concern to defend and maintain Prussia's position as a major power that brought about the last great test of strength that he was to face.

This interpretation is admittedly contested. Several eminent historians of the last century regarded the Seven Years' War as a further attempt at conquest, with Saxony and West Prussia as the prize. The scholarly controversy on this subject need not detain us, but it does suggest that the state of the world in 1756 deserves closer investigation. Given the prevailing circumstances was it at all possible for Frederick to believe he could make new conquests?

The Peace of Dresden had left Prussia without reliable allies. It is true that officially the Franco-Prussian alliance continued in force until 1756, but the bond was profoundly weakened by the numerous disappointments the two allies had visited on each other. It is equally true that Frederick remained in uncontested possession of Silesia, and that at the Peace of Aix-la-Chapelle in 1748 he even received an international guarantee of the new borders. In the negotiations he had very ably exploited his position as a neutral who held the balance of power between the belligerents. But as soon as peace was concluded this advantage disappeared, and Prussia faced the eastern powers almost in isolation. At first Empress Elizabeth of Russia had admired Frederick; but her vain, changeable nature, her sensuality and indolence, made her vulnerable to court intrigues, and under the influence of Austrian diplomats and her chancellor, Bestuzhev, she turned against Frederick. For years Russia's foreign policy had shown little energy; now it was growing more ambitious. Like Austria, Russia had no wish to see a new power emerge east of the Elbe, which, for one thing, might interfere with her designs on Poland.

From the time that French influence had been eliminated in Poland, Russia had viewed that country as a satellite and future acquisition. Elizabeth could not forgive Frederick for having supported Poland–Saxony against Russia at the end of the War of the Austrian Succession, nor his alliance with France, which had led to a Swedish attack on Russia. Since 1746 Russia and Austria were bound by a defensive alliance, not unlike the Franco-Russian alliance of 1894. If Frederick should again attack Maria Theresa, Austria could count on Russia's help to reconquer her lost province. Henceforth Elizabeth and Bestuzhev waited for an opportunity to strike, even trying to goad the hated rival power into taking up arms. In 1749 they nearly succeeded in unleashing a war over the succession to the Swedish throne; as a brother-in-law of the Swedish crown prince as well as an ally of France, Frederick could scarcely have remained uninvolved. The attempt failed thanks to his intelligent and energetic reaction: by ostentatiously placing his army on a war footing he dispelled the danger with unexpected speed. But from then on the Russian threat permanently darkened the political horizon. Diplomatic relations between Berlin and St. Petersburg were not resumed, and every spring Russian armies gathered on the East Prussian frontier.

The alliance between Russia and Austria was the first step in the political and military encirclement of Prussia, which now had to be prepared for war on two fronts. Frederick sought to meet this eventuality by gradually increasing his army to 180,000 men. When fighting began in 1756 its strength had actually risen to about 154,000 men, not counting waggoners and second-line troops, but including trained reserves that for the time being could not be uniformed and equipped. If the Russians, as Frederick still hoped in 1756, committed no more than 45,000 men, and if the Austrians remained at their former level, Prussia would be a match for their combined forces. Frederick tended to have a low opinion of the ability of the Russian soldier—a serious error, as it turned out—and a few years before the war he still thought Prussian training so superior that he was convinced 75,000 Prussians could defeat 100,000

Austrians. But with every passing year this calculation lost validity. The Austrian monarchy was rapidly increasing the efficiency of its administration and strengthening its army and financial position. By 1756 Maria Theresa had managed to bring her German, Hungarian, Italian, and Flemish contingents to 165,000 men, a figure that did not include the levies from the Balkan military frontier.

In short, a war against Austria and Russia was bound to be full of danger for Frederick; whether, for example, East Prussia could be held against the Russians was at least doubtful. As soon as one of the western powers combined with Austria to carry the war into central Germany it would become a struggle for life and death. But Frederick did not seriously expect such a turn of events. He counted on the continuing antagonism of France and England, which soon after the Peace of Aix-la-Chapelle had again intensified. Prussia should be able to ally herself with one of these powers, and thus keep the other in check. An alliance with France seemed at all events the more advantageous: the French army could be much more useful to Prussia—and also much more dangerous—than Britain's navy. Without French help Frederick could not have triumphed in the War of the Austrian Succession; an essential part of Prussia's new power rested on the alliance with France. Despite their disagreements during the past years, he felt that he had to do everything he could to regain French friendship. Frederick expressed the basis of their relationship by comparing Alsace Lorraine and Silesia to two sisters, one of whom had married France, the other Prussia: "This bond compels the two nations to follow the same policy. Prussia cannot passively stand aside if Alsace and Lorraine are taken from France, and Prussia is able to support France effectively, because she can immediately thrust at the center of Austrian power. Similarly France cannot tolerate Austria's reconquest of Silesia, since this would severely weaken an ally who is useful to France on the Baltic and in Germany, and who in case of unexpectedly grave danger could certainly save Lorraine or Alsace through diversionary actions."

This was the kind of pointed political thesis that appealed to Frederick. The eternal enmity between Habsburgs and Bourbons, from which followed France's need to secure Prussia as her German ally, seemed to him as inevitable and undeniable as any math-

ematical axiom. Political sense and the history of centuries demonstrated that it lay in the French interest to expand to the Rhine (at
times Frederick actually called the river France's natural eastern
frontier): in turn it was the natural interest of the German Empire to oppose this expansion. That this antagonism could ever be
bridged seemed as unthinkable to Frederick, as German statesmen
before the First World War found it inconceivable that England
and her rivals could one day become allies. Until the spring of 1756
Frederick relied on his equation; and for this reason did not especially exert himself to court France. He thought it preferable to let
the French make the first move; he wished to keep a free hand as
long as possible, rather than become involved too soon and without
necessity in the overseas conflict between France and Great Britain,
which did not directly affect Prussia's interests. With a show of indifference he at first responded to French inquiries about the terms
under which he wished to renew the alliance, which would lapse in
1756. He was convinced that even in the absence of a formal treaty
he could count on French aid in case of war.

And yet, in the end the apparently certain calculation turned out
to be deceptive. Neither French nor Austrian interests proved
immutable. Austria no longer was the imperial power that for generations had guarded Germany on the Rhine, often enough to the
detriment of her Balkan policies. As the emperor's strength declined in Germany—a decline to which Prussia's actions contributed more than any other factor—the Habsburgs concentrated
more and more on their dynastic interests in Hungary and Italy.
How passionately had the previous generation fought to block
French expansion on the borders of Lorraine and Belgium!
Twenty years after the War of the Spanish Succession Lorraine
was ceded to France in exchange for possessions in Northern Italy.
Now, after another twenty years, Vienna was prepared to sacrifice
large areas of the Netherlands, the Spanish legacy, which had once
been defended with such efforts—if in return France would help
her reconquer Silesia.

Count Kaunitz, the new Austrian chancellor and foreign minister,
and trusted advisor of Maria Theresa, had developed this unprecedented project during his service as Austrian ambassador in Paris.
Kaunitz, who was one of the ablest statesmen of his age, shared

with Frederick the rationalist concept of the modern, enlightened monarchy, which was ridding itself of outdated historical ties. He recognized that Austria's main task had come to be the recovery of her former dominance in Germany. All her strength should now be concentrated toward this end; remote possessions that handicapped her policies should be given up whenever necessary; above all, the traditional enmity of France must be overcome. He was able gradually to allay Maria Theresa's misgivings about such a daring reversal, which he pursued with every means of his subtle diplomacy, a diplomacy that was calmer, more consistent, and consequently more purposeful than Frederick's frequently shifting and nervous way in international relations.

The Austrian chancellor's project was facilitated by the fact that not only Austria's interests had changed but those of France as well. Versailles' traditional policy of conquest along the Rhine had attained its major goals; to continue on this path no longer promised great advantages. During the recent war French intervention in German affairs had required substantial sacrifices of men and money but brought far more disappointments than benefits. By contrast, the successful defense of North American possessions against Great Britain assumed new importance. The interests of the French nation were turning to the colonies, to the consolidation of her empire, to the expansion of her fleet and her overseas trade. But everywhere English rivalry interfered. In North America, Quebec and its vast hinterland had to be protected against British settlers. In the East Indies, British influence among the native princes needed to be undercut. In the West Indies, it was a question of raising the production of sugar, indigo, cacao, and coffee to achieve domination of the world market. In Africa, promising trading stations in Senegal and Guinea needed to be consolidated and militarily secured. In the Levant, British trade needed to be driven out. Neither the Peace of Utrecht in 1713 nor the Peace of Aix-la-Chappelle thirty-five years later had eliminated the numerous issues arising from the overseas expansion of the two great powers.

The eighteenth century was as intensely concerned with colonial and trade conflicts as the seventeenth century had been with religious disputes. Would England or France become the dominant maritime and world power? In particular, would the most impor-

tant of all overseas territories, the North American continent, fall
to the French or the Anglo-Saxons? This was the all-important
question that the next war would decide. The antagonisms of the
German princes, even the struggle over Silesia, paled to secondary
importance before these worldwide issues.

It is evident that in view of her imperial policy, the true enemy
of France was no longer Austria, but Great Britain. If the French
seriously intended to dispute English rivalry on the high seas and
in the colonies, they would be well advised to concentrate all energies on that goal, and put aside their old Continental disputes. It
was on this inherent need of France to limit her commitments that
Kaunitz based his proposals. The difficulty was that for the success
of his policy it was not enough to have French neutrality; he also
needed her military and financial assistance. Lacking such support,
in alliance solely with Russia, he would never risk war with Prussia. But was it really in the interest of the French state to help ruin
her old ally, who in former crises had proved so effective, and
to destroy the recently established balance of power in Germany?
Versailles was not convinced of this, and Kaunitz's first approaches
were rejected. Negotiations were not taken up again until a surprising shift in Prussia's position in January 1756.

In 1753 his agents had informed Frederick of the secret clauses in
the Russo-Austrian treaty, which referred to the reconquest of Silesia. Since that time he had expected war to come within a few
years. He increased his military preparations, but simultaneously
sought ways to postpone the inevitable for as long as possible. He
did not consider Prussia ready for war until his war chest contained at least twenty million taler, enough for four campaigns—by
1756, incidentally, he had been able to accumulate little more than
thirteen million. What particularly disturbed him was the great activity evinced in British diplomacy, the objective being to gain sup-
porters throughout Europe and turn them against France, and her
Prussian ally. This contrasted dangerously with the policy of Versailles, which he found hesitant and aimless—the constantly changing ministers were incapable or inexperienced, while the King, influenced by Mme. de Pompadour, was indolent, peace-loving, and
unwilling to make firm decisions.

As so often before Frederick feared that in a new war France would use Prussia as an auxiliary, who would have to carry the main burden of fighting on the Continent. For that reason he spurred the French on to greater activity when in the spring of 1755 fighting broke out in the Ohio Valley, and war in Europe became imminent. He advised France to check England with a strong attack on Hanover. Such a move, he presumably calculated, would place him in the position of the neutral who is courted by both sides—a situation similar to the one he had occupied after the Peace of Dresden. He was alarmed when Paris responded by demanding that as the ally of France Prussia should carry out the attack. His proposal had resulted in the very opposite of what he had intended. With the suddenness that characterized his diplomacy he immediately tried to divert French militancy to the Austrian Netherlands. In vain. He did not suspect that Vienna was now holding out the possibility of transferring the territory to France as part of negotiations which aimed at freeing France policy from its self-willed and dangerous Prussian ally.

Soon afterwards he learned that an Anglo-Russian subsidy treaty had been concluded, in which Russia agreed to protect Hanover with 50,000 men against France or Prussia. The news profoundly alarmed him: in case of war it would be intolerable to be faced by Russian troops on two fronts. But it was still possible to avert this prospect by immediately concluding an alliance with Great Britain. On 16 January 1756, in response to a British initiative, Frederick signed the so-called Convention of Westminster, in which both powers pledged peace and friendship to each other, and jointly undertook to prevent foreign troops from occupying or marching through German territory.

By a step that was as simple as it was surprising, the most pressing menace to Prussia had been dispelled. With the Convention of Westminster the Anglo-Russian treaty lost its purpose, English antagonism was put to rest, and the threatening encirclement was shattered. Or so it seemed. Frederick flattered himself at having scored a diplomatic triumph—above all, his agreement with England had "chained the Russian bear" and thus brought to a standstill Maria Theresa's plans for war. But never had he deceived himself more seriously. He underestimated Russia's desire for war, as he underestimated French sensitivity. What he had never wanted—indeed, had never believed possible—a complete reversal of the European alliance system, now became reality.

The French court had become accustomed to the willfulness of its Prussian ally; but this latest unilateral act, to put it crudely, broke the camel's back. In vain Frederick argued that France herself had refused to invade Hanover, and that nothing in the Convention precluded a French attack on the Austrian Netherlands. Versailles remained incensed—even more by the ruthlessness of Prussia's diplomacy than by the actual terms of the agreement. What could one expect of an ally who treated with the enemy behind one's back, and dared place restrictions on French strategy? The anti-Prussian faction at court, led by Mme. de Pompadour and her protégés, triumphed, and the Austrian proposals now found a receptive audience.

With great mastery Kaunitz made use of the favorable climate. Step by step, presenting increasingly far-reaching proposals, he entangled France deeply in the net of his military alliances. On 1 May 1756 he gained his first success by concluding a defensive treaty between the two states, which in case of aggression by Prussia gave Austria leave to reconquer Silesia (in contravention of the guarantee of 1748 of Prussian sovereignty) and promised her the support of 24,000 French troops. This agreement responded fully to the interests of French policy since it protected France on the Continent in her approaching conflict with England. Kaunitz found it much more difficult to negotiate the next step, that of an offensive alliance, having as its aim the destruction of the Prussian monarchy. Even the offer of extensive holdings in the Austrian Netherlands did not suffice for this purpose. Nevertheless, by 20 August Kaunitz believed he could count on French acquiescence in an attack on Prussia, and in her subsequent partition. The French also appeared ready to support the war with subsidies, which would enable Austria to obtain Russian help and raise German auxiliary contingents. No formal agreement yet existed on these points, and numerous French doubts remained, but slowly an offensive alliance was evolving. Moreover should Frederick be the aggressor, Austria could expect to receive the strongest possible support from France.

It proved much easier to win over Empress Elizabeth. Since the signing of the Convention of Westminister she no longer considered herself bound by the British subsidy treaty, and she agreed unreservedly to Kaunitz's proposals. On receipt of the French subsidies she was prepared, even without signing a new treaty, to join Austria in an immediate attack on Prussia. Her goal was the acquisition of East Prussia, which she intended to trade to Poland in return for Courland. Her eagerness was so pronounced that she became resentful when Kaunitz felt obliged to postpone the outbreak of war until the spring of 1757, since France continued to hesitate and Austria was not completing her military arrangements as rapidly as had been expected.

All in all, European politics had undergone a complete revolution. Frederick learned the full extent of the change only gradually through his secret agents. It is remarkable how long he continued to believe that with Great Britain on his side he need not seriously fear the anger of France or the aggressiveness of Russia and Austria. He found it inconceivable that against her true interests France was prepared to finance an attack on Prussia while she herself was engaged in an enormously expensive naval and colonial conflict with England. Not until June 1756 did Russia's overt mobilization and reports from his spies, particularly from Dresden, finally make it clear to him that a European coalition had formed against Prussia. At once he resorted to the same method that he had successfully employed in 1749: with deliberate publicity he began putting his army on a war footing to give his enemies pause. A succession of mobilizations and countermobilizations began, akin to the disastrous process in July 1914; in this case, however, it was not the military preparations that led to the outbreak of war.

After weeks of uncertainty, on 21 July, Frederick learned from neutral diplomats that the enemy attack had been postponed until the following spring. But instead of waiting patiently until the other side completed its military and diplomatic arrangements, he now mobilized completely and twice demanded assurances from Maria Theresa that she would attack him neither in this nor in the coming year. On 25 August his second, even more pressing inquiry again elicited an evasive response. In return, and without declaration of war, he invaded Saxony, which he suspected of being one of the centers of the conspiracy against him. Actually, Saxony was still neutral, though it was in the process of joining the great coalition. At the same time he offered the Dresden court peace in exchange for the use of Saxon territory and the Saxon army for the duration of the conflict—an offer that was naturally rejected. To Vienna he declared that even now he would pull back his troops if he were given the assurances he had demanded. The response was a proud refusal. Kaunitz had long waited for a rash move on Frederick's part, which now activated his system of defensive alliances.

Preventive war is always a highly questionable tool of international relations. Although the intentions of the other side could hardly be doubted, and although his own position was obviously critical, in the eyes of the world Frederick was a self-confessed aggressor. His policy had been less violent than in 1740; having learned a lesson from the events of those days he wanted to persuade everyone of his peaceful intentions, and on that account wasted an entire month in useless negotiations with Vienna. But the moral benefit of these attempts to buy the peace was lost as soon as Prussia took the offensive instead of letting her enemies make the first move. Not only was the still incomplete mechanism of the Austrian alliance system set in motion; the fact that the first victim of the attack was a country that was still officially neutral made it inevitable that European opinion would turn against him. Condemnation became even more severe when the invasion was followed by the full occupation of Saxony, and the royal family was subjected to humiliating treatment, behavior which clearly demonstrated Frederick's lack of dynastic feeling and his failure to appreciate the solidarity of the European ruling houses. Finally, when he forcibly broke open the Saxon archives so that he could document to the world the government's conspiratorial role, he committed what was regarded as yet another transgression of international law.

His minister Podewils had predicted that the invasion would cause universal outrage. The ambassadors of Great Britain and France had warned him against the step, the latter with an explicit reference to the treaty obligations of his government. Frederick was certainly aware of the possible consequences of his policy, and could hardly be surprised that all efforts to justify himself in the eyes of Europe would be in vain. Why, then, did he act as he did? Why could he not wait to see whether Kaunitz really would succeed in discovering a plausible reason to go to war, and in winning over the still hesitant French? Could he not hope that before the spring of 1757 the capricious policy of Empress Elizabeth might shift once again, and thus ease the crisis? The empress was ill; subsequently Frederick was to count heavily on her early death, as well as on the remote possibility of immobilizing Russia through a Turkish war. Might it not have been preferable to delay the war for as long as he could, and in the interval exert all efforts to disrupt the developing encirclement by diplomatic means?

Some German historians of the Wilhelmine era answered this question in the affirmative. They argued that Frederick's actions could be explained only by the fact that he himself was planning aggression and new conquests, and that his offensive happened to coincide with the attack of his opponents. This interpretation suggests that he welcomed Kaunitz's projected attack since it provided him with a cause for starting the war, and enabled him to set in motion the long-desired conquest of Saxony and West Prussia. But none of the scholars holding this view succeeded in finding even one item of supporting evidence among Frederick's countless public and confidential statements on his policy during the critical months of 1756 and in the preceding years. Evidence to the contrary is, however, considerable, and only the most willful of interpretations can ignore it. Nor indeed can we find any sign of military preparations for an offensive war in the summer of 1756. Today this historical dispute seems antiquated. It is obvious that in the situation of 1756 a war of aggression undertaken voluntarily with the aim of conquering Saxony would have been as senseless as the assumption that in 1914 Germany started the World War in order to conquer Belgium.

The similarity between 1756 and 1914 is after all not accidental. The threatened position of a state in the center of Europe, surrounded by hostile coalitions, demands rapid and forceful decisions. Even if it were more prudent to await the others' attack, the statesman charged with responsibility in such dangers will prefer to seek safety in action rather than remain passive, oppressed with the fear that by waiting he may give the other side an irreversible advantage. In 1914 Germany violated Belgian neutrality because that was the only way to win the decisive battle in France, and because Germany would have been lost if the enemy had penetrated the industrial complex along the lower Rhine. Frederick attacked Saxony because Berlin lay within 35 miles of the Saxon border, and because the later campaigns of the War of the Austrian Succession had shown that an offensive against Vienna could not be effective if the Saxon army threatened his lines of communication.

Some historians have asked why Frederick, instead of taking Saxony, did not immediately strike deep into Austria, the center of the menace? If in August he had penetrated the Austrian heartlands he would have found the Austrian army still unprepared. He did not choose this way because in 1744 his offensive through Bohemia had failed, and because the experiences of the winter campaign of 1741 to 1742 suggested that the alternate route through Moravia was probably too long for a successful thrust started relatively late in the year. Consequently he felt that he first had to acquire Saxony as a base for the defense of Silesia or for an offensive into Bohemia, and had to do it quickly before French and Russian armies could intervene. Having taken the first step he wished to organize the occupation of Saxony before moving on, since he believed he could not afford to pass up the rich military and economic resources of that country. But by advancing so slowly did he not lose the element of surprise—the intrinsic advantage of the preventive attack? And did not his purely military considerations conflict with the political realities?

Frederick undoubtedly miscalculated on one point. As in 1749 he hoped that energetic measures would intimidate his enemies and calm their militancy. But since they knew they were stronger than he, the opposite happened—bluffing without the requisite power has rarely achieved much in history. Nevertheless the courage with which he faced the emergency remains remarkable. "Great things are achieved only when we take great risks," he wrote to his heir. "With this consolation, and with the resolve to knock together the heads of all who stand in our way, we can defy hell and the devil, calmly read the news, disregard the empty boastings of our enemies, and possess the assurance that we will survive with honor. If our enemies compel us to fight, we must ask: where are they?—not, how many are there? Let the women in Berlin babble about treaties of partition, we Prussian officers who have experienced war have learned that neither difficulties nor enemy superiority can deprive us of victory." These sentences smack of self-conscious pathos; but, no doubt, they were meant seriously.

Actually Frederick was so far from fearing his opponents' superiority that he considerably underestimated their strength—the number and quality of the Russian troops as well as the financial resources and determination of France. And now that the conflict had begun he even raised his war aims as high as possible. If in spite of all he should triumph, and if the political situation were extremely favorable, he hoped to acquire West Prussia or Saxony. Marshal Lehwaldt, who was charged with the defense of East Prussia, was given instructions on how to conduct the relevant negotiations with the Russians after they had been defeated. The annexation of Saxony, with the Elector being compensated by receiving the yet-to-be-conquered Bohemia, was another early scheme. These optimistic expectations did not, however, affect the defensive nature of the war. The war was a struggle for the existence of the Prussian state. But it was in accord with Frederick's personality that he defended himself not passively, but by taking the offensive.

ii. The War for Survival

SEEN IN ITS broadest historical context, Prussia's struggle for survival was only part of a global conflict, fought on both sides of the Atlantic, with the fate of the North American Continent as the central issue. In the narrower context of European affairs, however, the essential meaning of the war was that a parvenu retained by force his newly won position in the circle of the established major powers. The aspect of *force* is decisive here. In the light of the Seven Years' War, Prussia appears as a deliberately created power, indeed as an artificial structure whose claim to influence and equality with other great nations seems to run counter to the nature of things. Unquestionably, Fredrick's policy went beyond the art of the possible; in this war, at least, he wanted to being about the seemingly impossible. It was a war waged by a state of five million inhabitants against ninety million—for with the exception of her British ally Prussia fought alone. And the involvement of the island kingdom in Europe was limited; she devoted the greater part of her energies to the war in the colonies and the fighting on the high seas. Only during William Pitt's resolute leadership did London recognize that the French will to fight could not be broken without energetically pursuing the war on the European continent. In general, however, the English dislike of Hanoverian dynastic politics was too pronounced, the fear that it might involve the country in matters remote from her true interests too great, for the government to be willing to embark on sizable military operations in Europe. Apart from subsidies, which were stopped before the end of the war, and a Brunswick–Hanoverian army which needed some years to become effective, Frederick received little help. Indeed at the beginning of hostilities it would not have taken much for Hanover to declare herself neutral and stay out of the war altogether.

In the meantime, the superiority of the opposing side became overwhelming. Frederick's worst expectations, were far outdone by the military and financial efforts of France, and by the vast Russian armies that flooded East Prussia and advanced on the center of the monarchy. On the motion of Emperor Francis, the Diet at Regensburg proclaimed the Empire at war with Frederick, and raised an army of German contingents as an auxiliary force of the French. Sweden recalled her old alliance with Versailles, and invaded Pomerania. As always happens in world affairs when a preponderant majority coalesces, everyone else joined to share in the safe booty. By January 1757 Frederick could compare himself to a stag pursued by a pack of kings and princes. However, he did not lose courage. His famous secret instructions to his minister Count Finckenstein provided for the worst contingency: if he were killed or taken prisoner, the Prussian government should pay no heed to his fate, but should carry on as though nothing had happened. He was an absolute monarch who believed that the state took precedence over himself.

Had his opening campaign met with greater success he might possibly have prevented the formation of such a vast coalition against him. But overpowering the Saxon army required more time than he had expected; when this was accomplished the year was too far advanced to risk a push into Bohemia. Incorporating the Saxons into his own units, an unusual and dangerous step, on the whole led to disappointments. And the first serious clash with the Austrians at Lobositz showed that during the years of peace they had turned the experiences gained in earlier Silesian campaigns to excellent use.

Still, with Saxony as his base of operations Frederick could await with some degree of confidence the thunderclouds of war gathering about him from all sides. A considerable augmentation of his forces during the winter would enable him in 1757 to face any one of his opponents with superior strength. Initially he lacked any plan for offensive operations—which confirms his defensive purpose; he wanted to wait until he could be certain where he would be attacked first. It was not until March that he was persuaded by the most gifted of his generals—the young, volatile Winterfeldt—to adopt an exceptionally daring offensive scheme. The plan called for his major opponents, the Austrians, to be attacked in their Bohemian winter quarters before they had completed their preparations for the coming campaign. Their stores were to be captured, concentric attacks were to weaken their resistance, and a few weeks should see them expelled from northeast Bohemia.

In the middle of April, long before spring campaigns customarily began, four Prussian armies invaded Bohemia from north, east, and west, completely surprised the Austrians, and almost without fighting drove them back to Prague. Plan and execution of this enterprise resemble the bold yet methodical offensives of the elder Moltke more than a century later. In the first flush of success Frederick hoped to engulf the Austrian field forces and destroy them with one more hard blow. But the extremely costly victory at Prague did not quite lead to this result. The main Austrian army saved itself behind the walls of the city. To encircle the fortifications, and starve out the garrison or overwhelm it, would immobilize large numbers of Prussian troops for weeks, perhaps even months, and might require more artillery than the army possessed. Besides, Frederick's temperament was ill-suited for such a long-drawn-out process, and the grave military situation in western Germany seemed to demand a more rapid decision.

In the hope of depriving the encircled troops of all possibilities of support, and of concluding the campaign with a second major battle, Frederick allowed himself to launch a hasty and ill-prepared attack on the Austrian relief army. Its commander, Daun, had drawn up his vastly superior forces in an exceptionally strong position on the heights of Colin, and dealt Frederick the first real defeat he had ever suffered in a full-scale battle. The day at Colin had disastrous implications, it was a turning point in Frederick's life. His aura of invincibility suddenly vanished, the siege of Prague could not be maintained, his hopes of quick victory were destroyed. For a time he seemed drained of all psychic energy. Exhausted in mind and body he delegated command of the retreat to his cautious, methodical brother Henry, who now triumphantly gave voice to his envy and malice: "Phaethon has fallen!" But soon the king pulled himself together. "My heart is broken," he wrote to one of his generals, Moritz of Dessau, "yet I am not dejected, and at the first opportunity I shall try to make up for this defeat."

His opportunity, however, was slow in coming. A long succession of further misfortunes descended upon him. First he learned the grievous news of his mother's death. Then followed a difficult retreat from Bohemia to Upper Silesia, at times degenerating into a rout, which was aggravated by the poor generalship of his brother August William, the heir apparent. The harshness with which Frederick removed this incompetent from all positions of command, while raising his gifted younger brother Henry to new honors, despite their deep mutual dislike, is one of the most impressive signs of the uncompromising realism that characterized his rule. But for him, too, nothing would now succeed. He failed in every attempt to regain the initiative and force the Austrians to risk another major battle. The news from the western theater of war was calamitous: the French defeated the Brunswick–Hanoverian corps, pushed it back to the lower Elbe, and at last compelled it to surrender. The whole of northwest Germany lay open to the enemy. On the Baltic, Pomerania was nearly defenseless against the Swedes, who bypassed it and were already advancing through the area of Prignitz, while the French marched across the western edge of Brandenburg and into the bishoprics of Halberstadt and

Magdeburg; both forces sought to combine for a siege of Magdeburg.

In vain Frederick tried to stave off disaster by diplomatic means: the French felt certain of victory and rebuffed his discreet peace feelers. Equally useless was his military advance against the combined armies of France and the Empire: they refused to give battle, and he only exhausted his troops by thrusting now against one front now against another of the slowly tightening ring. His position worsened from week to week. From East Prussia came the news that the Russians had beaten Field Marshal Lehwaldt at Grossjägersdorf, from the Lausitz that the corps there was withdrawing to Silesia, and at best hoped to be able to defend Breslau. In Silesia, too, his friend Winterfeldt—perhaps the only one among his generals who really understood him—was killed. His death, following the death of Schwerin in the battle of Prague, was a doubly heavy loss. In October an Austrian detachment penetrated to Berlin, occupied the capital for several days and levied contributions. The flow of taxes to the Prussian treasury from the Westphalian provinces, from East Prussia, Magdeburg, the best part of Pomerania, and much of Silesia ceased, and Frederick's resources rapidly diminished. Uneasily he arrived at the conclusion that even if he survived the winter he could not finance another campaign. For weeks and months he lived under extreme tension; feasible means of saving himself were nowhere at hand. He recognized that the world now took him to be an adventurer who had gambled and lost. How did his psyche overcome this crisis?

His feelings can be most clearly observed in his correspondence with his sister Wilhelmina. After so many friends and companions of his youth had been killed—most members of the Rheinsberg circle had died long ago—the close relationship between sister and brother grew even more intense, and finally reached heights of almost violent affection. It seemed as though the two wanted to cling to each other to keep from being psychically paralyzed by the storms of fate. At first, after Colin, Frederick's letters are still characterized by cold determination. Encouraging his troubled, almost desperate sister, he wrote: "Those who cannot survive disaster do not deserve success. We must rise above events, do our duty, and not complain about misfortune, which is the lot of all mankind." But as the skies darkened, his detachment seemed increasingly artificial. He called on the solace of fatalism, on the Stoic heroes of Rome, Cato and Brutus, as he tried to control his own agitation.

In lengthy odes filled with pathos, in rhymed epistles to his friends, in spirited poetic imagery, Frederick wrote of the tempests that pursued him and threatened to hurl the ship of state against a rocky shore. He depicted the horrors of the violence that all of Europe had unleashed against him; and he proclaimed the duty of the hero who would fall, sword in hand, fighting like a lion to the end. Above all, he praised the sweet rest to be found in the arms of self-chosen death.

> Et sûr de l'appui d'Atropos,
> Je vais m'élancer dans la barque
> Où, sans distinction, le berger, le monarque,
> Passent dans le séjour de l'éternel repos.

A rare picture indeed: the embattled commander-in-chief sitting at night in his tent or in some miserable peasant's hut, refining his verses by candlelight, lauding his own heroic fate and toying with thoughts of death! His restless, sensitive mind required such means to rid itself of depression. "Often I want to get drunk and drown my sorrows," he writes in one letter. "But I dislike drinking, and the only thing that diverts me is to write verses. As long as I can distract myself in this way I am not conscious of my misfortune." What was sincere and what was rhetoric in these rhymed confessions? Undoubtedly genuine was the constantly recurring wish to escape the "dog's life" of the soldier, to return to the quiet, pleasant life of the mind at Sans Souci, to renounce the "sad glory" of the general, and to usher in a period of truly humanitarian and peaceful rule. An emotional and sensitive spirit forced itself to assume the posture of martial heroism and Stoic calm.

In the evenings when Frederick declaimed his sorrowful verses to his reader, de Prades, he could rise to such peaks of excitement that tears covered his manuscript. But not for a moment did these emotions interfere with the realm of action. Excitability and feeling were not as powerful in his make-up as perseverance, which

Clausewitz has called the most important quality of true generalship.

> La stoique raison dont le flambeau m'éclaire
> M'apprend a me roidir contre un malheur vulgaire,
> A calmer le chargin, a dissiper l'effroi
> D'un désastre qui ne peut n'influer que sur moi.

To be sure, there were periods when Frederick was shaken by the desire to end his life, to throw off the unbearable yoke of existence.

> D'un regard intrépide envisagez la mort,
> C'est notre seul asile et notre dernier port.

There is no doubt that he was serious. Repeatedly during these years he thought of suicide; at times it became a dangerous temptation—when he was exposed to enemy fire, or at night in hours of despair, when he knew that a vial of poison lay within reach in his field equipment. But by seeking to justify to himself and to others the morality of committing suicide, by praising the gentle peace of death in verses, by considering all aspects of suicide, he liberated himself from its compelling power. Above all, he was never prepared to choose death to escape from his duties. "If I had been willing to act on my feelings," he wrote to his sister, "I would have ended things immediately after the unfortunate battle. But—I interpreted my mood as weakness, and considered it my duty to make good the misfortune. My devotion to the state was aroused. I said to myself: when things go well it is easy to find strength, but not when they go badly. And so it became a question of honor to redress the situation."

This is how he always reacted after a lost battle. First he despaired: everything was hopeless. Immediately afterwards he felt that he was responsible not only to himself, but also to his state and his people. Such an awareness can become moral torture when it includes recognition of one's own disastrous mistakes. Frederick once said to his reader, de Catt, that the only fear he knew was the fear of his own conscience, and he tried to overcome that by doing better. An inflamed sense of pride drove him to make up for a defeat by winning new victories. From one campaign to the next he hoped for the end of the fighting. If only he could survive this last phase, he would be rid of the unbearable load, he would be free to lead his own life. Again and again he was disappointed; but each time he recovered the determination demanded of him by a monarch's sense of duty, a soldier's honor, and a king's feeling of responsibility to history.

After the defeats of the summer of 1757 many men advised him to make concessions and end the war. His determination to die rather than renounce Silesia struck his coldly realistic brother Henry not as heroic but as extravagant. He shook his head over this strange daredevil who was unable to maintain his composure whether things went well or badly. At times even Wilhelmina feared the rigidity of his sense of honor, and Voltaire observed that after all even the Great Elector had yielded some of his conquests without losing the world's respect—Frederick would always retain enough possessions "to play a very handsome role in Europe." This advice by the private citizen "from his retreat" amused Frederick. Every class has its own obligations, he replied; it so happened that "accident of birth" had called him to the throne:

> Pour moi, menacé du naufrage,
> Je dois, en affrontant l'orage
> Penser, vivre et mourir en roi.

His spine, he said, "was stiffened by misfortune." He was determined not to survive the shame of Prussia's fall; he would fight on "whatever the price." He was driven by a dogged stubbornness, which found its clearest poetic expression in his ode to Prince Henry:

> Au courage obstiné la résistance cède,
> Un noble désespoir est l'unique remède
> Aux maux désespérés;
> Le temps termine tout, rien n'est longtemps extrême,
> Et souvent le malheur devient la source même
> Des biens tant désirés.

His resolution, closely tied to rhetorical appeals to the great heroes of the past, lends a romantic, exalted note to the verses written during these critical months; but it never interfered with the sober evaluation of his military position. In the end it was because he had the strength to maintain his courage without illusions that he led Prussia up the steep road toward political greatness.

The extreme tension of the last months of 1757 was suddenly relieved by a near miracle: the triumph of the Prussian cavalry at Rossbach on the afternoon of 5 November. It was an exceptionally daring decision for Frederick's inferior, worn-out force to attack the combined armies of France and the Empire as they were preparing to envelop his positions. But it succeeded. In one hour the enemy was scattered, and Frederick had won the most popular of his victories, the first triumph gained by German arms over the French in generations. From this day on the French leaders never again dared to engage a force led by the king in person. A first breathing spell had been won, but the more difficult task of reconquering Silesia remained. While Frederick hurried east in forced marches, the Silesian towns of Schweidnitz and Breslau capitulated, the Duke of Bevern commanding the Silesian covering force was defeated, and soon afterwards made prisoner. Only a great victory could save the day. It was a new miracle that Frederick won this victory, too, in the battle of Leuthen, which in its harmony of planning and execution is the most brilliant of his battles. Silesia was liberated. By a sudden turn of fate Frederick's military glory reached its apex. For many months he had not shown the confidence that now possessed him and that lasted through the winter—spent in Breslau—into the spring campaign. The British, too, were now spurred on to greater activity. Prince Ferdinand of Brunswick succeeded in liberating Hanover and Westphalia, and threw the French back across the Rhine. But what Frederick has always resisted—becoming dependent on British policy by accepting English money—could no longer be avoided. Care was taken to bind him so firmly to his contractual obligations that henceforth he did not dare pursue the independent diplomacy and separate peacemaking of his earlier wars.

Filled with new hope, and as always eager to attack, he opened the campaign of 1758 by thrusting deeply into Moravia, seeking to draw the Austrians out of their strong positions on the Silesian border and lure them as far as possible from the Russians. But as in the preceding year he was disappointed. Olmütz could not be taken, and the Austrians, who had learned a lesson from their defeat at Leuthen, evaded a decisive encounter while paralyzing his offensive by maneuvering against his flanks. The Prussians were forced to retreat first to Bohemia, then back to Silesia. The Russians in the meantime posed a strong threat to the heart of the monarchy. After taking the undefended province of East Prussia, they had advanced to within fifty miles of Berlin, and were besieging Küstrin. With a few of his best regiments Frederick hurried north. He hoped to destroy the Russians in a vast outflanking battle; but they proved to be extremely tough on the defensive. In the end the costly battle of Zorndorf was only a partial victory. The Russians left the battlefield to Frederick and broke off their advance; but they withdrew unhindered, the Prussian troops were too exhausted to press the pursuit.

Without respite, Frederick returned to Saxony to save Dresden from the Austrians. Again Daun evaded him, and assumed an unassailable position on the rocky slopes along the Elbe. Frederick took the greatest risks to dislodge him from the heights, finally encamping his army at Hochkirch, close to the enemy, in an unfortified and tactically unfavorable position. It was a move of fateful irresponsibility. A surprise night attack by Daun became a Prussian catastrophe. Frederick's army lost over one hundred guns and one third of its infantry; the most capable generals he still possessed were killed or captured. But with admirable energy he reorganized the beaten formations, and only a few hours after the defeat he again stood ready to fight on the heights near Bautzen. He managed to maneuver around Daun's army, reenter Silesia, relieve the fortresses of Neisse and Kosel, cover Dresden against a new Austrian assault, and by late fall had again cleared all of Silesia and Saxony.

Once more his restless activity, his quick jabs against one opponent after another, left him in control of central Germany. In the north, too, his generals finally succeeded in halting the Swedish and Russian offensives; the fortress of Kolberg was relieved and the Russians withdrew to the Vistula. In Westphalia Prince Ferdinand again defeated the French. France was growing tired of the war as England's ponderous might gradually asserted itself on the high seas and in the colonies, and the prospects of a French victory dwindled everywhere. A peace party formed at Versailles, and though it could not yet determine the course of events, the French government now deemed it necessary to loosen its ties with Austria while concentrating all efforts against Great Britain.

In sum, the outcome of this campaign gave Frederick greater reason for optimism than had the two previous years. At last his determination seemed to bear fruit. But he himself felt bitterness, growing horror, and disgust at the butchery to which his royal office drove him. His depression had returned after the costly battles of Zorndorf and Hochkirch. "I tell you in confidence," he said to his reader and companion, de Catt, "the affairs of the state are not desperate, but my heart is despairing. Oh, if you could see into its depths!" The news that his favorite sister Wilhelmina had died on the disastrous day of Hochkirch, struck him harder than the loss of his best commanders. She had been the only intimate companion of his unhappy youth. "Grand Dieu, ma soeur de Bayreuth!" with this cry he opened the floodgates of uncontrollable grief. "I am sick of this life," he now wrote, "the wandering Jew himself was not as tired of life as I am. I have lost everything that I loved and respected on this earth. My surroundings consist of unfortunate souls, whom I am prevented from helping by the misery of the times." We gain an insight into the nature of his feelings when we read in de Catt's diaries that for some time after his sister's death Frederick occupied himself with theological works and funeral orations, that he speculated on death, immortality, and the last judgment. Later he admitted that Stoicism had failed him during this deepest of his psychological crises. Consequently he sought firmer ground elsewhere—without, to be sure, finding it.

The uninterrupted hardship of life in the field had begun to affect his basically delicate physique. Since the previous winter he had been suffering from attacks of colic, which now occurred more frequently. His rheumatism became worse; in the later years of the war it reached such intensity that at times he was partly paralyzed, and had to be carried from place to place. He was often depressed, irritable, moody. For weeks he was unable to sleep. In Breslau during the winter of 1757 to 1758 he had returned to his accustomed musicmaking, and had assembled a small group of sophisticated companions. After Wilhelmina's death he found society unbearable. He buried himself in work, and ate alone. "I don't feel like operas, but like tragedies," he said. And, "if one is sad it becomes difficult after a while to hide one's sorrow." Evening after evening he could be overheard declaiming entire scenes from Racine. By immersing himself in these tragedies he overcame his shock and recovered the sense and awareness of his royal mission: "I have no time to weep for my sister."

Peace remained distant. For the waning energy of the French, Maria Theresa found a substitute in the increasing combativeness of the Russians, who promised to enter the next campaign in even larger numbers than before. On the Prussian side the problem of replacements became critical. Casualties and desertion had gravely weakened Frederick's regiments. By drafting adolescents, and by hiring and forcibly enrolling soldiers in Saxony, Mecklenburg, and Anhalt, it once more was possible to assemble a force exceeding 100,000 men. But most of these were naturally of inferior quality. The *esprit de corps,* drill, discipline, and experience of the elite units, which had formed the basis for Frederick's military superiority, could not be recreated overnight. And as the character of his troops changed, Frederick's relationship to them took on a new tone.

He had never felt true warmth for his men. In return his severity and lack of pathos tended to produce strict obedience rather than awake ambition or enthusiasm. Men did their duty—on the whole nothing more was expected of them. No doubt their allegiance often reached the highest level of heroic self-sacrifice for the king. And when he dropped his authoritarian tone and warmly appealed to the comradeship, the personal honor, and fealty of his officers, he would sweep them off their feet. Especially at one climax of the war, on the eve of the battle of Leuthen, he was able to exploit his charismatic charm in a famous address to his officers. But these were rare occasions. To repeat such appeals would have been out of character. It is here, perhaps, that the matter-of-fact Prussian king differed most strongly from Napoleon. He was incapable of consciously posing. Strict command and punctual obedience characterized his army, not the dynamic bond between leader and followers. Besides, the average Prussian officer was mystified and frightened by the king's personality and culture, and by his secret disdain of the brutal business of war. Covert criticism and mockery were the fashion—especially at his headquarters. It is true that during the early campaigns shared experience had led to a kind of comradeship, which helped overcome much mutual misunderstanding. This sense of community was strengthened by the personal friendship that linked Frederick to such generals as Schwerin, Winterfeldt, and Fouqué. But the most gifted of his commanders were killed, talented replacements were difficult to find, and the king became increasingly isolated from his officers. How many of them did he insult with just or unjust criticism, with suspected or real inequities in promotions! How many officers were embittered by his court-martials of fellow noblemen who had failed, either because their professional abilities were inadequate or because they lacked courage or perseverance? Apart from that, his audacious strategy, which ran counter to accepted rules, aroused the instinctive resistance of a large segment of his officer corps. Their opposition found its focal point in his brother, Prince Henry. More and more often Frederick had cause to complain about the "despicable lamenting and arguing" of his officers.

The long duration of the war had an even greater bearing on Frederick's relationship with the rank and file. He had marched into Saxony with pride in his incomparable troops, and in turn, the better elements among them had looked up to their victorious ruler with touching faith and almost filial loyalty. The spectacle of a monarch who as a matter of course shared their discomforts, who in almost every major battle forced his swollen, rheumatic feet into boots and rode with his men against the enemy, was bound to arouse feelings that bridged the deepest divisions of rank and personality. He knew, and his military writings emphasized the point, that it was important for the commander to be popular with the common man, that he should occasionally talk to his soldiers, walk through camp at nightfall to see if the stewpots were full, encourage his men before battle with a few cheerful words, and so on. There is a well-known incident after the victory at Zorndorf, when in his euphoria he called the cavalry together, patted troopers on the back and embraced them. Equally characteristic is the episode during the battle of Rossbach when musketeers in a front-line battalion called to him to "move out of the way, father, so that we can fire!" But he never fully recognized how the charisma of his personality affected his men.

As the war continued, the quality of replacements naturally declined. Frederick became embittered when whole battalions and regiments failed to do their duty, when he saw men in the thick of the fight throw away their cartridges, refuse to draw new ones, and slink to the rear on the pretext that they had run out of ammunition. Increasingly he cursed them as unreliable scoundrels, *canaille,* plunderers, rabble of every kind. To bring the undisciplined bands back to reason he ordered his officers to increase such extreme punishments as running the gauntlet as well as the use of the stick. The time came when he said, half in despair, that he feared his own troops more than he feared the enemy.

No doubt such impatient comments were unjust, as is shown by the behavior of his troops at Liegnitz and Torgau, and in many other engagements in the second half of the war. But it is true that neither in strength nor in discipline and training were the later armies suited for the sweeping offensives of earlier days. With each campaign Frederick found it more difficult to achieve clear-cut victories. The Prussian infantry lost its old impetus, while the Austrians were becoming masters in exploiting terrain and artillery for the defensive. Consequently after the spring of 1759 the character of Frederick's operations gradually changed. Much as it went against his temperament, he, too, was compelled to shift to the defensive. He still sought decision by battle whenever possible; but as his resources diminished, and as the Austrians entrenched themselves ever more securely, the mobile warfare of old, with its forced marches and set battles, increasingly turned into a war of fixed positions. Certainly it did not resemble the trench fighting and the mechanical artillery duels of the First World War; nevertheless, the Prussians and Austrians would now face each other for months, inactive except for minor skirmishes, until the frozen campaign was again brought into dramatic motion by some external factor.

Frederick's gravest task continued to be to keep the main Austrian and Russian armies apart. Once they succeeded in combining their superior strength, they could mount a decisive assault on the heart of the Prussian monarchy. From year to year it proved more difficult to prevent their union. As the ring of his opponents closed more tightly around Frederick his freedom of action was reduced until he could scarcely hope to do more than to save his field army—by means of feints, night marches, and sudden advances—from being encircled and crushed. He was safe against attack only in the west, where the proud marshals of France with their superior armies were being kept permanently in check by the corps under the command of his young cousin Ferdinand of Brunswick. The defense of Pomerania and Mecklenburg against the Swedes, and of Saxony against the forces of the Empire, presented greater difficulties: in Frederick's position even weak opponents were a threat since they compelled him to disperse his forces.

In the summer of 1959 an Austrian corps under Laudon succeeded in reaching the Russians. Together they advanced on Berlin. Frederick had no alternative but to give up Saxony for the time being and to face the combined enemy armies. Numerically far weaker and operating in extremely unfavorable terrain, he tried once again the desperate solution of outflanking and annihilating the enemy. His attempt failed. The battle of Kunersdorf ended in the most disastrous of his defeats. In despair he threw himself into the thick of the fight, as he had at Colin, to prevent disaster, or at least to cover the retreat with the few thousand men under his immediate command. With the words, "I must do my duty like everyone else," he rejected all pleas to leave the danger zone. Two horses were killed under him; a bullet was deflected from his coat, he was nearly captured by Cossacks. "Won't some accursed bullet hit me?" he cried during the battle. At dusk he watched the disorganized remnants of his army flee toward the Oder and thought that the end had come.

He now suffered a physical and emotional collapse that was more severe than ever before. At first, because of strain and physical exhaustion, he saw the defeat in even darker colors than was justified. He felt near death, unable to continue in command. "I no longer have any resources," he wrote to him minister Finckenstein; "and to tell the truth, I believe all is lost. I shall not survive the destruction of my fatherland. Farewell for ever!" The familiar thought of suicide must have been much on his mind. He ordered the army to swear allegiance to his young nephew, the son of his brother August William, who had died in disgrace. Prince Henry was to assume supreme command of all the forces, while General Finck reorganized the remnants of the ruined army. "If I still had the means," the king wrote to Finck, "I would have remained at my post." But once again he recovered with amazing speed. After only two days he resumed command, assuring Prince Henry that so long as his eyes were open he would maintain the state as duty demanded.

If the Austrians and Russians had at once decided to deliver a final blow, they could have destroyed the beaten army and conquered Berlin and the Mark Brandenburg. But even now they were held in check by their fear of the Prussian ruler's ability to strike back. How often had officers of the old school, Prince Henry at their head, complained about the reckless daredevil, who knew only how to fight battles, who led his troops to the abattoir, not to war. Now the full extent of the moral capital he had accumulated in victory after victory became evident. At this juncture nothing but Frederick's personal reputation saved the state from extinction.

It was, as Frederick called it, the "miracle of the House of Brandenburg" that the expected advance on Berlin did not take place. Soon the allied commanders separated again because they could not agree on their next moves. Frederick was able to raise new forces. With the assistance of his brother Henry, who now proved his great ability, he secured Silesia, he even tried to retake Dresden, which had fallen in September. He failed, despite risky maneuvers against the Austrian lines of communications by which he hoped to speed Daun's retreat. The forces sent against the enemy's rear were badly led, and an entire Prussian corps of 15,000 men was captured—something that had never before happened in open country. In vain Frederick tried to achieve his goal despite this setback by continuing operations far into the winter. He concluded "this cruel campaign" in constricted winter quarters on Saxon soil, close to the enemy, always facing the possibility of a surprise attack.

Slowly the war in Europe approached the stage of universal exhaustion. France had suffered serious defeats wherever she fought: in western Germany, on the high seas, in the colonies. Her last fleet was scattered, Canada was in danger of being lost; everywhere the superiority of England was becoming evident. Yet England, too, was growing weary. The winter of 1759 to 1760 therefore saw several cautious attempts on the part of British and Prussian diplomats to achieve peace, at least with Versailles. But in spite of her ruinous setbacks France continued to be held in thrall by Austria's diplomacy, and in the end all peace feelers collapsed in the face of Austrian determination to fight on.

The strategic balance was not significantly altered in the campaign of 1760. Nevertheless it was a considerable achievement that Frederick managed to retain Pomerania, Silesia, and a part of Saxony. In the spring he had considered his position to be hopeless. "Unless a miracle occurred," he figured that he could not continue the war for more than a few months. He himself was to bring this miracle about: at Liegnitz he evaded just in time the concentric attack of three Austrian armies, and changed certain defeat into a brilliant victory over vastly superior forces. Equally miraculous was his personal survival in the battle. A bullet pierced his coat, his horse was wounded; soon afterwards at Torgau he was struck by canister shot but suffered only a contusion. At times his situation was so perilous that he had to change his quarters nightly to escape Austrian raids. Once again only respect for his incomparable energy kept the main Russian force immobilized on the Silesian border; but he was unable to prevent a Russo-Austrian corps from penetrating to Berlin and levying contributions. With a costly victory at Torgau he secured the capital against further surprise attacks. To do more, let alone bring about a decisive turn to the war, no longer lay within his means.

Nevertheless, the war dragged on for another two years, and Frederick still had numerous opportunities for those "painful meditations," which he had once compared to the broodings of a man ill with the dropsy: "Day after day he follows the progress of his disease, in his limbs he already feels the cold premonition of death, and he can estimate in advance the moment when at last his heart will stop." Essentially, of course, it was his own stubbornness that kept the war from ending. France was exhausted, militarily and financially; now that she had lost Canada and India she wanted peace. In England, Pitt maintained himself only with difficulty against the peace party, which was ready to sacrifice the Prussian king to bring an end to the war. But negotiations between the two countries foundered on Frederick's refusal to turn Prussia into a passive object of diplomatic barter. He would not cede Prussian territory on the Rhine to help the great powers balance their accounts. That his position lost him popularity in England, he knew, but he did not waver, even though his army was melting away.

Frederick's officer corps now consisted in part of students or adolescent cadets; the rank and file was made up largely of forcibly impressed recruits from the occupied territories and of international mercenaries. With such a force it was scarcely possible to do more than toil from one relatively secure position to another. The fortresses of Schweidnitz and Kolberg finally capitulated to the enemy; for weeks the combined Austrians and Russians besieged Frederick at Bunzelwitz; each night could bring an enemy assault, he was cut off from all contact with his diplomats. For the first time the Allies established their winter quarters on Prussian soil— the Russians in Pomerania, the Austrians in Silesia. The territories of the Prussian monarch had shrunk alarmingly. He grasped at a last faint hope: for years he had negotiated with the Turks and Tartars to induce them to attack Austria as a means of deflecting Habsburg energies from central Europe. At times his imagination painted the prospects in the most glowing colors: Ottoman support would at last enable him to return to the offensive. But months passed and the Turks did not move.

In the meantime France was heartened by Spain's entry into the war against England, and Pitt, Frederick's firmest ally in London, fell to party intrigues. Again and again Frederick fought against thoughts of death. Could he continue to risk the future of his state in a hopeless cause? He remained determined not to make peace by surrendering. He would never put his signature to his "disgrace" but would rather allow himself to be "buried in the ruins of the fatherland." He recognized that his life's work stood or fell with the conquest of Silesia, and it was his salvation that he never doubted the justice of this conquest. But what if his achievement could not be preserved? In that case would it not be his duty to quit the stage in time, and let someone else carry on? If his ministers negotiated in the name of the young successor to the throne it might be easier for them to save whatever could be salvaged from the wreck. He decided to wait to the end of February 1762 for the Turks to declare themselves. If by that date no means of rescue had emerged he would like Cato, end his life: "Having sacrificed my youth to my father, and my maturity to the state, I believe I have the right to dispose of my old age as I wish." But he added, "should I see the slightest indication of a way out, I shall pursue it with all my energies. It would be cowardly to despair without compelling reasons."

In the midst of these tortured reflections, before the deadline Frederick had set himself was at hand, he was unexpectedly saved. On 5 January 1762 his bitter enemy, Empress Elizabeth, died. Her successor Czar Peter, was an enthusiastic admirer of the Prussian king. With one stroke everything changed. Prussia and Russia concluded peace; soon afterwards another separate peace was signed with Sweden. East Prussia, which Elizabeth had counted on as her spoils of the war, was saved. Peter's adulation even led him to offer Frederick a treaty by which the Russian army would be turned from an enemy into an ally. To be sure, the military alliance between the two powers remained in effect only for a few weeks; in July, Peter's German wife, Catherine, deposed him, had him imprisoned, and eventually murdered. But even under the new regime Russia remained out of the war. The great coalition had broken up once and for all.

For Frederick its ruin came just in time. At the moment that Russia detached herself from Austria, the bond between Prussia and England also broke. Pitt's successor, Lord Bute, sought an immediate peace with France since this would help solidify the position of the king's party. To render France more receptive to his proposals he would have liked to negotiate with Austria as well. But Frederick's stubbornness stood in his way. Henceforth Bute dealt with Prussia only "with his stick threateningly raised," as Frederick angrily put it. Bute raged about the obstinacy of this ambitious militarist, who was not prepared to sacrifice a single one of his provinces. He approached Vienna, secretly stirred up the Russians; above all, he suspended payment of the subsidies. It is remarkable enough that this did not bring Prussia's operations to a halt; but Frederick managed to keep his coffers filled through the ruthless exploitation of occupied Mecklenburg and Saxony, and through an equally ruthless inflationary policy, centered on an enormous debasement of the currency, which he carried out with the assistance of Jewish financiers. Under such unfavorable circumstances, however, the campaign of 1762 could hardly go beyond a feeble defensive. Its greatest successes were the recapture of Schweidnitz and the retention of Silesia north of Glatz.

By the end of the summer all warring powers on the Continent were exhausted. France had lost her most important colonies; during the last months Prince Ferdinand had even compelled the French armies to quit their German bases. In the absence of further French help Austria was near financial collapse. Sweden and Russia had left the war. The smaller German powers were eager to negotiate with Prussia. Only Great Britain was in an advantageous position; if she had been prepared to pursue the war energetically, she could now have conquered the Spanish colonies as well. But nothing was further from Bute's mind. Without regard for Prussia he concluded a separate peace with France, which assured Britain control of the North American Continent, and left Frederick to his fate. We can understand Frederick's indignation at the rupture of an alliance, which, when he had signed it six years earlier, had brought him the enmity of France. But fortunately for him, Austria too had reached the end. With the help of Saxon intermediaries, peace negotiations were opened at the Saxon hunting lodge of Hubertusburg. In the course of the discussions Frederick was able to retain all the territory that he had gained in the first two Silesian wars. On 15 February 1763 seven years of conflict ended. Frederick's refusal to give in had finally led to success.

Was the war no more than an adventure, whose outcome was finally decided by a propitious change of Russian rulers? Such a view would be inaccurate. Though fortune finally smiled on the tormented king, she had been his determined enemy for most of those seven years. However often his energy and resolution seemed to triumph, she had always turned against him again. The miracle of 1762, too, was no real surprise—Frederick had expected the death of the gravely ill empress since the beginning of the war. And if he was at the end of his strength, so was Maria Theresa. His policies often touched the limits of the possible, but never really exceeded them. Even Prussia's continuation of the war after 1760 never entirely lacked prospects. In the age of enlightened absolutism with its severely limited resources, all major powers tended quickly to exhaust their finances and their manpower reserves, so that a weaker state enjoyed certain possibilities of success if it could

.y hang on. Must we add that as a political recipe for all times and all circumstances, the slogan "fight on at all costs" is not without risks? Modern war, in which moral factors are overshadowed by material forces, machines, and mass armies, can render even the most determined will helpless against the enemy's superior manpower and industrial potential. As Germans know, in the age of total war, which engages not only the soldier but society as a whole, the principle "fight to the end" may easily lead to disaster.

Frederick's efforts and sacrifices had important results even if they did not lead to the kind of victorious peace whose significance is measured by the square miles of annexed territory. He had long ago renounced the hopes for acquisitions that he had briefly entertained at the beginning of the war. As soon as he had recognized that Prussia's existence was at stake he fought only to secure the frontiers of 1756. Temporary success had not seduced him into expansive desires for conquest. He might occasionally allude to a "salve for our wounds, if this should be obtainable," referring to Saxon-Polish frontier districts, if necessary in exchange for possessions along the Rhine. But under no circumstances were such demands allowed to interfere with the peace negotiations; their main function was to exert diplomatic pressure and to forestall territorial demands by the other parties. Frederick never diluted the essentially defensive character of the war. Now he had achieved his aim: the influence and power of Prussia had been asserted in the face of opposition from most of Europe. That counted for more than territorial gain. That in the process the old hegemony of France had been destroyed—not, as once before, through the combined efforts of Europe, but in the main by Germans—awoke a new pride in the German nation even outside Prussia.

The man whose heroic achievement was now universally admired returned home without joy in his triumph. His appearance and his feelings had changed radically. He still wanted to enlarge and intensify his existence by moving in the vast and free realm of the spirit, by living with the works of the great creators of mankind. During the war he had continued his literary and musical studies, kept up with French literature, had himself written philosophic and historical essays as well as poetry, and had delved again and again into the works of his favorite authors—the Stoics, Racine, Bayle, Voltaire. But the tensions of these years had destroyed his serenity and optimism. With increasing indifference he had reacted to the disappointments that 1761 and 1762 had brought. "My last days are poisoned," he wrote, "and the evening of my life is as horrible as its morning."

He returned to Potsdam prematurely aged, in spite of his fifty years an old man, gray, desiccated, arthritic, shabby in a worn uniform, his face now deeply lined, though his magnificent eyes were as bright as ever: a man despising men, who spread coldness and fear around him. Whenever possible he avoided celebrations. He was ready to let the Berliners have their fun, he wrote to d'Argens, "but so far as I am concerned. . . . I am returning to a city where only the walls are still familiar, where endless labor awaits me, and where soon my bones will find a refuge which will never again be disturbed by war, misfortune, or human meanness." He found no words of gratitude for his helpers, for the sacrifice of his officers, the death-defying courage of his soldiers, the faithfulness of his officials. Nor was he much interested in being honored by them. Immediately after the conclusion of peace he went on an inspection tour to Silesia, to plan the reconstruction of the province. When he returned to Berlin he did not ride in the ceremonial coach that awaited him, but reached the palace through side streets. There, the following day, he received a deputation of county councillors. He roughly broke into their welcoming address: "Be silent and let me speak. Do you have a crayon? Very well, write down: the gentlemen must draw up a list of how much wheat for bread, how much seed, how many horses, oxen and cows are immediately needed in their counties. Think it over carefully, and come back the day after tomorrow." With sober determination, refusing to tolerate any digression, he proceded to the business at hand.

8
Frederician Warfare

FREDERICK'S personality and his historical significance come to
life fully only when we understand his military achievements and the
nature of his system of warfare. What was it that distinguished
him from the traditional strategists of his day. What enabled him
to gain such brilliant victories, and what caused him to suffer such
serious—at times ruinous—defeats. Few aspects of his life remain
as much in doubt as these.

To the most knowledgeable military critic among his contemporaries, Prince Henry, it was evident that the royal commander permitted his genius, his impetuous temperament, and his excitable
imagination to seduce him into committing constantly new errors.
According to this view, he owed his victories to the unusual courage
and reliability of his troops—it was only their quality and the prudent strategy of his most eminent subordinate (Prince Henry himself) that prevented his faulty maneuvers and self-administered
defeats from leading to disaster. This judgment was based on the
conventional point of view of maneuver strategy. Napoleon, the
military idol of a new era, showed a greater understanding of
Frederick's passionate offensive spirit. He extolled the arrangement
of certain Frederician battles—particularly Leuthen. He admired as
Frederick's greatest achievement the ability to fight on regardless
of circumstance. On the other hand he found much to criticize in
Frederick's strategy. In the meantime Napoleon's own campaigns
had brought about a complete revolution in the art of warfare and
in military institutions, but a full understanding of Napoleon's
strategy and tactics had to await the analysis of Carl von Clausewitz, whose insights were to contribute directly to the further development of German strategic theory. His experience in the Wars
of Liberation led Clausewitz to consider traditional Frederician
strategy and tactics as outdated, retarded by the thousand debilities

of a primitive and ponderous military organization, incapable of pursuing the war to its climactic ideal: the destruction of the enemy. Like Napoleon he thought Frederick's strategic achievements admirable, but necessarily limited by the narrow constraints of their age.

In the patriotic historical interpretations of the nineteenth century, Clausewitz's insight into the fundamental difference between the two epochs was largely lost. Moltke's general staff sought the inspiration for its daring strategy not in Bonaparte, but in the great king, whose spirit after all continued to be cherished in the Prussian army. People were indignant—and not entirely without reason—when toward the end of the 1870's Delbrück took up Clausewitz's analysis and with doctrinaire exaggeration propounded a Frederician "strategy of exhaustion" in contrast to Napoleon's "strategy of annihilation." For several decades a debate raged between the Historical Section of the General Staff and the "academic strategist" Delbrück. As usually happens, it was never completely resolved, but it did bring about a certain mutual accommodation, and finally seemed to disintegrate into little more than a question of semantics. Actually, although the participants were not always clearly aware of it, a highly topical concern lay behind the scholarly dispute. Was the now classic "Napoleonic" method of seeking to destroy the main enemy army through the ruthless application of one's offensive potential the best in every circumstance —even against a greatly superior opponent who was pressing forward on several fronts at once? Or was another equally classic method available, that of exhausting the enemy through continued limited actions, pursuing the war with the least possible expenditure of force? And in a situation such as Frederick faced in the 1750's, might not this approach offer greater promise of success in the long run? Was the reckless offensive spirit a danger that could become fatal under such conditions?

The experience of the First World War lent additional weight to these questions, and stimulated even professional soldiers to renewed study of Frederick's strategy. We cannot follow them in their analyses. But we can learn from the previous dispute that the nature of Frederician war is clearly understood only if we first see how it differs from war in the Napoleonic era.

What Napoleon established was, in its general features, the now familiar kind of war waged by modern nation-states with the mass armies that universal conscription provides. The leadership of such armies may hope to achieve the highest goal of all strategy: breaking the enemy's will to resist by short, rapid, and destructive strokes against his main force. Napoleon's strategy, which derived less from theoretical studies than from the violence of his nature, from practical experience, and the instinct of his genius, can be outlined by mentioning a few simple principles. First, the resolute concentration of all available force on the decisive point, without anxious concern about such non-essentials as provinces that require protection, fortresses that must be kept under observation and rear areas that must be secured—in short, no fragmentation of the main force. What matters above all is to have superior forces available or at least near at hand at the decisive moment. Second, a determined advance on the center of enemy power, the direction of attack masked by cavalry; whenever possible the opponent is outflanked by forced marches that cut his lines of communication. Third, on the day of battle itself, concentration of the attack against the key sector of the enemy's position; preparation of the assault with massive artillery fire; attack in deep columns, which can continue to commit new reserves into the fight. Fourth, immediately after the decision, ruthless pursuit of the enemy until horse and man drop. If such a major stroke succeeds, the end of the war is generally in sight. What is still lacking to shatter the opponent's self-confidence is provided by a purposeful and flexible diplomacy that is especially adept at constantly driving new wedges between the partners of an alliance.

Most of the major wars of the nineteenth century were waged according to this general scheme, not least the campaigns of Moltke, though his creative imagination was far too rich to be restricted by any particular pattern. This type of warfare completely surprised Napoleon's opponents, who were helpless so long as they lacked its political and social preconditions, which in France had been created by the great revolution.

The first of the new prerequisites was the mass and relative cheapness of the human material at the disposal of the post-revolutionary army, in contrast to the far smaller resources available to the professional forces of the previous periods. Frederick had been forced to finance most of his campaigns, especially the first two Silesian Wars, out of a painstakingly accumulated war chest; the largely agrarian Prussian economy could not accommodate sizeable loans, and foreign credit was unobtainable. After the supply of money became almost limitless, war could grow far more encompassing. Until 1809 Napoleon never felt handicapped by fiscal concerns. His sizable armies enabled him to make deep advances, whose offensive thrust was scarcely diminished by the inevitable detachment of units for security purposes. The manpower now available permitted a more rapid replacement of disabled and wounded, which in turn made possible unheard-of improvements in march performance; it permitted attack in massive columns rather than in thin lines, and the ruthless employment of troops to pursue the beaten enemy.

A second factor was the national character of the revolutionary armies. They no longer consisted of mercenaries, foreign scoundrels that were kept in line by the corporal's rod, but of citizens defending their fatherland. To be sure, not too much should be made of this very obvious difference. France in the Napoleonic era was still far from having genuinely accepted the idea of universal military service. Usually the well-to-do bourgeois freed himself from this obligation by paying for a substitute, who then tended to remain permanently with the colors. Every year only a part of the able-bodied males were actually conscripted—far fewer than a third between 1799 and 1804—and of the conscripts a good number always managed to desert. On the whole France found it difficult to accustom herself to the concept of universal military obligation; she did so unwillingly and never completely. On the other hand, desertion in the Prussian army had significantly dropped since the days of Frederick William I. After the first Silesian War it often came to be a matter of pride even for a simple peasant's son to serve in the victorious army of the great king. Patriotism, at least in an early form of development, was awakening in the country. The French jest, that in Prussia one half of the garrison was needed to guard and whip the other, had long since lost its justification. The Prussian troops of the Seven Years' War, especially in the early campaigns, were something more than hordes of forced, rebellious mercenaries lacking any sense of public morality. If consciousness of Prussia as a state was still absent, the men nevertheless possessed traditional regional pride, which Frederick knew better than to discount. "The enemy has no Pomeranians," a grinning musketeer told him as he rode through the camp on the eve of Leuthen, "and you know how good they are!"

The discipline of the Pomeranians and the men from the Mark stemmed from local and regional comradeship, the patriarchal loyalty that the peasant owed to his squire, whose sons or brothers led him in the field, and of confidence in the great and victorious king. But above all it was formed by the strict religious obligation to obey, which Lutheranism had for centuries imposed on the north German peasant. Again and again we are told that on the march Frederick's soldiers sang the chorales that they had learned in their village church. The solemn "Now thank we all our God" rang out not only on the evening of Leuthen, but also after the triumph of Rossbach and on other victorious days. "We fight for religion, for you, for the fatherland," replied a veteran of the school of Leopold von Dessau to the king's praise after the battle of Liegnitz, and his words suggest the order of precedence of the ethical motives that animated the best elements in the army. Even in the revolutionary wars of the 1790's an intelligent observer still thought that for the Prussian mercenary faith took the place of the more developed sense of honor and military ambition found among the French.

In general, however, these moral obligations affected only native soldiers. They were scarcely felt by hired or forcibly recruited foreigners, by prisoners of war forced into Prussian uniform, least of all by the pillaging mob in the Free-Battalions that waged guerrilla warfare or was used as cannon fodder to clear the way for the regulars' attack. It should be added that the number of foreigners in the Prussian army has often been exaggerated. Studies by the Historical Section of the General Staff have shown that foreigners formed a majority only in those regiments that lacked their own native draft districts—the so-called cantons. At Frederick's accession, the army contained 26,000 foreigners out of 76,000 men; his intention to raise the foreigners' strength to two-thirds in each company was never achieved. In 1752 Frederick estimated that one-half of his troops were foreign born, but the regimental rolls show that during the Seven Years' War the elite regiments were almost entirely made up of Prussians. In February 1763 the entire army consisted of 103,000 natives and 37,000 foreigners.

Even so, the admixture of foreign elements was not insignificant. It was far larger, for instance, than in the armies of populous France, even in the days of the monarchy. The changes the Revolution brought about in manpower procurement gave the commander an unaccustomed freedom of action, because he was no longer dependent on unreliable and laboriously drilled foreign mercenaries. How many possibilities had Frederick shied away from because they seemed to facilitate desertion: night marches, marching through forests, marching in open formations—especially through so-called *defilées*—camping near woods, sending out small detachments for water or straw. Everywhere he had to post hussar patrols, officer pickets, guards, and even fence in the camps to prevent his men from running away. With the disappearance of mercenaries, service in the field became far simpler. Above all, it was no longer necessary to march troops against the enemy in closely ranged lines, with officers to the front and rear; now men could be sent forward as *tirailleurs,* that is, in skirmish groups that could exploit concealment and cover. Casualties declined. The greater reliability of the rank and file made possible greater initiative on the part of the tactical commanders. Such initiative had in any case become essential since the great numbers and dispersion of the combatants precluded Frederick's close order of battle and firm central control.

March security, cooperation among separate units, the gathering of information—all were greatly facilitated once patrols and security detachments could be sent out over longer distances. One eyewitness of the Prussian campaign of 1745 reported that one did not dare risk sending patrols out for even a few hundred feet at that time. As a result, Frederick's army operated with a highly defective intelligence service; repeatedly the king found himself in situations in which he was for weeks cut off from communication with his distant corps, and learned of their fate only through rumor. Particularly during his early campaigns he lacked both reliable cavalry patrols and light cavalry that could be employed in small units

—only after some time, and then never completely, was this weakness remedied by his hussars. His mounted troops were essentially battle cavalry, useful only for massed attacks in closed units. His infantry, too, lacked light troops that could disrupt the enemy's advance by fighting, as the Austrian Croats and Pandurs did, behind trees and hedges, in gardens, and other obstructed terrain. His Free-Battalions were too poor, his *Jäger* numerically insufficient, to achieve much. His infantry was unmatched in the impetus of its closed linear attack, but it was not suited to fight in open order and in small formations. The battle of Colin was lost partly because the advancing Prussian infantry proved unable to clear Croats from a small stand of tress in its flank. The serried ranks were obliged to avoid, rather than seek, obstructed terrain. Forests, hills, sunken roads were considered dangerous because they afforded possibilities for desertion. Even today's commander must fear that some of his men will be immobilized in such terrain; but the danger was infinitely greater for mercenaries. Under certain conditions even a hundred-yard gap between two wooded areas counted as a *defilée* that inhibited the attack, because to negotiate it the infantry lines had to break up into marching columns. Only gradually did the Prussian troops learn to master such obstacles. In Frederick's early campaigns he considered unobstructed plains as the ideal field of battle; later the successful repulse of the surprise attack in the hills of Soor taught him that battles might also be won on irregular ground.

The use of mercenaries also contributed to that extreme slowness of the baggage train and of the supply services, which constitutes a basic difference between Frederick's military system and that of the Revolution. The French revolutionary armies made no distinction between noble officers and plebeian troops; all were sons of the fatherland who could be called upon to suffer the same exertions and hardships. Keeping the men in good humor was no longer the concern it had been for Frederick, whose army enjoyed a particularly high reputation for its good rations (one pound of beef per man weekly), and therefore attracted many deserters. The defenders of the fatherland of a later age might sometimes go hungry; if things got too bad nobody hesitated to resort to requisitions. Had Frederick permitted this to his mercenaries there would have been no end to looting, deserting, and pillage—abuses that had horrified every responsible government since the Landsknecht era. Aimless destruction also conflicted with the new concept of the *raison d'état*. Wars were waged without national passion. So far as possible, occupied enemy territory was treated considerately, if only because wars could be expected to continue for long periods, and armies were not self-sufficient. But as we shall see, purchases in the zone of operations could only rarely satisfy the armies' requirements. The magazine system—which was to play a major part in shaping the warfare of the period—developed as a consequence of this.

In the zone of operations depots were established at easily accessible localities, at most five or six days' march apart, preferably near navigable streams. Saxony and Silesia were Frederick's favored bases because here the Elbe and Oder facilitated heavy traffic. Large quantities of grain, flour, and livestock could be accumulated in the depots, whose possession, together with control of the supply roads, came to be among the most important objectives of maneuver strategy. The fate of a campaign—or even, as Frederick once wrote from Moravia, the future of the state—might depend on the arrival of a great transport. But by no means all necessities could be stored and shipped to the troops. Particular difficulties were created by the cavalry's vast requirements of hay, straw, and oats. In order to have an adequate supply of fresh fodder, campaigns were postponed, if possible, until June. Often skirmishing broke out over stands of oats for the horses. Other needs, too, could not always be met without forced requisitions or the supplementary purchase on the spot of rations and spirits. But while Napoleon had enough men to garrison entire provinces, and to make the civil administration work for him, Frederician armies were rarely strong enough for an effective occupation. In Moravia and Bohemia Frederick's army remained limited to local foraging, which the peasants, especially in the Czech areas, could frequently evade. As they had for centuries when enemy soldiers approached, the peasants buried their valuables, drove off their animals and fled to the forests or to fortified towns and castles. It was in any case poor country; the standard of living of the serfs was miserable. Frederick thought Bohemia "not much better than a desert." The foreign invaders were hated, and the Prussians had to proceed with great circumspection to acquire any supplies at all. On the whole they remained dependent on their own transports, which were handicapped, especially during the wet season, by a lack of good roads and navigable streams. After the experiences of 1744 Frederick considered a prolonged occupation of Bohemia with Silesia for his supply base as highly dangerous: "A chain of mountains, created by nature to irritate us, separates these two areas—if you penetrate deeply into enemy territory, the aforementioned mountains choke off your supplies, the enemy cuts your lines of communication, and you risk having your army starve to death!" Saxony was thus essential to him as base of operations.

Napoleon possessed sufficient manpower and money to build military highways across Europe; Frederick's campaigns often became bogged down in the mire of country roads, which prevented any supplies from reaching the troops. In rainy weather the breadwagons might take days to move a mile to two, and still they had to throw away half of their loads. To minimize the consequences of such conditions, military theory taught that an army should not move farther than five days' march from its depots.

The soldiers of the revolutionary armies camped under the open sky if they found no quarters; Frederick's mercenaries rarely did, except before battle. At other times they slept in tents taken along to protect the precious human material. This added enormously to the baggage train; on the march each infantry regiment was accompanied by sixty pack-horses that carried the tents. Another burden was the personal baggage of the still largely aristocratic officer corps. Every company commander was entitled to a carriage and two saddle horses, every lieutenant to a pack and a saddle horse; staff-officers and generals took along five or ten times as much for their personal needs, as well as coaches and equipment carts. Wars were expected to last a long time, and sanitary conditions on campaign could be counted on to be very poor. The Prussians carried only a modest fraction of the baggage that the court-generals and noble gentlemen of the royal French armies considered indispensable—but even so it was a mighty burden.

Equally ponderous was the artillery train, which Frederick did not seriously attempt to improve until the Seven Years' War. Prussian artillery consisted of heavy guns (pulled to the battlefield by requisitioned farm horses) and light battalion guns (used particularly with case shot) which the soldiers themselves dragged from position to position. To match the superior Austrian gunnery, Frederick augmented his artillery until there were seven guns for every thousand infantrymen, whereas in 1809 Napoleon at Wagram had only somewhat over two guns for each thousand. By introducing horse artillery, Frederick sought to raise the mobility of the arm, and to lessen the danger that a cavalry charge might silence the guns. But to achieve the massive artillery fire which was often to prove decisive in Napoleonic warfare, significant technical improvements in carriage design and driver training were needed, as well as the reduction of calibers, an increase in range and accuracy, and better roads to assure the supply of ammunition.

The problem of pursuit perhaps most clearly demonstrates the limited mobility of eighteenth-century armies. It has always been particularly difficult to reorganize exhausted troops at the conclusion of battle and to set them in motion after a retreating enemy; but the reorganization of units was understandably far more essential with mercenaries than for a citizen army. To avoid uncontrollable flight, the defeated general frequently broke off battle while his command still retained a measure of cohesion—thus making it much easier for him to take up a strong position at the next obstacle, to disrupt the pursuer with his cavalry reserves, and to prepare other surprises. For these reasons, pursuit after victory rarely went beyond the next *defilée*. Frederick benefited from this limitation after the defeats of Colin and Kunersdorf; but in turn it prevented him from exploiting his successes. Among his major victories, only Leuthen and Rossbach led to energetic pursuits of the enemy.

All this suggests that the size of Frederician armies and their freedom of movement never sufficed to attempt the far-reaching strategic thrusts—aimed directly at destroying the enemy's center of power—that Napoleon was to undertake. In particular, Frederick condemned deep penetration into enemy territory without secure lines of communication and assured supply—actions that he called *pointes*. His *General Principles of War* of 1748 stated this clearly: "On the whole, those wars are useless in which we move too far from our borders. All wars that others have led in this fashion we have seen end in disaster! The glory of Charles XII vanished in the wastes of Poltava. Emperor Charles VI could not maintain himself in Spain, nor could the French remain in Bohemia. All plans that call for long advances should therefore be condemned."

This recognition resulted even more from experience than from theoretical studies. At times during the first Silesian Wars Frederick had considered a thrust to the gates of Vienna—only of course if it should be possible for the Prussians and Saxons to advance from the north while the French and Bavarians moved against the capital from the west. In practice he never attempted to execute such schemes, partly from suspicion of his allies, perhaps also on political grounds (as long as he acquired Silesia he was not at all interested in defeating the Habsburg monarchy) but mainly because such a distant goal as Vienna soon proved to be unattainable. Even to advance on Vienna was much too dangerous; for the Prussians alone to isolate and besiege such a strongly fortified city was unthinkable. Although Frederick in later years also worked out schemes for marching on Paris in case of war against France, all invasion plans of this type remained pure theory. Not one of the campaign plans of the Seven Years' War aimed for more than the occupation of Saxony, and for thrusts into Bohemia and Moravia. The most daring among them was the plan of 1757, which with some reason has been compared to Moltke's offensive of 1866. But closer study shows that this plan, too, originally did not intend the destruction of the enemy, but only the disruption of his initial deployment, the seizure of stores, and, under the most favorable circumstances, the capture of considerable terrain. In short, a rapidly executed stroke, a *coup de main* of the first magnitude! That this surprise move almost decided the war was an unexpected success.

Frederick owed this achievement, at least in part, to the fundamental changes he made in Schwerin's and Winterfeldt's schemes, by means of which he turned an operation that ran the danger of being fragmented over separate areas into a concentric advance on the enemy's center. But it remains doubtful whether he made the changes with the conscious intention of bringing about a decisive battle or simply in order to reduce the danger of the whole enterprise. The background of this campaign shows more clearly than any other the barriers of military reality that constrained Frederick's energy and strategic imagination after the unpleasant experience of the 1744 offensive. Much as Winterfeldt's daring plan attracted him from the start, he found it difficult to accept. If it had not been for the counsel of the two generals he would have restricted himself to a strategic defensive with various limited advances, he would even have dangerously divided his forces to cover as many positions as possible against enemy attack. After Colin he risked a major offensive only in Moravia—in accordance with the arguments developed in his theoretical writings. But the enemy needed only to evade him, refuse to give battle, interfere with his supplies or capture them, for this undertaking, too, to end in failure before the walls of Olmütz.

It follows that Frederick's war aims had to be entirely different from Napoleon's. In the Silesian Wars the issue was the conquest and retention of Silesia, not the enemy's military and political destruction. We have seen how Frederick tried to achieve his aims through nearly simultaneous military and diplomatic actions. During the Seven Years' War when he fought on three or four fronts at the same time, a decisive blow that would end the conflict was no longer a serious possibility. Now it was a question of making oneself as formidable as possible in the strategic defensive by maintaining a tactical offensive, and—if this could be managed—to keep control of a piece of enemy territory as a pawn in the peace negotiations. Remaining passively on the defensive, simply awaiting enemy attacks, would have resulted in the loss of one Prussian province after another, until the strangulation grew unbearable. A simple defensive could never protect this monarchy of border zones. But to achieve the "destruction" of his enemies, to fight campaigns that forced a quick decision, was beyond Frederick's means. He was already aware of the fundamentals of the Napoleonic strategy of annihilation: force must be concentrated and superior power must be available at the decisive point—he repeatedly impressed this on his generals. But he was not in the fortunate position of Napoleon, who wished to seek a decision by battle only when he could count on a 70 percent chance for success. Prussia's geographical position, and all the limitations of strategy that have just been discussed, mercilessly forced him to divide his troops, to cover at least the key provinces, in order to secure his communications and supply. Consequently he often had no choice but to risk battle even when he faced a clear superiority.

Thus his strategy was not based on the great decisive stroke, but on reducing the enemy's will to fight by lashing out with repeated blows. Whether or not this is called "strategy of attrition" does not really matter if it is understood that in this position no other strategy could have succeeded. Daring *pointes* in Charles XII's fashion would soon have led to catastrophe. Prudent maneuvering, cutting lines of communication and overruning depots in Prince Henry's fashion might perhaps have postponed the catastrophe for a long time, but such methods could never have sufficiently impressed his enemies and kept them from the center of Prussian power. Even waged in Frederick's spirit, this war remained a highly uncertain risk, and no one will deny that haste, impatience, and underestimating the enemy several times led Frederick into fatal errors. But the same temperament that caused these mistakes also made him superior to his opponents, not least to the most capable among them, the clever procrastinator Daun.

A defensive strategy that wears down the enemy with repeated blows—that was also the system which Germany was forced to adopt in the First World War, after the attempt to destroy the opponent on the Marne had failed. By then it was no longer only the cabinets that faced each other, but the peoples themselves, with their national passions, their immeasurable material and moral reserves. That rendered the task of hanging on even more difficult for Germany. Frederick could still expect that, in the eyes of his enemies Prussia's struggle for existence was little more than another episode of cabinet politics. Disagreements among the allied governments and their generals, court intrigues, change in rulers, opposition of interests and war aims, limitation of his enemies' finances —all these could, indeed would, one day improve his situation. Without such fortunate incidents he would eventually have been lost. Not that the allies during the First World War were without their internal differences—certainly England's true interest in the complete defeat of Germany soon became doubtful. But the peoples' enthusiasm and passion—a political factor that was still unknown to the eighteenth century—in the long run overwhelmed all else.

Our analysis has attempted to expose the limitations that Frederick's epoch placed on his military policies. We can now see how his system differed from that of later wars, and that it cannot be turned into a direct model for modern strategy. What did constitute its greatness?

Frederick's military genius goes far beyond the unique moral energy that permitted him to fight on regardless of circumstances. We can most readily identify it by relating it to the military theories and commanders of his own age, not by measuring his achievements against those of later periods. The first characteristic that sets Frederick apart is the unflagging offensive spirit, pressing for rapid decisions, which we have already discussed. The limitations of its military means had led the Baroque age to develop a so-called "methodical" strategy. The commander risked as little as possible and left few things to chance; instead he carefully weighed all probabilities and tried to predict them rationally. The greatest achievement of the methodical strategist lay in outflanking enemy positions and winning territory rather than in destroying enemy forces. To gain limited successes by surprising the opponent and masking one's own intentions, by careful exploitation of the terrain when choosing field positions and encampments, by cutting off the enemy's lines of communication and capturing his depots and forage areas and thus forcing him to quit his strong points—that was the true purpose of this strategy, which was neither risky nor too costly. Decision by battle was to be sought only in certain well-defined emergencies, or under unusually favorable circumstances.

Frederick was familiar with all these techniques; their discussion is prominent in his military works, especially in the earlier writings. But in practice even more than in theory, he outgrew them. The location of his state and the character of his army, above all his own turbulent genius led him to counter the considerations of cautious methodicalness with the principle: "Our wars must be short and active. . . . Those who lead the Prussian armies must be clever and careful, but must try to bring the issue to a decision."

He acted according to this rule, despite criticism by his brother and many of his generals, even in situations in which a cautious defensive appeared the only salvation. He knew that he could never win wars simply by maneuvering. For him the true purpose of maneuvering was not to gain ground, but to force the evasive opponent to give battle, if possible under favorable conditions.

The other important characteristic of Frederician war is the methodical cultivation of the offensive battle as the core of Prussian tactics, in contrast to the Austrians, and especially Daun, who developed the defensive battle to a high level of sophistication. In practice the scope of Frederick's strategic offensives remained limited; but he brought the tactical offensive to a state of perfection far beyond the standard of the day. He realized that the superiority of his small army rested almost wholly on its tactical drill, its ability to maneuver quickly and precisely, and on its spirited attack. He, too, was at his best in combat.

What is the nature of the Frederician battle? First, it differs from the battles of a later age in that there are relatively few participants. Rarely were more than 30,000 to 40,000 men committed in combat; only at Prague did the total reach 90,000. With the tightly ranged formations of the day the battle did not take up very much space. At Leuthen, the unusually extended Austrian front measured about four and a half miles, the Prussian attacking lines probably not more than half that distance. If the terrain was relatively open, the whole battlefield could be pretty well observed from one elevated point. Battles of such limited extent could be centrally directed even without the means of modern technology. The action developed from a pre-arranged order of battle, with landmarks designated to the wings of every battle line as guides for their advance. In crises, much still depended on the initiative of the subordinate commanders, especially of the cavalry leaders, whose actions not infrequently decided the outcome. The heavy cavalry with its massive attacks remained the most valuable support of the infantry. Despite all its improvements, artillery was still incapable of seriously weakening a strong position for the assault. At least in the early period of the Seven Years' War, its greatest contribution was made by battalion guns in close combat.

Infantry tactics had entirely changed since the end of the seventeenth century, when the flintlock with paper cartridges had replaced the old matchlock. The efficacy of fire had increased enormously; fire rather than close combat with the pike now constituted the true strength of the foot-soldier. In the seventeenth century pikemen, in conjunction with musketeers had still played a major role; they advanced in close squares, lances extended—a method of fighting that was very strong in the defense but possessed little offensive force. Subsequent development reversed this relationship. Frederick raised the offensive power of the infantry to the highest level of the age, while the Austrians could not entirely free themselves from the old defensive approach. The infantry's fire is best exploited by linear formation: the more rapidly the men load and fire, the thinner the line can be. The complex loading drill performed with the old musket had necessitated a formation of at least six ranks, one of which fired while the other five were recharging. The Prussian line had been reduced to three ranks and was correspondingly longer. On the drill fields firing was practiced with great ingenuity; each battalion line was divided into eight *Pelotons* which fired in turn with great speed, all three ranks at once, the front rank kneeling, the other two standing, so that an uninterrupted rolling volley resulted. In battle such artifices quickly broke down; an irregular flickering fire was generally all that could be achieved, and the more one tried to volley strictly according to command, the more the attack was delayed and the troops' impetus paralyzed. Frederick soon recognized this. He enjoined his men to advance on the enemy with long strides, fire a good volley into his face, and then as rapidly as possible shove the bayonet into his ribs. At the beginning of the Seven Years' War he even had his men shoulder their muskets during the advance, and forbade all firing in order to get them more quickly to the enemy. Already at Prague this proved to be impracticable, since it asked too much of the troops' courage and casualties rose dreadfully. But the offensive spirit and dash of the Prussian infantry remained the secret of its success.

The Prussian infantry attack ideally took place in the following manner: the men advanced in carefully aligned ranks, in cadence to the beat of the drums, led and surrounded by officers and NCO's. Volleys were fired on command, at the earliest 300 paces from the enemy—muskets being ineffective at longer range—more usually at 200 paces. Rather than striving for accurate aim Frederick wanted rapid and massive volleys at this point. Then bayonets were fixed for the final assault. Frederick thought he could guarantee that the enemy would rarely be able to withstand a bayonet attack executed by this human wall.

This scheme naturally varied considerably over different terrain. At Kunersdorf, for example, forests, swamps, ponds, and ravines narrowed the main offensive thrust to such an extent that the formation of an extended line was impossible, and there was no opportunity for supporting cavalry attacks. The Prussian army bled itself white in hopeless frontal assaults of limited width against the well-fortified and safely anchored Russian positions. On other occasions the commanders lacked sufficient time to arrange the order of battle: Hochkirch, for instance, degenerated into wild struggles of separate, disconnected units. But basically the method of attack was always the same: an advance in line without depth. It is true that the attack formations were arranged in two lines of battle, each of three ranks, the second line perhaps 150 to 200 paces behind the first. But the shortness of the distance between them indicates that the second line of battle was not really a tactical reserve and could be used for little else than filling the gaps caused by enemy fire.

Such thin lines were needed to stretch the front as far as possible, and thus prevent its being outflanked. The flank was the weakest feature of the linear order of battle. Even bending back the extreme wings or inserting additional troops at the flanks between the two lines could not completely solve the problem. This was especially true of the original type of Frederician battle, in which the attack unrolled as a frontal assault parallel to the enemy front. The main object of such attacks was to outflank the enemy. That could be done by quickly forming from the marching columns into the line of battle, and by rapid and accurate deployment of the attacking lines, so that the enemy had no time to take countermeasures. To this end the advance was commonly made in several columns marching side by side from which a solid attacking line was formed. The rapid execution of these two phases constituted a primary objective of Prussian training. But in theory the opponent could be outflanked only if one's own lines were longer than his. What could be done if the Prussians were merely of equal strength, or even numerically inferior to the enemy? Would this put them in danger of being themselves outflanked? How could this threat be avoided?

To meet this problem Frederick developed the oblique order of battle. The concept evolved from his experiences at Mollwitz and other battles of the first two Silesian Wars, from his studies of military history, and above all from his tactical experiments. It consisted of withholding or "refusing" one wing of the attacking line, while the other wing was strengthened with additional troops, assault units, a tactical reserve, massed guns, and cavalry. This reinforced wing closed with the opposing enemy units, and if possible outflanked them. Its local success could then provide the starting point from which to roll up the entire enemy front. Even a weaker force could thus overcome a far stronger opponent, as was brilliantly demonstrated at Leuthen.

In theory the oblique order of battle is simple, but its execution in the field leads to great difficulties and complications. If the enemy perceives the purpose of the attack he can take countermeasures: he can reinforce the threatened wing, or bend back his front—as happened at Colin, or he can counterattack the refused wing and attempt to outflank it in turn—as was done at Zorndorf. Everything hinges on the enemy's not recognizing the direction of the true attack, or being deceived about it. Both occurred at Leuthen: a feint induced the Austrian commanders to make false dispositions, after which the true approach march was hidden from them by a rise in the ground. At Colin, by contrast, the Austrians from their positions on the hills could observe the entire maneuver in time to take remedial action, though they did not go so far as to counterattack. It is also essential that the attackers' withheld wing keep the opponent sufficiently occupied without itself becoming too deeply involved in the battle—above all, it must not take the offensive prematurely. Otherwise the oblique battle turns into a battle of parallel fronts with unequally distributed forces, a situation which can have serious consequences and deprive the commander of his last reserves. Frederick experienced this more than once. The tendency of his generals to advance too soon, in line with the main attack, was almost always intensified by the fact that in oblique advances the solid front tends to break, so that dangerous gaps can easily appear between the attacking battalions. Frederick tried to diminish this danger and insure that the refused wing was actually held back. At Leuthen his solution was to advance his attacking battalions not in an oblique line but in echelons—a formation which later, in the years before Jena, was taught and practiced with doctrinaire zeal, as if such methods, which might succeed once, could guarantee victory. Frederick himself knew that the battle should be shaped not by doctrine but by the intellect of the general and his exploitation of the specific situation. He also knew that complex maneuvers rarely succeed under fire. In his eyes, drill simply served to give his troops the mobility and precision that enabled them to carry out any maneuver in any direction.

Early forms of the oblique order of battle were discussed in the theoretical literature long before Frederick's time; the concept was already known in antiquity. But Frederick first made its actual employment possible. In general his achievement lay not so much in inventing new complicated methods as in simplifying those that were too complex, and in recognizing a few basic rules—his "General Principles"—which could guide the commander's decisions and actions in the pressure of events. To be sure, he too attempted to subject war to the power of rational analysis, and to restrict the scope of chance and accident as much as possible. But he never surrendered to the rigid demands of theory. He proved himself in the rapid exploitation of the changing aspects of combat, in his rich inventiveness, and in the promptness and decisiveness of his leadership.

The advantages and flaws of Frederick's tactics are apparent. Usually a well-planned and energetically executed attack soon led to a decision. Because Frederick's opponents were not his equal in quick and determined action, and because their troops were better trained for the defense than for the attack, he was able to overrun even a very much stronger enemy within a few hours. But his system suffered from certain defects. The best troops were expended in the first attack, and sufficient reserves could not be retained—a weakness ameliorated but never eliminated by withholding one wing. Even though Frederick could support his infantry's first assault with cavalry charges, he was unable to bring additional infantry to bear and could not maintain the battle for long periods. Because of this inability he foundered at Colin and at Kunersdorf, where—as already mentioned—the terrain also ruled out effective cavalry attacks. Finally, the rigid Prussian drill could sometimes prove a handicap: battalions moving in line and firing volleys were easily thrown into disorder by difficult terrain; they were not trained for fighting in open formations. But these were limitations that sprang almost inevitably from the structure of the military institutions of his day; what his troops could do Frederick exploited to the fullest. The scope of his tactical and strategic inventiveness would become wholly apparent to us only if we could trace the design of his battles from one campaign to the next. The difficulties constantly increased, his attempts to solve them became steadily more daring. As his enemies learned to perfect their defensive methods, he further expanded his enveloping tactics. At Rossbach he attacked the flank of an enemy envelopment; at Zorndorf and Kunersdorf both armies reversed their positions in attempting to outflank one another. At Torgau the flank attack was raised to a dual attack: two separate corps simultaneously moved on the enemy from north and south; the main assault proceeded from an enveloping march that led in a semicircle about the Austrian right wing.

In the final analysis, what proved decisive for Frederick's success was that his practical genius matched the clarity and profundity of his theoretical understanding. The rationality of his thought neither handicapped the soldier's determination nor reduced the self-confidence of the political leader. And so it was possible for him to raise the art of war of his period to its highest possible level. After the Seven Years' War he occupied the same position among the generals of Europe that once had been Prince Eugene's: Frederick was now the universally admired, studied, and emulated preceptor of modern war. But in the military realm as in the field of political theory his efforts constituted an ultimate achievement, a high point from which there could only be a decline. Very soon after his death a new age dawned for the military institutions of Europe.

9

The Character of Fredevician Government and Society

i. The Bureaucracy

WE HAVE SUGGESTED that Frederick's military policy relied on the methods of the absolutist state, which it perfected until they attained their highest possible effectiveness. Much the same can be said of his civil administration. Not that he significantly altered the bureaucratic organization he had inherited from his father, or changed the direction of his father's internal policies. He was clearly a man of action rather than an administrator, and in the main his domestic policies were conspicuously lacking in innovations; they were far more conservative than those pursued by his most eminent predecessors, his father and great-grandfather. Unlike Joseph II, whose enlightened absolutism is of a later variety, he never transgressed the special privileges of the Estates or of the provinces for the sake of a ruthlessly centralized uniformity. But in one decisive respect he broke with the policy of his predecessor: he deprived the ministerial bureaucracy, which his father had carefully built up, of all independence. In its place he raised the personal rule of the monarch to its highest potential.

Frederick William I's most significant accomplishment in reorganizing the structure of Prussian government was to combine the two distinct administrative groups that operated both in the provinces and in the central agencies in Berlin. He united the older administration of the royal domain lands with the newly established War Commissariats, which collected the war tax, but also supervised the economic administration of the army, policed the guilds, and dealt with other local matters. The customary tasks of government could now be expanded without compromising administrative homogeneity. Indeed, with this innovation an important start was made in overcoming the former regional fragmentation of the government's agencies. All provincial domain and tax bodies were subordinated to a central authority in Berlin, the General-Superior-Finance-War-and-Domains-Directory, commonly known as the General Directory, which combined the duties of today's finance, agriculture, and commerce ministries, and later was also to incorporate certain tasks of military administration.

In practice, to be sure, government was still far from centralized. Older judicial and ecclesiastical agencies, disposing of a considerable share of the state's power, continued to function side by side with the provincial war-and-domain chambers; they were not subordinated to the General Directory but came under a separate department of justice, ecclesiastical affairs, and education. Uncertainty about their areas of competence continued to cause friction among the various government bodies. But even more important, the General Directory itself was not organized into functional departments, each responsible for the entire monarchy, but into provincial ministries. Each of the four ministers who jointly headed the General Directory supervised the administration of several provinces. Some duties, to be sure, were already organized along functional lines: there were departments for frontier questions, postal affairs, the currency, the salt monopoly, and other matters. But these departments were unsystematically assigned as additional duties to a particular minister, which complicated the lines of responsibility and made departmental procedures rather cumbersome. It was not possible, for example, to reform the salt monopoly without encountering opposition from special interests in the provinces, for which the ministers themselves acted as spokesmen. Unfortunate experiences of this kind later induced Stein to include the introduction of modern functional ministries as the first step in his reform program.

Frederick did not modernize the organization which he took over from his father. He was content to expand on it by makeshifts and improvisations. A number of additional departments were created with responsibility for military administration, mining, forests, and trade and commerce—subsequently he himself took charge of this office. But as was the case with the older departments, the new creations were not organically connected to the General Directory.

With the conquest of Silesia the conduct of domestic affairs became even more complex. Frederick did not place the government of Silesia under the General Directory, but appointed a separate provincial minister, who resided in Breslau, and reported directly to the royal cabinet. For a time a similar arrangement prevailed with West Prussia. Such measures seriously diminished the cohesion and responsibility of the General Directory, and in the end the ministerial council no longer held joint meetings. It was even easier to do without them since the council was also losing its old function as the central agency of Prussia's financial administration.

Frederick William I had restructured Prussia's antiquated and extremely complex treasury organization into two main bodies: the General Finance Directory, disposing over the income of the royal domains (which was primarily charged with the costs of the civil administration), and the General War Treasury, into which flowed the so-called "war taxes", consisting of the excise and rural contributional taxes (which defrayed the war budget, namely, the requirements of the military). Both directories were subordinated to the General Directory, which issued the annual budget, and to the General Audit Office, which saw to it that all boards and offices kept accurate books. A fixed annual budget was even given to the royal court, the king personally receiving a "pension" permanently set at 52,000 taler, which to be sure, was considerably enhanced by other income. The main advantage of this system lay in its thrift and accuracy. But it lacked flexibility. To give himself a freer hand, Frederick began to withdraw large sums from the control of the General Directory and the General Audit Office, placing them in a secret fund. In time this "Royal Disposition Fund" received the surplus from the central provinces, from Silesia, and West Prussia, the entire proceeds from new sources of income which the king had introduced—taxes on lotteries, banking, and the mails, and the tobacco and coffee monopolies—and finally even the proceeds of indirect taxation, the administration of which he removed from the General Directory in 1766. The unity and clarity of the financial administration, which his father had achieved with such difficulty, was destroyed. But Frederick gained what he wanted: unhampered, creative disposition over the state's income.

He employed his secret fund with great practicality, not capriciously but according to firm principles. The most important of these was never to waste a penny, so that resources were always available for the pressing demands of the state, and so that he could afford to be generous whenever it seemed really necessary. He was always conscious of the fact—which he stressed to his successor—that the income from taxes was "the blood and sweat of the people" which should be spent only for the benefit of the state. The fund paid not only for his magnificent palaces, but financed his extensive projects to improve the rural areas of the monarchy, the rebuilding of the provinces that had been devastated by war, the settling of thousands of foreign immigrants—indeed, it defrayed all extraordinary expenses of the state. At the same time the war treasury was increased until it reached 51 million taler, in contrast to the ten million, which the vault of the Berlin palace had contained at the outset of his reign.

The king, in short, was his own minister of finance. The ministers heading the General Directory were reduced to the status of treasurers responsible for different areas of the exchequer, who lacked any real knowledge—let alone control—of the overall budget. Income and expenditures of the state remained the king's secret. The unity that Prussia's administration had once found in a central agency it now found only in the person of the monarch. More often than not he communicated over the heads of ministers directly with their subordinates, the provincial officials, receiving their reports and issuing orders. He sent instructions directly to his ambassadors, often without even informing the two ministers who jointly headed the foreign office. In the same way, no intermediaries screened the extensive correspondence between the monarch and his subjects. An immense number of memorials, complaints, and appeals was daily presented at the Potsdam Palace, and forwarded by the king with instructions to the appropriate agency, which often labored endlessly to achieve an acceptable settlement.

Ministers were granted a private audience only in exceptional cases. The king saw them in a body once a year, at the time that the budget was drawn up. Communications among the ministries and between ministries and the royal cabinet took place in writing, a policy that had been introduced by Frederick William I. The ministers submitted their proposals to Potsdam, where the king made the decision, generally by writing a few words on the margin of the file. His cabinet secretaries, subordinate officials of middle-class descent, expanded these brief comments into so-called Cabinet Orders. The advantage of this form of government—government from the king's study—was that rapid personal decisions took the place of complicated deliberations in committee and decisions finally arrived at by majority opinion. Frederick despised great councils of state, formal ministerial meetings under the king's chairmanship, which were the custom elsewhere. On campaign he had never called a council of war, but decided everything himself. That was the approach he also preferred at home. Council sessions, he said, "simply provided opportunities for mutual intrigues and for the introduction of hate and passion into the affairs of the state." He was also aware that his own temper might have betrayed him in such meetings. But the main consideration, of course, was that he wanted to have sole responsibility for all decisions. The four ministers of France, he wrote on one occasion, governed side by side like four kings: in the process the cohesiveness of government was lost, besides, every state secret became public. He himself did not want to lay bare his reasoning to anyone: "I lock my secret into my own heart." It seemed to him that the dignity of true kingship demanded no less. He would not admit the need for publicly justifying or explaining his actions; he never tolerated public comments or suggestions in any form on his management of the government's business.

Personal rule driven to such extremes was made possible only by constant, intense activity, and an almost unlimited versatility. Frederick's military correspondence during the Seven Years' War shows us that, assisted only by his confidential secretary Eichel and a few adjutants, he personally read and answered the daily mass of incoming troop reports, news of the enemy, messages from secret agents, and the countless queries of subordinates down to the commandant of a garrison or the officer in charge of an outpost. Beyond that he dealt with an enormous diplomatic correspondence, and with the whole business of supply, troop replacements, and other essentials of military administration. He accomplished by himself what today would be handled by an entire general staff. In much the same way he governed the state. Together with the great issues of foreign and domestic policy, he concerned himself with details down to the least significant problem: the lease of a royal farm, the budget of a town, municipal appointments in some provincial nest, and the private complaints of any subject who chose to raise them. From every inspection tour he returned with bundles of notes on the state of repair of buildings in towns and villages, needed road construction and reforestation projects, particulars of the local nobility and officials, and the condition of the peasants. He observed everything, wrote everything down, and everywhere wanted to interfere, encourage, and supervise.

Certainly his energy and activity were admirable. We see a monarch who rules his state in the true sense of the word, surveys all branches of government, gathers all reins in his hand, and despises all pomp and ceremonial as empty externals. But the bureaucracy with which he worked had reached such complexity that he alone could manage it properly—just as the imperial constitution that was devised by his spiritual heir Bismarck could be guided only by its creator. Furthermore, Frederick's successors could hardly be expected to match his energy and industry. Immediately after his death the system of personal rule began to waver. Under Frederick William II favorites gained influence, waste and corruption became rampant, and within a few years the great financial reserves Frederick had accumulated were scattered. The next ruler, Frederick William III, well-intentioned but only moderately gifted, became dependent on his cabinet councillors, who were subordinate officials lacking personal responsibility and a broad view of state policy. Even in Frederick's time, personal prejudice or insufficient knowledge had often led to mistakes. The monarch could not be infallible in all areas. His successors usually lacked even the courage to make important decisions. Vast issues remained unresolved, or were settled—but not decided—through an unhappy compromise of opposing views. Thus the judgment of history on Frederick's administrative policies must remain in doubt. Their great practical results will be analyzed later in this chapter. We admire his system as the personal achievement of a highly gifted man. But the system of personal rule as such was necessarily impermanent. Frederick's work did not coalesce into lasting institutions because, like Bismarck, his impetuous creativity tolerated only subaltern assistants, not independent and capable collaborators.

"Man must labor like the ox must pull the plow." This motto—half sigh, half good-humored encouragement—with which Frederick resumed his work after the Seven Years' War, aptly describes the spirit of punctual execution of duty that permeated all branches of the administration. Basically this spirit—the spirit of the absolutist state in its purest form—expected everything from compulsion, little or nothing from free will; men on the whole were considered a "mean race," and its own officials in particular it regarded with deep suspicion. The voluntary offering of advice and cooperation by subjects who were not servants of the state was easily viewed as presumptuous interference in official business. Even Frederick's correspondence with his ministers and senior officials contains numerous passages that revert to the harsh and despotic tone of his father.

The severity of Frederick William's regime is explained in large part by the need to compel the self-assured nobility, which still tended to oppose the government in its provincial assemblies, to work for the crown. It required great effort to turn the obstinate gentry into unconditionally obedient "royal servants" in army and administration, and in the process the king did not shy away from the most rigorous measures. Insubordination, embezzlement, and blunders in office led not only to dismissal but directly to the dungeon in Spandau. A disloyal noble official was hanged "as an example" in the town square of Königsberg, before the eyes of his colleagues, in spite of all the appeals of his influential family and the indignation of the East Prussian nobility. Two royal domain councillors in the same city, who did not want to be transferred to Tilsit, were promptly incarcerated for one year. "One must make short shrift," Frederick William commented; "the people want to force my hand. They must dance to my tune, or the devil take me: I will execute and burn like the tsar, and treat them as rebels. . . . I command my army, and should not command these damned scribblers! I would be a scoundrel if I were to tolerate that: I am master, and the gentlemen are my servants!"

Since Frederick William's reign the discipline of the Prussian bureaucracy had improved remarkably. The zeal of the native nobles in the service of the state had proved itself in twenty battles and in the administrative labor of several generations. More than once Frederick warmly acknowledged their loyalty and willingness. But the great distance separating the ruler from his servants had increased even further. We recall the self-assured irony with which the young king had shunted aside his ministers, grown old in the state's service, when they voiced objections to his first reckless moves in foreign affairs. The only difference between this and the previous era was that now icy ridicule usually took the place of abuse and bluster. But this was mockery against which no one was permitted to defend himself, the effect being particularly cruel when both ridicule and rudeness were combined in the expressions of royal disfavor. Only once did the members of the General Directory dare humbly to criticize a royal decision—one that concerned economic innovations which the king had introduced after the Seven Years' War. The response was a highly ungracious Cabinet Order: "I am amazed at the impertinent memorandum that you sent me. I excuse the ministers on the grounds of their ignorance, but the malice and corruption of the actual author calls for exemplary punishment, otherwise I shall never force the rabble into proper subordination." As a result, the Privy Financial Councillor Ursinus, an able and highly regarded official, was sent to Spandau. The king's suspicions that Ursinus had been bribed by economic interest groups was not confirmed, but some minor irregularities in the conduct of his duties led to a one-year imprisonment and his dismissal from office. Better known is Frederick's intervention in the suit of the miller, Arnold. Today it is clear that Arnold was a quarrelsome and litigious individual, whom the king wrongly thought to be a victim of aristocratic injustice. The minister of justice and the judges of the high court were ordered to report on the case in a personal audience; Frederick barely listened to their explanations, the judges were taken directly from the palace to prison, and when the minister opened his mouth he was shown the door with the words: "March, march! Your position is already given to someone else!"

We must not overlook such episodes if we wish to understand the stern reality of personal absolutism. But we must also be careful not to see them solely as expressions of a royal whim, or to confuse them with the despotic caprice of minor princelings. An element of the *raison d'état* is active in these confrontations, though it is obscured by the impatient outbursts of a highly excitable individual. Frederick's anger was always caused by the suspicion that his officials were venal and corrupt. At times his distrust expressed itself in a truly grotesque manner; most extravagantly perhaps when, on the occasion of an insignificant matter, he wrote to the West Prussian government: "with good conscience one can always hang ninety-nine out of a hundred war commissaries; it is already saying a good deal if a single honest man is among them." Such outbursts insulted and discouraged their recipients, and could only do harm. But the motive behind them—Frederick's eternal concern for the integrity of his officials—was anything but superfluous.

The danger of political corruption, and of the biased manipulation of the state's authority, exists in every form of government. In modern democracies the most effective counterforce is the free expression of critical public opinion, which ultimately has the decisive voice in the affairs of the state. The struggle of pressure groups and political cliques is revealed by the searchlight of the press, and the disagreeable picture of constant party conflicts is seen by all. Political life seems to consist of a mass of mutual recriminations and public accusations and it is only in rare moments of patriotic exaltation that the nation recalls its common values. In the absolutism of the eighteenth century, self-interest and ambition fought for power with equal viciousness, and the natural conflict of interest of different economic groups was by no means absent. But their battles took place behind the scenes, barely visible to the public. In particular, a thousand ways were found in the administration and the courts to satisfy the economic egotism of the nobility, the most powerful of the Estates, as well as the capitalist interests of the entrepreneurs. The remedy of public opinion being out of the question, the responsibility of the absolute monarch became doubly heavy. He alone could rise above the contesting groups, and was therefore obliged to prevent the interests of any one faction from usurping the place that belonged solely to the interest of the state. He alone was the guarantor of justice.

Actually Frederick was surprisingly successful in detaching his senior officials from the special interests of the nobility—to which the great majority belonged—and in turning them into obedient instruments of his rule. Military discipline and promptness, competence and complete integrity were the glories of the old Prussian bureaucracy. As long as the monarchy existed, the population never completely lost faith in the reliability and impartiality of this body —even though under weak or incompetent rulers the influence of court cliques and of interest groups at times assumed dangerous proportions. Frederick had taught his administrators the virtue of conscientiously performing their duties for the good of the state. But he did not know how to arouse and nurture the courage to assume individual responsibility, and consequently the talent for political action. The mechanism of his administration remained without a soul, politically passive, unable to act on its own. Its achievements depended almost wholly on the energy and will of the king.

A few capable and independent personalities could be found among Frederick's ministers: Finckenstein and Hertzberg in the foreign office, Heinitz in the industrial, economic, and commercial realm, Zedlitz in ecclesiastical and educational affairs. But such men were rare, and as long as the old king lived they labored under a heavy hand. It is true that even during his lifetime his great reputation and the opportunities offered by a vast administrative organization attracted young and able officials from all corners of Germany to the Prussian service. But not until he died, and the rigor of personal rule diminished under his successors, could they develop their talents freely. Even then the forms of Frederician administration continued to handicap them. Only when government from the king's study was destroyed in the days of Stein and Hardenberg could the system of royal absolutism be replaced by a system of bureaucratic absolutism, which in some periods at least was also able to demonstrate initiative and creativity.

ii. The Structure of Society

LIKE the bureaucracy, the population as a whole was trained to render scrupulous service to the state. During Frederick's reign the organization of society remained essentially as it had been under his predecessors. Nobility, middle class, and peasantry—each Estate had its own tasks, and the character and vitality of each was therefore carefully preserved. Even after its political privileges had been eliminated, the nobility still constituted the most powerful support of the crown. From their estates its members governed the rural areas of the monarchy on behalf of the state, wielded police and judicial authority, kept the peasants in order, supervised the punctual payment of their taxes, and enjoyed their services and tithes. On the other hand, in times of need the landowners were responsible for seeing that the peasants retained their livelihood, and that there was no reduction in the district's revenues or in the number of peasant families. Those sons of the nobility who were not needed to work the estates were enrolled in cadet academies or entered the royal administration.

The nobility's pride in family and class formed the basis for the officer corps' sense of honor. The aristocratic background and early training at home stood the government in good stead in the diplomatic service and the higher ranks of the bureaucracy, where self-possession and good manners were desirable. For these contributions, the nobility was rewarded with the sovereign's special solicitude. The government protected the *Junkers'* exclusive right to own "noble" land; only in exceptional cases was a commoner permitted to acquire a *Rittergut*. The debts of the large landowners, which had grown considerably during the Seven Years' War, Frederick reduced by donations worth many millions, by new mortgage regulations, and by organizing credit unions supported by state subsidies for the nobility in Silesia, Brandenburg, and Pomerania. The creation of entailed estates sought to assure the preservation of the nobility's landholdings. In most provinces the noble estates were exempt from taxation. Frederick William had tried to enlarge the royal estates by means of numerous lawsuits with the neighboring gentry; he sought to repossess former state property, and to buy up estates that had run into debt. Frederick discontinued these policies. The sons of the nobility, he said, "are the ones who defend the country; they are a breed so valuable as to merit preservation by any means possible."

Promotion to senior positions in the bureaucracy was almost without exception reserved for the aristocracy, though now and then a commoner of outstanding ability might be appointed from abroad. The army, after the end of the Seven Years' War, accepted only young nobles as officer candidates; commoners who applied were turned down. The sons of cultivated bourgeois families who during the war had rushed in great numbers from schools and universities to Frederick's colors, and had earned their commissions in the field, were now ruthlessly weeded out. Inferior officers among them were simply discharged, while the more valuable and deserving ones were transferred from the Guards and the line regiments to the artillery and the second-line garrison troops. In the cavalry, only the hussars were not too particular about a man's pedigree. Later on, when the nobility could no longer fill all available posts, the opportunity of acquiring the particule of nobility by long-term service in the artillery or in garrison regiments was held out to sons of bourgeois estate owners. But barring these exceptions the king maintained that the aristocracy alone was to be considered as the country's true military elite.

On principle the middle class served the state not by bearing arms but by increasing the national income. Commerce, trade, and the academic professions were permanently exempt from military obligations. The peaceful bourgeois was to be affected as little as possible by the wars of his king. In return, he carried the greater part of the tax load, made up largely of tolls and a number of indirect taxes, which increased steadily as the middle-class economy grew, while the rural land taxes remained fixed once and for all at a given level. This explains the zeal with which the government fostered the development of trade and industry; it is characteristic of mercantilist economic policy in general. The economic security of the bourgeois was protected from outside encroachment no less than that of the noble landholder. The aristocrat was forbidden to engage in commerce and trade; competition by rural artisans was reduced to an indispensable minimum—smiths, wheelwrights, millers, and tailors; commerce and brewing were prohibited outside town limits. The rural population was expected to buy its goods in the towns, and thus assure an adequate livelihood for the urban artisan.

The peasants carried by far the heaviest burden in state and society. Their sons were recruited for the army. On their farms lay the oppressive weight of the land tax, to which the nobility made a small contribution only in Silesia and East Prussia. Counting the billet money and other payments to the army, the average amount of a peasant's taxes has been estimated at about 40 percent of his net income, to which must be added his compulsory labor for the state, his obligation to supply relays for officers, officials, and troops marching through the district—all for negligible compensation. Even more oppressive than all these duties were the burdens imposed by the squire—the tributes and compulsory services of various kinds, rarely stipulated in writing, often of unlimited amount and duration, which the peasant owed to his master, a noble landowner or the tenant of a royal domain. Frederick himself admitted that the peasant was truly the "beast of burden within human society." His attempts to improve the peasant's lot met with some success only on the royal domains. There most of the peasants received their lands as hereditary holdings; in some provinces they were relieved from compulsory domestic labor; in many cases the amount and type of their obligations was established in writing, and occasionally even reduced. Finally, the colonists in the new settlements were given greater privileges.

On the other hand, Frederick was unable to do much to improve the lot of the so-called "private peasants" on the noble estates. At most, his prohibitions of senseless beatings were of some use because occasionally he underlined them by vigorously punishing a despotic squire. But otherwise his attempts at reform gave way before the protests of the landowners, who cited their services to the state, economic need, and inherited prerogatives. He was inflexible only on one point, his refusal to permit the enclosure of peasant land, which at that time was being carried out on a grand scale in neighboring Mecklenburg and Swedish Pomerania. The vitality and productivity of the third estate, like that of the others, was to be preserved for the monarchy. The *raison d'état* even more than common humanity made this essential.

In short, the Prussian monarchy under Frederick, like all European monarchies before the French Revolution, was still an aristocratic state. The nobility had lost its claim for sharing the country's government with the prince; its constitutional rights inherited from feudal times had disappeared. But it remained the dominant class. Noblemen could no longer make use of political privilege for unlimited exploitation of their subjects; but together with the manorial claim on the peasants' services, they still disposed over parts of the state's power in their possession of patrimonial justice, local police authority, and church patronage—all forces that they could utilize both for their personal benefit and that of their class. They no longer had the right to expect a monopoly of state benefices, but it was granted them voluntarily by the king. Frederick was even more warmly disposed toward the nobility than his predecessors had been. Their struggle to "destroy the authority of the *Junkers*" and, in his father's words, "establish the king's sovereignty like a rock of bronze" had long been forgotten. As Frederick declared in his first political testament: "In Prussia one need not fear political factionalism and rebellion; it is necessary only that the ruler governs with moderation, and bewares of a few debt-ridden or disgruntled nobles, or some titled prebendaries and monks in Silesia. But even these are not outright enemies. . . . Strictness is needed only on a few occasions." In his writings he praised the Prussian nobility—in spite of sharp criticism about particular aspects—as incomparably the best disciplined and best trained on earth. He considered it to be the real "foundation and pillar of the state."

Surely this evaluation was not without good cause. Even an absolute monarch cannot accomplish great deeds merely by physical coercion. Like any autocrat who wants to be a true leader he needs the personal confidence, if not of the entire population then at least of a group of closer adherents, who are tied to him by ethical forces, by mutual loyalty. The King of Prussia found this following first of all in his noble officers, and more generally in the aristocracy as such. He felt certain that their preferential position would not deteriorate into the enjoyment of privilege without actual achievement, as in France, or into a self-serving class government and the brutal exploitation of the peasantry, as in Mecklenburg and Poland. Strict supervision by the state and the severe discipline of army and administration served as effective antidotes.

At the same time Frederick strove—not without success—to bring the rural noblemen out of their narrow provincialism and to liberate them from their lack of education and their particularist egotism. The experience of military service did much to awaken for the first time the consciousness of a national identity in men whose origins lay in different provinces of the state. The blood that was shed in the Silesian Wars forged a bond of comradeship between them. Frederick deliberately pursued their political education: the *Junkers* were to lose the habit of entering foreign service, they were to consider the collective term "Prussia" as their name of honor, in place of Pomerania, Silesia, or the Mark Brandenburg; they were to know no higher aim in life than devotion to the service of their country. His letters on patriotism, discussed earlier, were addressed to their sons. Frederick wanted to develop the nobility into the nucleus of a new nation and not solely into a personal following. And it was the Prussian military and bureaucratic aristocracy that became and remained the principal representative of the Frederician concept of the state.

During Frederick's lifetime the bourgeoisie and peasantry, far from considering the inequality of the social groupings as an injustice, saw in it a preordained condition to which one must patiently submit. It was not until shortly after his death that Prussians too at last began to apply a political interpretation to the familiar Enlightenment doctrines of the natural equality of man. These views were expressed first perhaps in Königsberg, where Kant taught his listeners, among them aristocratic officials of senior rank, that the misuse of man as a mere means to an end, and the disregard of his moral dignity, violated the commandments of ethics and reason. Had Frederick been told of this he would presumably have agreed in theory, being convinced that the favor in which he held the aristocracy had nothing to do with supposed advantages of noble birth, which could not possibly imply any kind of human superiority. He had often enough ridiculed such views as barbaric. He believed that he preferred the nobility not because it was superior by birth, but because it actually was the most competent and useful of the three Estates. In the same way he deplored the fact that he had not succeeded in improving the lot of the peasants on the private estates. Even the best intentions, he thought, must founder on the impossibility of changing existing "contracts for service" without compensation, which would lead to the ruin of the nobility. In this regard too, despite all apparent contradictions, he felt himself to be an enlightened, humanitarian ruler.

And yet, Frederick was not as unbiased as he believed. He hardly noticed that during the last years of his reign a genuine sense of national identity had begun to stir even the middle and lower levels of the population. The innumerable signs of loyal affection and of an often childlike trust, which were daily shown him by men of all classes, seem to have made only the slightest impression on him. He regarded the great majority of the citizenry simply as politically immature subjects, who must obey whether they liked it or not. Certainly he no longer caned men on the street as his father had done, and he evinced a great deal of sympathy and understanding for people's troubles. In his personal dealings with the lower classes he was able like a true soldier to enter persuasively into their manner of speech, and his unassuming, completely unceremonious ways quickly made him a popular figure, inspiring—particularly in Silesia—countless legends and anecdotes. But basically he was an aristocrat, despising the *canaille,* elevated in lofty solitude high above the masses. And around this industrious, outwardly plain Prussian soldier flowered the world of courtly rococo: a world whose serene radiance and splendid beauty must be imagined against the dark backdrop of millions of hopelessly toiling peasants. The possibility that this world could one day be overturned from below no more occurred to him than it did to any of his French associates.

In Prussia, to be sure, there was no immediate reason for him to anticipate anything like this. Revolutionary tremors, uprisings of the bourgeoisie and peasants in protest against aristocratic privilege, did not occur in Prussia until 1848, and even then lacked permanent force. But during Frederick's last years it was already forseeable that the Prussian aristocracy was not destined to become the leading representative of a higher culture and of new political vitality, and that the old separation of the Estates, made more rigid by the Frederician system, would soon be obsolete. A new middle class, wealthier and less easily intimidated than its predecessors, was coming to the fore, reaping the benefits of the king's economic policies. As yet it made no political demands, but it was most receptive to new political ideas. A new German culture, whose existence Frederick did not suspect, was being nurtured by this bourgeoisie. In its name, Lessing, the great light of Berlin's bourgeois enlightenment, had already declared war on the aristocratic culture and civilization of the king. He dismissed it as antiquated, and even denied that it suited Germany. German national feeling began to rebel against the French preceptors, whom Frederick still admired. Two decades after his death, moreover, the monarchy experienced the most severe crisis in its history. Now it no longer sufficed for an aristocratic society to cultivate Prussian national consciousness. If the monarchy was to maintain itself in the storms of a new, revolutionary era, all of Prussia had to accept and be moved by the idea of the state. The artificial barriers between the classes had to fall before a new desire for national community. And further, Prussian patriotism needed to expand into German patriotism, and Prussia's drive for power turn into the German people's desire for liberty. In the period of gigantic conflicts which Europe now entered, the fate of the Prussian monarchy was inseparably chained to the fate of the German nation.

iii: Achievements of the Administration

WE HAVE SURVEYED the administrative organization and the social structure of the Frederician monarchy. What were the actual accomplishments of this administration? We need not consider the details, many of which are today of no more than antiquarian interest; but we should treat those general features that are remembered as the personal achievement of the king, and that have contributed to his fame, or at least have helped to determine his place in history.

A clear understanding of the new spirit that is expressed in the practical measures of his administration can be gained if we revert briefly to our earlier discussion of the reign of his father and of his own political philosophy.

Frederick William I was still dominated by the patrimonial concepts that the German territorial princes had developed as their authority over the Estates became firmly established in the seventeenth century. At the beginning of his reign, in 1713, he issued an edict that declared all territories of the state and all crown lands and forests to be an indivisible and unsalable entail; henceforth the king could not sell a single farm without the approval of all male members of the House of Brandenburg. The entire state—land, people, political authority, and royal possessions together—was transformed into a kind of private property of the monarch. For Frederick, on the other hand, the state was no longer the property of his family, but a power structure with vitality and demands of its own, an organism that existed side by side with the throne, as it were. His dynastic sentiments were feeble. His male relatives he regarded with suspicion, and was always inclined to interpret their behavior as political pretension without actual achievements. Most of his fellow rulers he ridiculed or despised. "The prince is the first servant of the state; he is well paid so that he can maintain the dignity of his office." This had been said before, but it was new for the state to be seriously placed above the dynasty. The unity of the Prussian kingdom was no longer based on the fact that all provinces belonged to the House of Hohenzollern, but on the proud consciousness of collective achievements, on an awareness of a common "fatherland." The new patriotic sentiment that Frederick hoped to develop in the nobility was to be more than a feeling of personal loyalty—*Fritzian* in Goethe's well-known term: it was to be Prussian. Above all, the king no longer owned the state, as he had in the time of Frederick William I, who quite simply proclaimed: "everything must be mine"; now the king had himself become an organ of the state. Since the monarchy no longer derived its claims to sovereignty from dynastic law, succession, or divine right, but like all other authority from natural law and the social contract, it could no longer be considered indispensable. The monarchical form of government was particularly suited to Prussian conditions; but in theory other types were also possible.

This new concept of the state had practical consequences in all areas of society. Even the kingship of Frederick's father had still been one of Christian authority as envisaged by the leaders of the Reformation. Under Frederick William I the Brandenburg–Prussian state still felt itself to be a Protestant realm. This had now come to an end. The acquisition of Silesia, almost half of whose inhabitants were Roman Catholics, was one factor that necessitated a new ecclesiastical policy. It is true that the addition of half a million Catholics did not at once lead to complete constitutional equality for the two faiths; for years to come Roman Catholics were not appointed to senior positions in the administration. Moreover, some disagreeable experiences during the Silesian campaigns caused Frederick to suspect the Silesian clergy of Austrian sympathies. When he appointed a new bishop to the Breslau episcopate in the 1740's he autocratically passed over the rights of the cathedral chapter—without, incidentally, securing the loyalty of the man he eventually chose. To counteract the anti-Prussian intrigues of Silesian monks he imported French Jesuit scholars as educators of the young Silesian nobility. But he granted both confessions equal freedom of public worship; the state protected the property of the Catholic church; and he was almost anxiously concerned to obliterate all signs of the Protestant traditions of his dynasty, and to demonstrate his "neutrality between Rome and Geneva" to the world. By erecting the magnificent church of St Hedwig for the Catholic community in Berlin in the immediate neighborhood of the royal palace and the new government buildings in the center of the city, he wanted to make clear to all that the enlightened monarchy treated the different confessions without prejudice.

His tolerance was of course far from being an expression of sympathy with the message of the churches; rather, it originated in complete indifference—not toward their activities, which in the nature of things he considered indispensable and necessary for the good of the state, but toward the distinctions between their teachings. To the Philosopher of Sans Souci all revealed religion was only "a nonsensical system of fables." He could scoff at his position as *summus episcopus* of the Lutheran church: "I am so to speak the Pope of the Lutherans." His own religious convictions were too far removed from the Christian tradition to allow him any understanding of the actual concerns of Lutheranism. Without hesitation he made use of the parson as a kind of spiritual control agent, who acted as spokesman for the authorities. When ecclesiastical bodies sought to prevent the introduction of radical rationalist sentiment into the sermons of the church, he considered them fanatics who should be rebuffed. On the other hand, he wanted nothing to do with the fanaticism of the Enlightenment. When four congregations in Berlin appealed to him for protection against the compul-

sory adoption of a new rationalistically diluted hymnal, he supported the congregations against their ministers.

We have already mentioned Frederick's refusal when Voltaire
and other French writers suggested that the Prussian state help
establish a new realm of reason and humanity. He shocked the entire French Enlightenment by offering the Jesuits an asylum in Silesia as the very moment when the Pope—bowing to the demands
of the Catholic courts—dissolved the Order and it became the object of persecution in most of the Catholic states in Europe. Frederick felt sufficiently certain of his authority not to fear Jesuit plots;
he valued the Order's educational work, and had no wish to secu-
larize its property. Besides, the best way to make Prussian rule
popular in Silesia was for the Prussian king to seem a greater
friend of the church than the Catholic court in Vienna. Better
proof of the total domination of the *raison d'état* over Frederick's
thinking is scarcely conceivable than the fact that this hedonist, the
feared heretic and scoffer, protected the former spiritual elite of the
Pope against its Catholic oppressors.

The Frederician monarchy was a purely temporal state, but its
secularity made no pretense of absolute authority. Frederick had
not freed himself from serving a theological view of the world in
order to place his power at the disposal of an "enlightened" philosophy of life. In contrast to the Catholic France of Louis XIV and
of the Revolutionary France of Rousseau, the Frederician state did
not claim to control all aspects of life. Because of this it did not
view the autonomy of religious ideology as a restriction of its own
power, as a limitation to the authority it claimed over man. The
state was enlightened, but not opposed to religion. It had no need
for such opposition since it felt too secure to demand more than
the ready obedience of its subjects in concrete matters—in contrast
to the revolutionary people's states of a later epoch. The souls of the
people could belong to another supragovernmental community so
long as this allegiance did not alienate them from their temporal
fatherland.

A connection probably exists between the Frederician state's voluntary limitation of its powers and the almost complete absence of
educational reforms during Frederick's reign. Frederick's mind was
too proud and too skeptical, his education too aristocratic and es-

tranged from German ways, for him to believe that comprehensive education of the masses was possible or even desirable. In any case, a thorough reform of public education could not be financed with the limited means available to the Prussian treasury. Nor was education the most pressing task of a state that first needed to work its way from economic backwardness and political impotence to European significance. Indeed, the rigorous concentration on this aim may strike us as one of the advantages that Frederician administration enjoyed over the rule of other German princes, who spent the resources of their states on what were often rather dubious cultural purposes.

It has justly been pointed out that in his old age Frederick showed increased interest in pedagogic and moral problems; but the effect of this development on educational policy was slight. In education, as in all other social activities, he demanded that the differences between the classes be strictly observed. For the peasant children he thought that on the whole some instruction in religion and reading—mainly from the Bible—should suffice. But even this modest aim was rarely achieved. After the Seven Years' War Frederick did make a start on reducing illiteracy in the countryside and implementing the law on compulsory primary education, which had been on the books for years. The training of village school-teachers was improved, their salaries were raised, new elementary schools were built, and school inspections became more rigorous. In West Prussia alone Frederick founded about 750 new village schools. But the actual results were limited because money was always scarce, and the local authorities—the gentry and the parsons—usually showed little zeal.

Reform of the secondary schools and the universities is discussed several times in Frederick's writings. He urged doing away with scholastic traditions and the teachings of Leibniz, which still dominated German universities, and favored instead increased study of the Latin classics and better preparation of students for active life, in accordance with contemporary French and English standards and the ideas of the European Enlightenment in general. His minister Zedlitz was able to gain widespread acceptance of these views; universities and schools relinquished much antiquated matter, and new subjects were introduced to the curricula; but the one-sided concentration on the practical world and on the courtly ideals of French classicism could not survive the very different concerns of the next generation. Frederick played no part in the great German intellectual awakening, which, commencing in the middle of the century, sought out new and more elevated ideals of knowledge and culture, and in particular a more profound understanding of classical humanism. Indeed, it might be said that by the time he finally returned home from the Seven Years' War, he had become estranged from the intellectual currents of his epoch.

The Academy at Berlin, which he had at the beginning of his reign raised from decay to new luster, was now increasingly isolated in its German environment. Since Maupertuis' death in 1759, Frederick had personally guided its affairs, with d'Alembert's confidential letters from Paris as the only source of advice. Not surprisingly the Academy turned into a society of French wits and *littérateurs,* joined by a few Swiss and German scholars, who were paid less than their French colleagues though their scholarly achievement was far superior. When it seemed possible in 1765 to lure the great archaeologist Winckelmann to Berlin, Frederick wrote that "for a German one thousand taler are sufficient"—and thus himself ruined the opportunity. The Academy's election of Lessing, after Voltaire had maliciously represented him as a dangerous antagonist of French literature, apparently annoyed Frederick so deeply that he even deprived the body of the right to choose its own members. Herder, whose works repeatedly gained prizes in the Academy's competitions, never was admitted to membership.

And yet Frederick's reign exerted a deep and lasting effect on German culture. Indirectly—in the sense of a much-discussed observation in Goethe's *Dichtung und Wahrheit*—Frederick's military triumphs became the glory not only of Prussia but of the entire nation; they swelled German pride, and for the first time in generations provided German writers with a monumental patriotic theme. Frederick's influence on his immediate environment was more direct. Under his eyes, though frequently in opposition to his views, the Berlin Enlightenment developed as a social and intellectual force of marked individuality. Even today its character can be sensed in the intellectual life of northern Germany. Foreign elements—members of the French Protestant and Jewish upper bourgeoisie—contributed to its growth; but fundamentally it was sustained by senior officials of the Frederician bureaucracy in alliance with enlightened theologians and scientists of the Academy. The problems of ethics for which the old king showed a preference in his disquisitions before the Academy, and which he liked to set as themes for its public competitions, also formed the favorite themes of the Berlin salons. They were discussed without restraint, just as complete freedom prevailed in all Academy publications.

It was this freedom which made possible the emergence of a specifically Berlinese form of the Enlightenment, and to the most progressive minds in Germany it was a special asset of the Prussian monarchy. Kant believed he could characterize its essence with the motto: "argue as much as you wish, and about whatever you like, but obey!" And it is, of course, true that freedom in Prussia found a definite limit in the *raison d'état*. No one should presume to meddle in the king's business by publicly speaking his mind on foreign or domestic affairs, or even by printing political news without approval of the authorities. Defamation of the army, spreading false rumors, and similar acts were ruthlessly prosecuted. Foreign books and newspapers antagonistic to Prussia were stopped on the frontier and their authors occasionally beaten up at the instigation of Prussian agents. Within Prussia's borders Frederick's frequently quoted remark that to be interesting newspapers must be left alone had hardly any significant consequences. After a brief period of leniency at the beginning of his reign, newspapers were again placed under strict political censorship, with the result that their political contents did indeed become extremely boring. To prevent public scandal, scientific and scholarly writings were also subject to censorship, but on the express order of the king this control was applied with extreme mildness. In practice everyone, in Lessing's irritated comment, was free "to spread as many stupidities against religion as he wishes." Attacks on his own person, even those of the lowest sort, Frederick ignored with amazing tolerance and self-assurance.

All in all, enough scope remained for the growth of a vigorous and independent literature, which shaped the spirit of the Enlightenment in Berlin. It was rational, concrete, extremely critical, industrious, filled with a sense of duty. Generations of Prussian bureaucrats, until far into the nineteenth century, were animated by this spirit. For an example of its strong points we need only look at the diligent and severe art of Adolf Menzel, the great interpreter of Frederick's epoch in crayon and oil. Germans beyond Prussia's borders have not been sparing in their criticism of the weaknesses and limitations of the Berlinese style. But who would deny that the German people, always too prone to romantic daydreams, needed a strong dose of this sobriety and rationality if it was ever to achieve political self-determination. The spirit of Weimar and Jena alone could not create a new nation.

In the totality of Frederick's administrative work, the culture of Prussian society, its churches and schools, occupied only a modest and marginal place. Next to the army, Frederick's greatest daily concern was the economy of the state.

In its principles Frederick's economic policy was similar to that of his father, but it was both more methodical and more ambitious. Frederick William had pursued fiscal aims so single-mindedly that he did not hesitate to resort to such questionable methods as exaggerating the value of a royal domain in order to receive the highest possible rent from his tenant. His trade policies had brought the antiquated guild system under close state control and had modernized it; but attempts to develop modern industrial enterprise had never gone beyond the modest beginnings of a partly state-controlled wool industry, which worked primarily for the army. No great progress was made in turning his territories into a single economic whole. The most significant achievement of Frederick William's economic policies was the rehabilitation and resettlement of East Prussia's depopulated areas; the greatest asset of his financial administration was its rigorous frugality.

Frederick did away with the narrow fiscal point of view of the royal domain administration, convinced that in the long run the state would not profit from the ruin of its tenants. More important, with far greater energy than his father had shown, and with a better understanding of economic theory, he set to work creating a systematic trade policy. Its guidelines were the then dominant principles of mercantilism, and their exemplary implementation in France under Colbert.

The goal of mercantilism was the liberation of the national economy from the pressing confines of largely agrarian local economic systems. Besides eliminating or reducing local obstacles such as internal tolls and staple stations, its most important measure was the methodical cultivation of modern industry, or at least of technologically advanced crafts, which would rapidly increase the wealth of the population and the amount of gold and silver currency in the country—the significance of which was overestimated. To achieve this goal in a traditional, underdeveloped, and undercapitalized economy called for state intervention of the most varied kind: The medieval guild organizations must be restricted or even abolished in favor of state supervision of artisans. The state must advance loans and subsidies to competent manufacturers and merchants, and must recruit and settle in the country technically trained workers and master craftsmen. The production of raw materials in one's own country must be systematically developed, and their export restricted or prohibited altogether—in Prussia particularly the export of wool. The price of foodstuffs must be kept low. The government must purchase and store goods, particularly those intended for export. Entrepreneurs and merchants must be guided by comprehensive trade regulations; wages and working conditions must be strictly controlled. Market for goods and agricultural products must be guaranteed by purchases for the army and the court. Export must be encouraged by subsidies and trade treaties with other powers; foreign competition of local manufacturers must be restricted by tariffs and import prohibitions. Finally the creation of capital and credit must be facilitated through state banks and state monopolies. In most European states the early stages of modern industrialization were based on these measures of state capitalism—the old, static, essentially agrarian economic conditions could never have been overcome by any other means. This was particularly true of the eastern provinces of the Prussian monarchy.

In 1749 Frederick personally assumed the direction of the state's commercial and trade policies. He applied himself with enormous diligence to these tasks. The detailed knowledge he amassed is amazing: the discussion of economic questions in his first political testament extended to the manufacture of shoelaces and the problem of guild opposition to modern looms. He devoted particular

care to the silk industry, which he raised from insignificant beginnings to considerable—if somewhat artificial—prosperity. Exact
regulations on the treatment of silkworms, the spinning of the
thread, and numerous other details were printed and in rural areas
even announced from the pulpit. In his concern for his favorite
industrial project, the king sometimes appeared like the head of a
large business, who observes the actions of his foreign competitors,
plans new and attractive designs for his products, weighs prices
and costs, and is on the lookout for new markets. Nor was he content to improve already existing industries, such as the Silesian
linen weavers. Studying the trade balances of the various provinces,
which were regularly submitted by his local officials, he deliberated
on what might be done to manufacture articles that were presently
imported. Luxury goods as well as necessities—fine damask and
cotton fabrics, paper, sugar, porcelain—were to be produced at
home to weaken foreign competition (particularly from Saxon
industry, which he hated) to bring export to the eastern markets
under Prussian control, and to save Prussia from the fate of Poland, which in Frederick's opinion was being ruined by heavy im-
ports that were not balanced by domestic production.

Not all of his projects succeeded or achieved permanency. But on
the whole he accomplished a great deal; for some industries that
subsequently gained great importance, like the Silesian mines, he
actually created the conditions necessary for growth. Cadres of
trained workers and competent entrepreneurs settled in Prussia;
commercial ability and ambition were awakened everywhere. His
greatest pride was that Prussia's passive trade balance was con-
verted into an active one. By the most conservative estimate the
surplus for 1783 amounted to 3 million taler, and the total value of
industrial production three years later to 29 million taler.

This assiduous encouragement of industry need not be discussed
in detail. The methods were those employed by all governments in
the age of mercantilism, an age which was at that time coming to
an end in Western Europe. Even during Frederick's lifetime a new
school of French economic theorists, the Physiocrats, was beginning its criticism of his economic policies, which the younger
Mirabeau developed in his multivolume work on the Prussian
monarchy. Frederick was shown to have committed numerous

blunders of the sort that can never be avoided when the state tries to direct industries that are rapidly expanding, increasing in complexity, and consequently becoming more difficult to supervise with each passing year. Poor investments of all kinds had been made; incompetents and foreign adventurers had received subsidies while able men were held back by red tape and prejudice; trade and agriculture had been injured by prohibiting the export of raw wool and the import of manufactured goods, and by the whole system of protective tariffs and transit duties. But the most important criticism was the one raised against the political system of absolutism in general: the free initiative of the people was not sufficiently trusted, while too much was expected from rules and regulations. Similar objections were raised by Prussian officials from the 1780's on, and became more urgent when the University of Königsberg began to disseminate the teachings of Adam Smith throughout Prussia.

The tragedy of Frederick's position in history—that he represented the apogee and at the same time the end of his epoch—is once again apparent. Not until the last decades of the nineteenth century did the need of the state to intervene in economic affairs again meet with sympathetic understanding. Indeed, Frederick's laws for protecting the peasants and his regulations of wages and working conditions in industry were appealed to as a historical justification for Bismarck's social legislation. But on the whole this is misreading history. If we wish to understand Frederick's actions in the economic sphere we must remember that like mercantilist policies in general they were less concerned with raising the economic well-being of the population—which was to be the first goal of the liberal age—than with increasing the power of the state. The true intent of Frederick's policies was to liberate Prussia in peace and war from dependence on the Dutch money market and on English and French goods, to satisfy the needs of the population, and above all of the army, with native manufacture, to retain sufficient currency in the country so that millions could safely be put aside as a war chest. The interest of the state was more important than any consideration of economic welfare. In addition, his policies were characterized by the belief that the country's economic forces could be strengthened only in conflict with one's neighbors, not by peaceful collaboration. Frederick expected Prussia to rise at the expense of her weaker rivals, among which Saxony appeared the most dangerous. To this end, Frederick waged bitter economic wars for decades, accepted the ruin of Silesia's transit trade, and crippled the commerce on the Elbe River by resorting to the age-old tactics of imposing tolls and restrictive warehouse and marketing controls. These were brutal measures, which in the end failed to achieve their purpose. Later generations condemned them as shortsighted. Today when it is more difficult than it was in the nineteenth century to master the severe conflicts among vast economic interest groups, Frederick's methods may again meet with greater understanding.

Frederick also tried to organize banking and commercial activities into a unified, significant force that served the state. Prussia's export trade, based on the country's rising production of goods for foreign markets, was to be expanded and brought under native control through the establishment of a state bank, which would regulate the money market, and of a number of state monopolies in such areas as the lumber trade, maritime insurance, and trade with the Orient. But these vast projects were only partly realized, and many failed. A European economic recession soon after the Seven Years' War shook the companies that Frederick had founded, and ruined some of them. The state bank survived, but it passed through years of fluctuating fortunes before achieving stability and winning general confidence. It proved to be much more difficult than Frederick had imagined to wrest control of Prussia's foreign trade from the stronger and more experienced West European competition. Their traditional ways, inexperience, and lack of working capital made Prussia's merchants reluctant to face the dangers of long-term foreign projects. Even the time-tested technique of reducing risks by founding joint stock companies holding government monopolies could not overcome Prussia's natural weaknesses. Repeatedly Frederick found that granting a monopoly reduced rather than stimulated initiative. But as interim measures, monopolies were necessary—a point not grasped by the later criticism of the Physiocrats.

In general Frederick's commercial policy, especially during the last years of his reign, suffered from the fact that his primary concern was the rapid development of industry. A complicated system of protective tariffs and transit tolls simply could not be combined with the best interests of commerce. In the Prussian monarchy, the "Kingdom of Border Zones," which sat astride the lines of communication between east and west, commerce could have flowered only if frontier controls had been reduced to a minimum. The barriers to import and export were particularly damaging to Silesia which had lost her old ties with Austria and Galicia as well as the commercial traffic between Saxony and Poland that had once passed over her roads. Nor did Frederick succeed in imposing uniformity upon the domestic market—something that no government before the French Revolution was able to accomplish. Nothing was done to reduce the sharp customs divisions between town and country in the eastern provinces. On the highways crossing the monarchy a thousand different tolls continued to be collected, though their scale was significantly reduced. And at least a start was made on a uniform customs system when the king established an excise and customs administration under the direction of French specialists. But the most important progress in the country's commerce was achieved by the opening of the Oder River, the only river which in its entire navigable length flowed through Prussian territory. Old obstacles to shipping were removed, as were local commercial restrictions, the streambed was regulated and the estuary was dredged. Again following the French example, the work on the Oder was complemented by a number of important canals, which connected the various rivers.

The encouragement of trade and commerce formed only one part of Frederick's economic policies. He was never a one-sided mercantilist, who discounted the significance of agriculture. On the contrary, in accordance with the economic structure of his country, agriculture received the greatest share of direct state support.

We have already mentioned Frederick's eagerness to help manorial estates that had suffered in the war by giving the owners sizable grants of money and by organizing credit associations. That at the end of the Seven Years' War he still possessed over 30 million taler—admittedly in debased currency—was remarkable enough. About one-fifth of this sum was immediately spent on the rehabilitation of the devastated provinces, peasants and the inhabitants of the small rural towns sharing in the distribution of grain, seed, livestock, and building funds. Apart from these emergency measures, Frederick sought to raise agricultural productivity in the same way in which he tried to help trade, through state education. Everywhere he pressed for improvement: increased plantings of feed crops and potatoes, rotation of crops in the English fashion, abolition of night grazing, introduction of stall feeding, better livestock breeding, modernization of vegetable production and tree culture. His efforts met with success on the royal domains, less so on the manorial estates, least of all with the servile peasants.

Beyond the realm of his immediate authority, the king encountered obstacles that proved difficult to overcome: poverty, lack of capital, distrust, most of all the power of apathy that stems from tradition. These forces also blocked his attempt to achieve a more intensive working of the land by redistributing the fields, dividing among individual peasants the land held in common by a community, and removal of crop restrictions. Agriculture differs from industry in that technical innovations can never be adopted quickly, and rarely without a temporary decline in yields. It was not until the decades following his death that the rationalization of agriculture after the English pattern gradually gained impetus in Prussia. The process took a course similar to that of the abolition of peasant servitude and of the reform of peasant ownership of the land. Policies that enlightened absolutism had considered desirable but had not implemented, were brought to realization by the needs of a new and revolutionary era.

Success was achieved more rapidly whenever the state could directly employ the might of its capital and authority: in the regulation of prices, for instance, and in the colonization of the country.

The control of grain prices by the state belongs among the greatest achievements of Frederick's agrarian policies. To assure the supply of the army in time of war, grain was stored even in peacetime. The amount was so considerable that it could also be used to help stabilize civilian supply and demand. In years when the harvest was poor, needy regions received grain from the government storehouses, which kept prices at a reasonable level—a matter of particular importance to those groups of the population working in trade and industry. In the years of oversupply, state purchases prevented the price from sinking below the farmer's cost of production.

Frederick's lasting achievements in the colonization of Prussia have played the greatest part in establishing the reputation of his rule among contemporaries and posterity. To the rationalistic spirit of the eighteenth century—always searching for clear concepts, which, if possible, could be mathematically proven—it seemed that the economic well-being of a country and the success of its government could be determined on the basis of statistical tables: how rapidly did population density increase? how many square miles of wasteland were made arable? Populating the country was therefore a primary objective of all enlightened governments. Each of the great Hohenzollern rulers had tried to settle foreign immigrants in their underpopulated, backward eastern provinces. The Great Elector had taken in 20,000 French Protestants, his grandson Frederick William I, the same number of refugees from Salzburg. Both groups were elites, native to old and rich cultures, whose coming to Prussia as a result of religious persecution was a particular stroke of good fortune for the country.

Frederick did not profit from similar episodes; he had to resort to a systematic campaign of recruiting. But in this area, too, his energy backed by the enterprise of some of his best officials led to results that greatly surpassed the achievements of his predecessors. It has been estimated that during his reign 300,000 individuals settled in Prussia, and that as many as 900 new villages were founded for the colonists. While the commission for colonization established in the Bismarck era could in the course of two decades bring no more than 11,957 families to the eastern territories, Frederick settled a total of 57,475 families. At the end of his reign every fifth person in Prussia belonged to a recently immigrated family. The extent of this colonization bears comparison with the great eastward migrations of the Middle Ages. It increased the German character of the population in the monarchy's provinces to a very significant degree.

But to suspect considerations of nationalism at work in Frederick's policy of colonization would be erroneous. It is true that his actions had the tangible result of extending German influence and power, and that he preferred his settlers to be Germans, partic-

ularly in West Prussia, the last territorial acquisition of his reign.
He did not, however, prefer Germans for the sake of their nationality but because they were better workers than the "slovenly Polish
trash." A new civilization could hardly be built up by the physically and morally ruined serfs of the Polish nobility and the
wretched inhabitants of the Polish country towns. Instead Frisian
peasants were to improve the area's animal husbandry and dairy
industry; Swabians, Mecklenburgers, and German Poles till the
more productive fields; specialists from the Palatinate teach modern methods of vegetable and fruit production; and artisans from
the whole of Germany raise the industrial activity of the towns. As
Frederick repeatedly emphasized, the race and religion of the new-
comers were of no concern to him. He was prepared to invite Mo-
hammedans and heathen, and build mosques for their worship, if
they were able and diligent workers, and he actually did attempt to
settle Tartar horsemen in East Prussia. Not interest in the race but
solely the interest of the state guided him in this as in all of his
political behavior. With some reason it has recently been pointed
out that in the matter of colonization, too, Bismarck was his heir;
but it must be kept in mind that in Bismarck's time it was no
longer possible to draw a clear division between the interests of the
state and the interests of the German people.

Frederick did not break up manorial holdings to provide land
for his settlers, not even in West Prussia where he wished to drive
out the Polish nobility and bring as many of their large estates as
possible into German hands. Instead he made use of the extensive
crown lands, which occupied nearly one-third of the monarchy. He
no longer held to the narrowly fiscal views of his father, who had
never tired of buying smaller farms to round off the great crown
estates. Frederick released over 300 of these farms, on most of
which entire villages were built. The crown also disposed over
more than enough woods and fallow land suitable for settlement.
Finally, new land was won by extensive drainage projects and
other improvements. The drainage of the Oder Valley and of the
districts of the Warthe and Netze belongs to the best-known acts
of Frederick's colonizing policy. From these and other melioration
projects the state gained a new province without firing a shot.

These successes were scarcely affected by certain flaws, becoming more noticeable in time, which attach to all colonizing that is carried on entirely under state control. Not enough scope was given to the initiative of the settlers, and too much dependence was placed on government regulations. For the sake of a rapid increase in the population, too many small farms lacking sufficient acreage to support their owners were established. Nor was adequate care taken to determine the knowledge, suitability, and character of the recruited settlers. Subsidies were paid to men who did not deserve them, who soon ran away, or who proved unable to work the land. Using the police to prevent settlers from leaving their farms—a device frequently resorted to—failed to achieve its purpose. Later generations learned from these errors, in particular recognizing that only personal labor truly links man to the soil, and that the peasant considers only those lands his own over which he can dispose freely, without the tutelage of the state.

The distance that separates Frederick's domestic policies and attitudes from those of his father is most evident in the field of justice. In his own way Frederick William had tried to improve the state's administration of justice, but he lacked a clear sense of what needed to be done, and he had no respect for the dignity and independence of the legal profession. It was Frederick who placed Prussian law and its administration on an entirely new basis. To his great credit he gave such gifted men as Samuel Cocceji, Johann Heinrich von Carmer, and Karl Gottlieb Suarez sufficient scope in their work, and once he recognized their ability he retained and supported them against all opposition.

Certain grave miscarriages of justice in France, which Voltaire had exploited for his attacks on the state and the church, opened Frederick's eyes to the need for reforming the traditional methods of administering justice in criminal cases. Immediately on his accession to the throne he had tried to illuminate this bleak sphere with the light of humanitarianism and common sense. The barbaric penalties of an earlier age were modified, the rights of the defendant were strengthened, above all torture was abolished.

Modernizing Prussia's civil law proved a gigantic task, on which several generations of jurists labored under Frederick. Cocceji's attempt to create a unified code fell short of success; all the greater was his achievement in simplifying and expediting court procedure, in settling thousands of protracted lawsuits, and in creating a uniform and centralized judicial system for the entire monarchy. The bench was purged of unworthy and incompetent members, candidates for judgeships were required to pass government examinations; and the judges became salaried state officials, which rendered them independent of fees and bribes. It remained to do away with the confused mixture of common law and particularist traditions, and draw up a modern uniform code of laws valid for the entire monarchy. This was finally accomplished toward the end of Frederick's reign by Carmer and his associate Suarez. Their Prussian Law Code, a highly significant synthesis, parts of which remained valid for more than a century, developed with exemplary clarity the principles of enlightened absolutism to their ultimate logical conclusion.

Before Cocceji's reforms the Prussian judges felt themselves to be members of a guild, which could encounter the state with a degree of independence. Now they had become true government servants. The temptation lay near to treat them simply as instruments of the state, as organs of the political executive, or even as minions of the arbitrary will of the monarch. That this path was not chosen is probably the most impressive proof of the genuineness of the "enlightened" principles that Frederick extolled. He deliberately took as his own Montesquieu's maxim that in the true monarchy the law reigns, and that even the monarch must subject himself to it. His two political testaments open with discussions on the administration of justice. In 1752 he wrote; "I have decided never to interfere with the legal process; in the courts the law should speak and the ruler must be silent." He gave this thought even greater emphasis in the testament of 1768: "the sovereign must not interfere in legal proceedings. The laws alone must rule. The duty of the sovereign is restricted to the protection of the laws."

To fulfill this duty, to prevent injustice, the ruler must supervise the judiciary and mercilessly punish unfaithful judges. Frederick's mistaken belief that he had discovered such malfeasance explains the only example afforded in his reign of the monarch intervening in a pending action; namely, in the previously noted case of the miller, Arnold. It can be argued that Frederick's interference, though mistaken, was not really a violation of his principles, but actually their indirect confirmation. To be sure, Frederick did not apply the principles of judicial independence as fully as the authors of the Prussian Code desired. He was reluctant, especially in criminal law, to relinquish to the courts his power as the supreme judge of the state. He was even less willing to grant the courts the right to control his policies. The Prussian Code did in fact go much farther than establishing norms of criminal and civil justice. It contains a definition of the entire system of the three Estates prevailing in the monarchy; it sets out the general rights of all citizens, such as freedom of belief and of conscience, and the privileges of each of the different Estates. In short, the Code approaches the nature of a constitution. Its authors believed that the courts should be called on to watch over the observance of these general laws, in the same manner in which the French *parlements* guarded the *lois fondamentales*.

By the end of the century, Prussian jurists and senior officials, including the king's cabinet councillors, were in far-reaching agreement with this view. But they no longer thought in Frederician terms. Frederick never permitted the courts to limit the political power, sovereignty, and administrative authority of the absolute monarchy. A formal division and separation of powers was far from his thoughts. But he was in earnest about limiting political arbitrariness through law. He regarded his exercise of supreme judicial authority as a function of the state, not as an expression of the sovereign's personal power. Even the monarch must accept the concept of objective, impersonal justice. And further, even the state itself was bound by its judicial norms, since only this acceptance made the rule of law possible. The sanctity of justice was a part of that natural reason—eternal and superior to the subjectiveness of all human intent—in whose validity the king implicitly and religiously believed. "Security of property is the basis of society and of every good government," he wrote in his *Political Testament* of 1768. Freedom of belief and conscience were equally fundamental to all justice. In applying the objective legal norms it should even be possible to hand down judgments contrary to the fiscal interests of the state; Frederick was therefore prepared in principle to deprive his administrative agencies of their judicial powers, and was dissuaded from doing so only by objections—of a largely technical nature—raised by the bureaucracy.

With this theoretical separation of legal and administrative power, of justice and policy, a new force was emerging, one of the grandiose achievements of the nineteenth century: the rule of law. In its application of the laws Frederick's reign did not mark the conclusion of an epoch, but a beginning.

10
The Old King:
Foreign Policy in the
Last Decades of his Reign

"*GLOOMY,* cold and hard, like a sunless winter day," so Frederick's biographer Koser described his hero after his return from the Seven Years' War. And certainly, the serene light of self-confidence which had gilded the days of Frederick's youth, the classic days of Rheinsberg and Sans Souci, no longer brightened the second half of his reign. An infinite amount of resignation and bitterness was now interlaced in each day's work for the state. All the more remarkable is the greatness of Frederick's actual achievement.

More than anything else, the foreign relations of the monarchy after the Seven Years' War seemed to warrant pessimism. Prussia had maintained her position as a great power; but she had lost her former allies and gained an implacable foe. The feeling of constantly being threatened never left the king—in contrast to his successors. This was the reason for his unceasing effort to increase the state treasury, and above all to strengthen the army, which soon after the Seven Years' War was raised to a first-line force of 200,000 men. The main danger, in Frederick's view, continued to be the enmity of Austria, which pressed on Prussia's newly acquired position like a heavy, practically irremovable mortgage (to use a well-known Bismarckian phrase). It was no longer possible to ease this burden by allying oneself either with France or Britain. A resumption of the former friendship with France after all that had occurred during the great war was out of the question, even though the fundamental antagonism of British and French policy, on which Frederick had once based his calculations, was not terminated by the peace of 1763. Prussia and France faced each other with deep reserve.

Prussia's alliance with England, on the other hand, had ended in shrill discord. Frederick did not intend to keep on playing the part of the continental satellite, who "pulled the chestnuts out of the fire" for the British Empire. His unwillingness was underscored by the events of 1761 and 1762, after which—exactly like Bismarck a century later—he lost faith in the ability of Great Britain's parliamentary form of government to pursue an alliance policy that could survive a change of ministry. Only one way remained open to avoid the threatening diplomatic isolation: an approach to Russia. Russia's defection from the Grand Coalition had saved Prussia; the "Kaunitz Coalition" of 1756 must under no circumstances be allowed to recur. Russia and Austria must be kept apart permanently. Frederick was prepared to make considerable sacrifices to attain this goal.

But here too memories of the war interfered. Empress Catherine had risen to power by opposing her husband's Prussian alliance; in the first manifesto after her accession she declared the King of Prussia to be the "mortal enemy" of Russia. Even more worrisome was the fact that in her restless ambition she threatened Europe's peace both in Poland and at the Turkish border. Full of dreams for expanding her empire, counseled by ambitious soldiers and politicians, she pressed toward the west and the south at the same time. Could it ever be to Frederick's advantage to support such ventures? Would Prussia's situation deteriorate even further if the empress succeeded in bringing Poland completely under Russian influence? And if her ambitions really could be diverted toward Turkey and she became entangled with Austria, should Frederick bind himself to support her in the possible military conflict that might result? What was the Near Eastern question to the King of Prussia? Was it worth risking the bones of a single Pomeranian musketeer? The Prussian monarchy stood in dire need of peace, and a Russian alliance made sense only if it served to prevent war. To maintain peace on the basis of an alliance with the most belligerent of European rulers would certainly require diplomatic ability of an extraordinary kind.

However, Frederick succeeded! And not only did he preserve the peace, he was also able to gain a large, strategically important province without striking a blow—solely through peaceful negotiation. This accomplishment constitutes the strongest evidence of Frederick's diplomatic mastery, which was now at its peak. Cautiously and ingeniously he advanced by calculated moves toward his goal. None of his ministers and diplomats, only the old king in person directed the game.

The Polish question provided the point of departure for his approach to Russia. Formerly a great power, Poland had for over a century been in a process of dissolution, caused principally by the quarrels, selfishness, and political delusions of her nobility. The European powers for their part had become accustomed to taking advantage of this state of anarchy. They nurtured it by every means of corruption, by direct and indirect intervention, and managed to stifle every attempt at reform, whether originating with the kings or the diets. Each of the major power blocs maintained its own party of Polish nobles, which made its appearance chiefly at the elections of the king. During the era of Louis XIV, France had played the main role of ally and protector; later, Peter the Great had made himself the real ruler of Poland. He ruthlessly exploited the country's internal conflicts during the Northern War, shrinking neither from bribery nor brute force, and succeeded in turning the defenseless country into a satellite of Russia. Poland's former importance as the eastern ally of France practically disappeared. Louis XV's attempt to restore and revitalize the old connections by having his father-in-law Stanislaus Leszynski elected king, was defeated by an alliance of Russia and Austria in the War of the Polish Succession, in which Prussia participated as an auxiliary of the Habsburgs. Crown Prince Frederick himself had taken part in the campaign in Austrian headquarters as a pupil of Prince Eugene. When the death of August III, the Saxon Elector, shortly after the end of the Seven Years' War again raised the question of Polish succession, Prussia—now no longer a satellite of the eastern monarchies, but a neighbor of considerable power—advanced her own claims. Frederick, unlike his father, could not afford to leave the settlement of the Polish question chiefly to Russia and Austria.

He was aware of Catherine's ambitious plans to complete Poland's submission to Russia by elevating her former lover, the Polish noble Poniatowski, to the throne. What this might mean for Prussia had been demonstrated during the Seven Years' War, when the Russian armies had used Polish territory as a base for their operations. From the days of Peter the Great, Russian troops had occupied Polish soil as the guarantors of Poland's freedom, or of her "fortunate anarchy," as Catherine called it. If Russian domination became even more entrenched, her position on the lower course of the Vistula would at any time enable her to separate East Prussia from the main body of the monarchy. Frederick's sole alternative lay between joining Russia in her interference in Polish affairs, or of impotently observing the dangerous colossus advance to the Prussian border, and possibly even intrude itself between the Prussian provinces. The idea of supporting the shaky gentry republic with an anti-Russian alliance would have been downright utopian. There was nothing left to support in Poland: at least nothing that was truly viable; any such effort would only have led to a new war without prospect of victory. Moreover, in Prussia too it was a traditional axiom of statecraft that Polish impotence worked to the advantage of all her neighbors.

On the whole, a Russo-Prussian alliance was far more important to Frederick than to Catherine. Nevertheless, by an extremely subtle combination of level-headed reserve and personal flattery, and by cleverly utilizing the conflicting interests of the major powers in the Polish question, he was able to steer Russian policy in the desired direction. He was considerably helped by the diplomatic skill of his brother, Prince Henry. In the end Catherine, whose candidate for the Polish throne had been rejected in Vienna and Paris, unwillingly agreed to secure Prussia's support in return for a formal defensive alliance. By the terms of the treaty of April 1764 the two countries recognized each other's territorial integrity; if one party were attacked it would call on its ally for military or financial assistance. Both powers henceforth appeared jointly as "protectors of Polish electoral freedom" and as patrons of Poniatowski.

Prussia had been saved from the dangers of isolation. What is more, an association had been initiated which proved to be the most durable of all alliances of the Prussian monarchy, outlasting every change in the European power constellation and surviving even recurring estrangements between the two states. Later, after the French Revolution, when the conservative eastern powers combined against the dangers which threatened from the liberal west, friendship with Russia practically became the basis of Hohenzollern foreign policy. Its particular advantage to Prussia, the rising power, was the strong backing the alliance provided against the might of the Habsburg Empire—so long as the Near Eastern question sustained continuous tension between Russia and Austria. Russia's and Prussia's common interest in keeping Poland weak, which had originated with Frederick, remained one of the strongest ties between the partners, down to Bismarck's time. Both the Near Eastern and the Polish questions, however, carried great dangers with them—especially in Frederick's day, when Russia was not yet the champion of conservatism, but comported herself like a conquering, warlike power. The possibility of Prussia being involved in oriental adventures which did not concern her has already been mentioned. It was even more difficult to prevent Russia's claim to domination of the Polish state—which Prussia now supported—from working to Prussia's disadvantage. Spheres of influence had to be agreed on that would be advantageous to Prussia. For good reason Frederick carefully avoided giving the empress the impression that he was the weaker partner, who stood in need of help. Very soon he encountered a tendency in his new ally to treat Prussia as a mere vassal—an experience which was to be repeated frequently during the next century, and which finally caused Bismarck to seek a counterbalance to Russia's far too demanding friendship by means of a dual alliance with Austria.

The brutality of Russia's action in Poland surpassed the worst expectations. The Russian ambassador, Prince Repnin, behaved like a dictator. Poniatowski, after being elected king, refused to act as a mere tool of the empress and even tried, by agreement with all parties, to eliminate the calamitous *Liberum Veto* of the deputies in the central diet. In return, the empress tossed the concept of "freedom of religion" for non-Catholic denominations as a bone of contention among the parties, and had Repnin instigate a virtual revolution of the nobility. Threats, bribes, and the arrest of political leaders added to the pressure, until the "silent parliament" of 1768 decided on the retention of the old anarchical constitution. It was highly inconvenient for the King of Prussia to be associated as an ally in these crude procedures, which were condemned by all of Europe: at the very least, he would have preferred different methods. The situation became completely bewildering to him when armed Catholic "confederates" rebelled against Russian domination. Catherine ordered the movement crushed by her troops and as further reprisal engineered an uprising of Ukrainian peasants and Cossacks against the Polish nobility. What were the ultimate aims of this policy? It was high time to consider a definitive solution to the Polish question.

Frederick never had any doubts about the region of Poland in which Prussia was mainly interested. As early as 1731, in the letter to Natzmer, he had discussed the necessity of gaining a solid corridor to link Pomerania and East Prussia. His political testaments repeated this idea more than once and elaborated on it—but as late as 1768 without the hope of acquiring, in one stroke and with the consent of the empress, all of what later was to become known as "West Prussia." In fact, he encountered a cool refusal when in 1769 he cautiously suggested a plan to her ministers by which the three neighboring powers would agree on the acquisition of certain Polish border provinces, and thus eliminate their conflict of interests. Catherine was not yet ready to share with others the booty that seemed secure in her grasp.

The situation became even more dangerous when France, in connection with the Polish dispute, instigated a war between Turkey and Russia. A series of rapid victories led to Russian control of the so-called Danube Principalities; her ascendancy in the east threatened to grow intolerable, and Austria's warnings of armed counteraction became more menacing. With deep apprehension Frederick foresaw the danger of being involved as Russia's ally in a new war against Austria, which would finally overturn the balance of power in the east, and was thus diametrically opposed to the true interests of Prussia. But in order to avoid losing his newly won friend, he had no alternative for the time being but to live up to the terms of the treaty. For years he reluctantly paid subsidies to Russia; if absolutely necessary he would even have been prepared to go to war with Turkey. He hoped this policy would establish his claim to important compensations in the future. For the present, however, his position was so weak that he voluntarily renewed the Russian treaty without stipulating anything for himself beyond the formal recognition of his hereditary claims to Ansbach–Bayreuth!

That is not to say that he did not try to improve his standing within the alliance. As Catherine's actions increasingly disturbed Europe, Paris and Vienna began to show new interest in the King of Prussia. Kaunitz, always the clever calculator, would have liked to entice him to quit the Russian alliance by means of such artful combinations as offers of Polish territory in return for recognition of future Austrian hereditary claims to Silesia if the male line of the Hohenzollern should become extinct. Not for a moment would Frederick consider such proposals, but he welcomed Vienna's approaches. Somewhat as Bismarck did later, he used them to bring pressure on Russia. Two meetings with Emperor Joseph II, his youthful admirer, and with Kaunitz, which otherwise produced no results, served the purpose of a demonstration. At the first meeting Frederick even drafted a kind of "Reinsurance Treaty" designed to protect him against Austria without loosening his ties with Russia. At least the negotiations served to strengthen the force of Austria's threats to the Russian Court, particularly after Austria occupied a strip of land in Polish Galicia as security for "claims of compensation."

Now even Catherine, in conversations with the Prussian mediator, Prince Henry, began to talk about dividing Polish territory among the neighboring powers. Frederick reacted to the first word of this suggestion with disbelief and suspicion, and even rejected the idea. It was characteristic of his pessimism that Prince Henry actually had to convince him that the hour to fulfill his long-cherished wishes was at hand. Protracted and fluctuating negotiations, in which Prussia took a very strong line, were still required before Frederick achieved his aim of being given the border area of the lower Vistula, with access to the Baltic. The treaties of 1772, known as the first partition of Poland, which the Polish parliament ratified under pressure of Russian arms, granted Frederick the territories of Ermland and West Prussia, without Danzig or Thorn.

In physical extent, this amounted only to one-third of Russia's gain and one-half of Austria's. But in political terms Frederick was the greatest winner.

To Prussia, her new territory brought the fulfillment of an undeniable and long-felt political need; the others simply enlarged their areas. Catherine was deeply disappointed: contrary to all her wishes, she had been forced to share the Polish booty after all, and, in particular, to cede the mouth of the Vistula. Moreover, the peace treaty with Turkey, forced upon her by Austria's threats, had snatched the fruits of the Turkish war, the Danube Principalities, from her grasp. Still, for the time being the appetite of the Russian giant was satisfied. At the expense of Poland the peace of Europe was secured.

The territories taken in 1772 made up about one-quarter of the area of the Polish Republic. That an act of brutal violence had been committed was acknowledged even by the chief participants. Austria gained the province of Galicia, a mere appendage on the far side of the Carpathians without natural connection to the Danube basin, and Maria Theresa at first vehemently opposed this acquisition. She was frankly indignant, indeed profoundly unhappy, that her son had joined in the partition, for which his occupation of the border zones had in fact provided the ostensible cause. In her eyes it was robbery, pure and simple. She felt that the partition destroyed the greatest source of pride in her life—the fact that Austria had always been on the side of justice. In the end, however, she consented, for the sake of the European "equilibrium"—prompting Frederick's malicious comment: "she cries, but she takes." He himself quite openly admitted in his *History of the Partition* that the manifestoes claiming putative "legal titles" to Polish territory were sheer deception on the part of the annexing powers. On the other hand, he had nothing but scorn for Poland's aristocratic anarchy. He considered it to be "the worst government in Europe with the exception of Turkey," and compared the country's level of civilization to that of the American Indians. In the task of introducing European culture to his new acquisition he saw the only moral justification for his claim. And it must be said that although formally the treaties of 1772 clearly constituted an open act of violence, their result—so far as Prussia was concerned—was not founded on force alone.

Today German historiography should be able to renounce its traditional retort to Polish accusations, namely, that it was the political ineptitude of Poland, or at least of her governing elite, that bore the blame for the downfall of the Polish state. No doubt this view was not inaccurate. Even without Frederick's intervention Poland could not possibly have withstood Russia's thirst for conquest. The Gentry Republic had proved itself incapable of protecting the states and culture of Europe against Russian encroachment. But we readily admit that the political downfall of this old and proud society was not solely a matter of "guilt," due entirely to the political and economic failings of a thoroughly corrupt aristocracy. As Stein shortly afterwards said with genuine sympathy, it was equally a matter of "misfortune," of extremely unfavorable geographic and political conditions. No one, however, can believe that the anarchic regime of the Polish nobility was able to contribute to the economic and intellectual life of the country even a fraction of what Frederick and his successors achieved in West Prussia. If a historical claim can be earned by constructive effort, the Prussian monarchy is surely entitled to it. Despite the harsh means employed, West Prussia's modernization—the replacement of primitive conditions by orderly government, a reliable legal system, and a sound economy—belongs among the brilliant achievements of Frederician administration.

Historians such as Recke have justly pointed out that the events of 1772 did not constitute a true "partition" of Poland. The three powers annexed border territories that the Polish state was unable to defend, a process recurring throughout history, which Germany in particular has frequently experienced without anyone calling it "partition." Poland's true partition, that is, her annihilation as a state, did not occur for another twenty years, in political conditions that had completely changed. National annihilation was never in Frederick's thoughts. For a time after the loss of its outlying areas, the Polish body politic even seemed to revive and regain its internal strength. Count Hertzberg, the Prussian minister of foreign affairs during Frederick's last years and under Frederick William

II, strongly wanted to support these efforts at reform in order to avert a total break-up, which he felt would be a misfortune for Prussia as well as for Poland. We should be careful, therefore, not to evaluate the acquisition of West Prussia in the same light as the outcome of the so-called second and third partitions of 1793 and 1795, in which Prussia, frightened by the prospect of Russia's ascendancy, annexed much more territory than she could accommodate.

It is even less advisable to regard these events from the nineteenth-century point of view. The era before the French Revolution still knew nothing of the right of ethnic groups to self-determination. Even Napoleonic France was not noted for its hesitation in imposing the most arbitrary governmental boundaries on the peoples of Europe. Only in one sense, but that a highly significant one, were the three so-called partitions 'of Poland related. As Maria Theresa clearly perceived—and as Friedrich Gentz was later to argue in a famous pamphlet—this was the first time the monarchies of the *ancien régime* collaborated in a revolutionary act. We must repeat, it was an act in the ultimate consequences of which Frederick did not participate; but he did help pave the way for it. The degradation, and finally the annihilation by brute force, of a realm which, though it was extremely weak, nevertheless was ancient and venerable in history, the ruthless destruction of historical rights for the sake of sheer political convenience, the overthrow of the traditional European balance of power by the forcible elimination of one of its members—all this is touched by the breath of a new revolutionary age, an age in which political authority is no longer based on historic tradition and divine right, but on concepts of political expediency and on cool, irreverent rationality.

Thus the last important act of Frederick's foreign policy, his acquisition of West Prussia, once again indicates his position on the border between two periods in history. Frederick's Polish policy is all the more remarkable since in other respects his diplomacy during the final years of his reign displayed a strict, even rigid, conservative character, particularly in relation to Austria and the Empire.

The faded dignity of the German Empire, which had declined almost to the point of empty ceremony, seemed to revive once more under Joseph II. Holy Roman Emperor and enlightened despot at the same time, he set out to strengthen and expand his rights as Imperial Sovereign with the youthful eagerness that characterized him, and with the easy confidence of a true son of the Enlightenment. In this quest he used time-honored means of imperial dynastic politics, as well as modern concepts of sovereignty, which he applied to the antiquated constitutional customs of the Holy Roman Empire. Important ecclesiastical principalities in the Empire were given to Austrian princes, while in Austria numerous convents were suppressed or secularized; diocesan unions were dissolved and reconstructed according to political convenience, without regard for Papal rights; and the sovereign powers of the state were ruthlessly exploited and expanded in dealings with the Church. The severe quarrel which presently broke out between the emperor and the Princes' Estate of the Imperial Diet brought the Ambassadorial Assembly at Regensburg to a halt, and markedly increased the emperor's influence on the imperial tribunals.

The greatest agitation, however, was caused by Joseph's plans to expand the power of the House of Habsburg–Lorraine in Germany by acquiring large parts of the adjacent state of Bavaria. When the main Bavarian line of the Wittelsbachs became extinct, Joseph occupied Bavaria—by virtue of a settlement of succession which in January 1778 his diplomats had secretly concluded with the childless heir, Charles Theodore, Elector Palatine. Should this venture succeed, it would more or less compensate for the loss of Silesia; the German character of the Danube monarchy would be substantially reinforced, and with it, Austria's interest in German affairs; while the dangerously growing dynastic power of the Bavarian and Palatine Wittelsbachs would again be dismembered, placing southern Germany completely in the Habsburg sphere.

Were the new north German power, Prussia, to permit this, she faced the choice of either continuing the existing rivalry with Austria, in which case a renewed struggle for the possession of Silesia would be fought under far less favorable conditions; or, of reaching an understanding with Vienna over a division of power in Germany. The Prussian statesmen of the next generation chose the second of these alternatives; soon after Frederick's death, Prussia sought an accord with Austria. The outcome was the great upheaval of 1803: wholesale secularization of ecclesiastical principalities, mostly for the benefit of the two major German powers; and sizable territorial exchanges to round off their lands and give them better cohesion. To be sure, such an upheaval required the most powerful of external shocks: the convulsions of the revolutionary wars. But Frederick's closest advisors would at least have liked to begin the great trade: Prince Henry and Count Hertzberg urgently counseled him not to make useless sacrifices to preserve the sovereignty of Bavaria and other smaller states, advising him instead to satisfy his own "convenience" by persuading the emperor to agree to various additions to Prussian territory in Germany and Poland. Only this, they argued, was becoming to a great modern power.

Frederick obstinately resisted such temptations, though they were also held out by Kaunitz and even by Joseph II. The more the young emperor played havoc with the historic privileges of the German Estates, the more zealously the Prussian king used his influence to defend the liberty of the Princes of the Holy Roman Empire, taking pains to avoid even the mildest suspicion that his eagerness might be prompted by selfish motives. He presents a remarkable picture: the man who had violated the peace in 1740, who cynically despised the ancient glory of the empire as "dust-covered trash," at the end of his life turns into a selfless champion of the imperial constitution! It seemed unbelievable, and for a long time the genuineness of his intentions was doubted in Vienna. Could it be merely an old man's desire for peace and quiet, his vexation that traditional values were being overturned, or was it peevish vanity that begrudged his young rival's success? For some time Kaunitz and Joseph flattered themselves that they were able to see through the "unpredictable" moods of the "morose old man": in the end, seeing that his military ambitions had vanished long ago, he would surely keep the peace if he were offered some small compensation. This seemed even more likely since Catherine, his only ally, was involved in a new conflict with the Ottoman Empire.

But they completely deceived themselves. When diplomatic negotiations failed to yield results, the old man unhesitatingly went to war once more. In the summer of 1778, allied this time with his neighbor Saxony, two powerful Prussian armies entered Bohemia. Was it really a quixotic undertaking for the benefit of powerless princelings, as his brother Henry disapprovingly thought? Not at all. Frederick was never motivated by interests other than the most dispassionate reasons of state. He went to war, in fact, not for the obsolete world of the minor realms of old Germany—which he continued to despise thoroughly, no matter how strongly his proclamations championed the Empire—but solely for the purpose of maintaining the equilibrium between the two great German powers. He felt that this balance was secure only so long as Austria's political ventures in Germany were constrained by the traditional, unwieldy forms of the imperial constitution—forms from which he, on the other hand, did his utmost to emancipate himself.

Frederick's policy was logical, and every step was carefully thought out. But it lacked dynamism. It wished only to save the *status quo,* not to achieve new goals; it was not buoyed up by great hopes. Consequently, the Bohemian campaign of 1778 followed a lackluster course. Prince Henry, who was given the most important mission, failed to exploit his brilliant opening successes; misunderstanding arose among the commanders in the field; and after a few months the whole enterprise ended in a Prussian withdrawal, without a major battle having been fought. Prussian leadership seemed to have lost its former aggressive spirit. On the other hand, no excessive efforts were needed to dampen the feebly burning fires of belligerence on the Austrian side. Maria Theresa, whose attitude once again contrasted sharply with that of her son, practically immobilized him with her attempts at mediation. Nor had Joseph been prepared for such a serious outcome to his Bavarian policy. Russia and France, the allies of the two antagonists, pressed for an early peace. Thus this "potato campaign," as it was called by the disappointed Prussian soldiers—the last of the old-style cabinet wars—ended in a compromise brought about by Russian and French mediation. By the terms of the peace treaty of Teschen of 1779, Austria received the district of the Inn, but had to relinquish her claims to the Bavarian succession. On the whole, therefore, the King of Prussia had achieved his purpose.

To be sure, only Russian support had enabled him to succeed. Without concern for national sentiment, Russia was now admitted to the European guarantors of the German constitution, joining France, which had held that right since 1648. Frederick wanted to secure European-wide support for his conservative policy in Germany once and for all. However, it remained problematical whether the restless and ambitious Catherine could stay faithful to such a self-willed ally. She was disappointed that the king would not back her latest plans for conquests in Turkey, but that here too he pressed for compromise. Joseph cleverly seized upon this new discord, and expanded it into virtual alienation. With the death of his mother in 1780, his diplomacy was liberated from the cumbersome fetters of her conservative opposition, and with greater energy than ever he renewed his attempts to enlarge the powers of his imperial office. At the same time he maneuvered so adroitly in the oriental question that he appeared at once as the savior of Turkey, the friend of Russia, and the ally of France. In 1784, the latest Russo-Turkish dispute was terminated by mediation in which all major European powers took a hand, except Prussia, which stood apart in complete isolation.

The time seemed opportune for Joseph to carry out the Bavarian plans that had foundered in 1779. He developed a scheme of transplanting the Bavarian electoral house to the Austrian Netherlands, which Vienna had long considered to be an inconveniently remote possession; in return, Austria would annex Bavaria, the Upper Palatinate, and the Archbishopric of Salzburg. Despite the obligations she had assumed at Teschen, Catherine was immediately won over to his project. But French opposition soon frustrated it, and it provided Frederick with the opportunity for his last diplomatic coup. His disappointment at the latest escapades of Russian policy was already prompting him to seek new support against Austria. From the early months of 1784 on he tried to extend Prussian leadership to a party of princes which was organizing to oppose Joseph's "encroachments" on the Empire. For some time the king was frustrated or at least hampered by the suspicions of the minor courts. His own ministers also opposed this move, which was entirely foreign to his customary policies. It appeared to them to involve Prussian diplomacy in the endless quarrels and litigations of the princelings, bind it to obsolete claims, and seriously impede its mobility. Only when the emperor's newest schemes of territorial exchange became known, did Frederick's negotiations gain impetus. The three great electoral seats—Prussia, Saxony, and Hanover—agreed to defend the threatened imperial constitution, if necessary by force of arms, and were gradually joined by fourteen small states.

The formation of this league had the remarkable consequence that Frederick, the great destroyer of the Empire, acquired during the last days of his life the aura of a mighty protector of ancient German traditions. How deep an impression this phenomenon made on the world of the minor German states is shown, for instance, by Goethe—minister of Saxe-Weimar—who described Frederick as the "lodestar around which Germany, Europe, and even the world seemed to revolve." The court at Weimar was especially taken with patriotic schemes to employ the League of Princes for a lasting reform of the Empire's constitution. The reorganization of the Empire under Prussian leadership—would this not be a desirable goal for Germany's future? But it turned out to be merely a soap bubble. Only fear of Austria had driven the minor princes under the wing of the Prussian eagle; they were moved by particularism rather than nationalism. And Prussia too sought only to further her own aims.

Frederick's League of Princes was to provide Prussian policy with the backing that could no longer be found elsewhere in Europe—a situation that was to be repeated several times in subsequent German history. The league was meant to perpetuate outdated constitutional forms in Germany, and prevent the increase of imperial power. It was not the tool of reform but of reaction. By 1790 a shift in Prussian policy had already rendered it meaningless. But even if the league had held together for more than a few years it could never have led to a recovery of Germany. It has no significance in the history of the growth of the German nation; and even in the context of Prussian history is should be interpreted not as an expression of political strength but rather as the symptom of a momentarily unfavorable political position. Still, the league scored a considerable tactical success by putting a stop to the emperor's plans. And it demonstrated the inexhaustible fertility of our hero's political imagination, which even in his last days allowed him to devise new and surprising maneuvers for extricating himself from difficult situations.

Our account of Frederick's life is drawing to a close. In the course of the many conflicts that he had fought to safeguard his life's work he had grown increasingly lonely. His former companions of Sans Souci had died. The spirit of the French Enlightenment as well as that of German literature had grown beyond his reach. The revolutionary ideas toward which France was turning were making him uneasy; in the writings of his old age he fought passionately against Rousseau's view of life and against the materialism of such thinkers as Holbach. As author and philosopher, the old king occupies a peculiarly isolated position in the cultural environment of his time. His life at Sans Souci shows this clearly enough. No new faces appeared who could take the place of the old friends. A few officers, an occasional Italian man of letters— that was the usual company. As in former times, the royal family maintained a respectful distance, far from the circle of intimates. But Frederick did not consider this solitude a burden; he felt oppressed only during the annual weeks of official court activities in Berlin, from Christmas to 23 January. Once he had escaped from these obligations, he found relaxation and intellectual stimulation in his books, his writings, in music, and in the enjoyment of his excellent collections of paintings and prints, among which he often spent hours by himself. He had learned to manage without his former companions. Empty talk was an abomination to him in any case, and he had never had any use for court poets and sycophants. Whatever tenderness and concern he possessed, was now lavished on his greyhounds.

Far beneath the lonely ruler lay the mass of humanity which he had been called on to govern. As time went on, the officers and administrators who served as his instruments found it increasingly painful to bear the harshness of his ways. In the army men grumbled about unjust and even insulting treatment of regiments to which for some reason the king had taken a dislike during the wars. They complained about his capriciousness, stubbornness, and impatience, about his unmercifully sarcastic criticism during inspections, about cuts in officers' allowances in the face of the constantly growing demands of the service, about the difference in pay between the guards and the line, and above all about his refusal to

grant sufficient autonomy to his senior officers, whom he confused
and made unsure of themselves by a ceaseless stream of orders and
regulations. The civil service felt particularly insulted by the introduction in 1766 of the so-called *Regie,* a special body in charge of
taxation, whose more important positions were occupied by
French experts. Derisively it was pointed out that the *Regie* by no
means matched Frederick's expectations, while alleged misappro-
priations by native tax officials were never substantiated.

The taxpayer for his part was indignant about the new ruthlessness with which taxes were now collected, about the snooping for
coffee, tobacco, and salt in private households by agents of the state
monopolies, and about the increased imposts on the necessities of
life. But none of this diminished the popularity of the great war
hero among the masses. To be sure, men complained and cursed,
and not merely in secret, indeed, it was done so openly that foreign
visitors were amazed; but not only were the king's orders obeyed,
admiration and even enthusiasm were evident whenever he appeared in public. Friedrich von der Marwitz has described the frequently repeated scene of the king's return to the capital from a
military review: tired, covered with dust, bent over his horse, an
unpretentious figure in a worn uniform—and yet everyone cheered.
Long after he had disappeared the crowd continued to stand silently,
bareheaded, staring at the spot where he had ridden past. Frederick's response to such scenes was skeptical, to say the least. A year
before his death, in a talk with the philosopher, Garve, he used the
term "rabble." When Garve objected that the crowd which the previous day had hailed the king on his entry into Breslau could
hardly be considered a rabble, he is supposed to have retorted
immediately: "put an old monkey on horseback, let him ride
through the streets, and the mob will gather just as quickly."

He was not concerned about popularity, about the approval or
dislike of the crowd. Long ago he had detached himself from the
warmth of human relationships, family or friends without which
the rest of us cannot exist. When his last illness came he no longer
stood in need of anyone. He died alone, in the arms of an orderly
on 17 August 1786.

Soon after his death it became evident that an era of world history had been buried with him.

Index